Paul M Lawrence
Box 128
East Point, Ga.
404-761-2686

AF800036

16

Catastrophes AND *Celebrations*

One Woman's Look at the
Ups and Downs of Everyday Life

by NANCY DENDY RYLE

with Illustrations by JUNE ANTLEY VREELAND
and an Introduction by EUGENIA PRICE

CHEROKEE PUBLISHING COMPANY
Atlanta, Georgia
1985

Library of Congress Cataloging in Publication Data

Ryle, Nancy Dendy.
Catastrophes and celebrations.

Bibliography: p.
Includes index.
I. Title.
PN4874.R85A25 1985 818'.5407 85-28025
ISBN 0-87797-097-1 (alk. paper)

This book is printed on acid-free paper which conforms to the American National Standard Z39.48-1984 *Permanence of Paper for Printed Library Materials*. Paper that conforms to this standard's requirements for pH, alkaline reserve and freedom from groundwood is anticipated to last several hundred years without significant deterioration under normal library use and storage conditions. ∞

Manufactured in the United States of America

ISBN: 0–87797–097–1

This material has previously appeared in the *Marietta Daily Journal* and the *Neighbor Newspapers*, published by Times-Journal, Inc., Marietta, Georgia.

Cherokee Publishing Company is an operating division of The Larlin Corporation, P.O. Box 1523, Marietta, GA 30061

To Dallas

Whose love,
encouragement,
quiet strength,
and ready humor

Make the bad times less catastrophic
and the good times more joyful

Introduction

If I'm honest, I confess that I don't always look forward to writing an introduction for another author's book. My own deadlines for manuscripts often make the extra effort of an introduction seem like work. I don't write one, though, unless I can do it with a clear conscience, no matter how much I might want to oblige a fellow writer or a publishing friend.

I give you that much background only to say this: all through the final stages of my just completed second novel in the planned Savannah Quartet of novels laid in the old city, I *have* looked forward to spending time setting down a few heart-deep comments about Nancy Ryle's *Catastrophes and Celebrations*. I find it pure delight to have been chosen to introduce readers to the meaning-filled yet humorous and natural work of this woman who calls herself "ordinary" but who definitely is *not*.

There are numberless talented writers, but Edmund Fuller was right when he contended that talent is the least qualification an author should be expected to bring to a book. One way or another, the author as a human being *stands behind the work*. With Nancy Ryle standing behind this book, no reader can miss. She and her work are warm, profound, and funny. But here is the nugget in what you are about to read: while her writing is at times truly humorous, there is enormous meaning in the humor itself. She thinks. She will not insult your intelligence, but will allow you to think along with her. And just when you're easing into what appears to be enjoyable humor, *meaning* will overtake you.

Here you will find evidence of bright and shadowed humanity—and shared faith. As Nancy wrote in a recent letter: ". . . there's no way you can separate your own values and beliefs from what you write about personal experiences." True.

Not only is this a book you won't have to pre-read before giving it to *anyone*, including yourself, *Catastrophes and Celebrations* is valuable in so many ways that it can speak for you—no matter who you are—with joy and sympathy and understanding. My own gift list for this book has already grown to 15 copies! An author cannot more highly recommend another author's work—nor with more enthusiasm.

EUGENIA PRICE
St. Simons Island, Georgia
JANUARY 7, 1985

Preface

The "Catastrophes and Celebrations" in this book are not front page news stories. They're just some of my personal experiences in the eight years I've been writing columns for the *Marietta Daily Journal*.

Marietta, Georgia is an ordinary, middle-sized town 20 miles from Atlanta. With the city's skyscrapers visible in one direction and a gentle, blue-scalloped border of Appalachian foothills in the other, we're about as mixed town-and-country as you can get.

I'm an ordinary, middle-aged woman with a husband, five children, two sons-in-law, two small grandsons, and various dogs and cats that come and go.

An ordinary town . . . an ordinary woman . . . so why a book?

Because nothing in life is ordinary. Judith Guest proved that forever with her haunting, beautifully written novel, *Ordinary People*.

Every place has a story. Every person is unique. And it's in the ordinary, everyday events of life that we do most of our living and find—or fail to find—meaning and happiness.

Understanding this truth has helped me realize that what I do as a columnist, by opening up and sharing personal experiences and feelings, can be of value to others if I do it with honesty and love.

Our individual catastrophes and celebrations differ—but we share the journey. We all know joy and sorrow, triumphs and failures, laughter and tears. Some of these we bring on ourselves; some just happen. A former First Lady of Georgia, Betty Talmadge, says, "Life is what happens to you while you're busy making other plans."

One person's most horrendous, traumatic ordeals may be completely insignificant to everyone else—like giving the world's worst cook-out (I did it); or forgetting where you parked your car at the shopping mall (it's easier to find Heathcliff on the moors); or losing just one piece of your nativity set (and it's the Christ Child).

Others are major passages and turning points. Your first little girl becomes a bride. Your parents die and you're not ready for that yet (are you ever?) You encounter the wondrous miracle of a perfect new baby. Or meet a shabby drifter who touches your heart.

I hope that by sharing my experiences, I can help affirm *your* efforts to hang in there through your own catastrophes, and to savor more fully the joys of life's many celebrations.

As for the place where I live and the people I write about . . .

Marietta began in 1835 when the Cherokees were banished to their Trail of Tears. For over a century ours was a small Southern town where everybody knew everybody else.

Today the city of 30,000 is the center of a booming metropolis. From 1950 to 1980 our Cobb County population has tripled. The 330,000 people living here come from up east, out west, all over. We're a real microcosm of America.

You don't hear as many southern accents any more.

But in a unique way Marietta has kept her small town friendliness and community identity. Surrounded by urban sprawl threatening to spread from Atlanta to Tennessee, we still have our park on the square. We go there at Christmas for carols by our bands and choirs, and in summer for art shows, barbeque suppers, and concerts under the trees—just as Mariettans did 100 years ago.

The Glover Machine Works is going strong under its sixth generation of Glovers. Many young families live in antebellum and Victorian homes built by their ancestors.

We're aware that this small town feeling in such an urban area is unusual. Newcomers seem to appreciate a sense of belonging as much as "O.M."s (Old Mariettans.) So far we're staying ahead of the danger Toffler warned of in *Future Shock*, that in the computer age people will become "modular man" or "disposable man," impersonal and alienated from one another.

As a columnist it's my privilege to write about this place and its people—not the big events and the newsmakers, but the community happenings and special individuals who add to the quality of our lives.

You may not know my children's friend, Clyde Kirk; or the gentle Hugh Spears, who helped so many in such a quiet way; or our beloved Miss Jennie Tate Anderson, Cobb County's unofficial First Lady.

But maybe they'll remind you of remarkable people you *do* know. Every place has them.

Someone has said, "The love story of the universe is written by the simple acts of millions of characters. That story is not fiction but fact—a huge book full of the goodness of people loving people."

These columns are my part of that love story. They are written in the belief that, in spite of the problems and painful hurts we all know at times, each day can hold extraordinary blessings.

My wish for you, the reader, is that you'll be granted the little prayer that hangs over our kitchen sink which I read each morning when I stumble in for that first cup of coffee . . .

Lord, make my ups longer than my downs.

Acknowledgements

My special thanks

To Bobby Nesbitt, Executive Editor, *Marietta Daily Journal* and *Neighbor Newspapers*, for giving me a chance

To Susan Miles and Lynn White, *Marietta Daily Journal*, for editing my weekly columns with patient understanding and a sharp red pencil, and to Susan for advising me on this collection

To Virginia Meldrum for thinking this book was a good idea

To Ken Boyd for making it happen

And most of all, to my children: Dixie and Ken, Patty and David, Buddy, Katie and Stephen, for their love and support for a mother who discovered at middle-age that she wanted to be a writer when she grew up.

Contents

WINTER

A New Year: Enjoy the Journey 3
Me and the Man of La Mancha 5
Looking Back with the Bard 7
New Year's Dieting: A Slim Possibility 8
Six Flags Auditions (The Grit Behind the Glory) 10
Oops, Not My Grocery Cart . . . and Where Did I Park My Car? 12
Budding Journalists at West Side Elementary School 14
Another Link in the Friendship Chain 16
True Confessions of a Crossword Puzzles Addict 18
Big Band Sounds—Can't Beat 'em 20
I'm a National Public Radio Freak 22
Side Effects: A House By The Side Of The Road 24
Twisted Words and Teen Talk 25
Why Mothers Should Never Have the Flu 27
How Can You Judge a Little Girl's Doll? 29
Memories of Lilian Sullivan 31
Strictly for the Birds 33
A Valentine for Garfield 35
A Formula for Love 37
Jury Duty 39
Old Friends 41
The General's Lady 43
Did Anything Exciting Happen While I Was Away? 45

SPRING

Spring Will Be a Little Late This Year 51
Don't Crack No Acorns for No Chickens! 53
Beginning Drivers, Hysterical Parents 55
Kaleidoscope: The Ides and Arts of March 57
Spring Celebrations 59
Leo Aikman 60
Being Middle-aged Means Always Needing Your Glasses 62
What, Exactly, Does a School Principal Do? 64
Parents Need Their Freedom, Too 66
I Love New York! 69
Spring Means the Cobb County Symposium 71
My Three Fathers 73
Windows Aren't the Only Things I Don't Do 75
Allergy Sufferers—Here's Looking Atchoo! 77
Sidewalks 79
Motherhood: Openings For Challenging Career 81
School Bands Earn Excellence the Hard Way 83
Help Someone Into A New Life Through Reading 86

SUMMER

June's Sweet Girl Graduates—Then and Now 91
Father's Day 93
You Know You're a Parent When . . . 95
My Perfect Father-in-law 97
Summertime—and The Livin' Ain't Easy 98
How We Gave the World's Worst Cook-Out 100
Mother of the Bride 103
A Modern Good Samaritan 105
The Varsity: "Three MKO Dogs and a Large PC" 106
Getting in Shape for the Peachtree Road Race 108

Under the Spell of Georgia's Golden Isles 110
Friendship Force Comes to Cobb 112
A Cat-Astrophic Summer for Liza 114
The Home of the Braves 116
Cobb Libraries Offer Children the Magic World of Books 118
Mountain Air at Sylva 120
Neonatology Is a Beautiful New Word 122
Joy Is Having Your First Grandchild 124
My Husband, the Pot-hunter 126
The Art of Cooking 128
Georgia Governor's Honors 131
The Girls Club: Bubbly, Black, White, Short and Tall 133
Family Reunion 135
Callaway Gardens: Georgia's Beautiful Get-away Place 137
A Message to the Ku Klux Klan 140
Hate Loses, Good Will Wins 142
Mr. Ruddell—Sunny Side Up 144
Please Remove Label 145

FALL

September Goodbyes 151
Off-to-College Advice from a Great-Great-Grandmother 153
Back to School at Candler Street . . . Remember? 155
Hemlock Inn 158
Clyde—Our Children's Friend 159
Autumn and Miss Annie 161
Car Pool Mania 164
How to Read in Bed 166
Memories of the Frances Virginia Tea Room 168
A Case of Mistaken Identity 170
Meals on Wheels Deliver Love 171
ALTA's Back in Town 173
Kindergarten Teaching: Not Much Glory but a Lot of Love 175

Hugh Spears . . . What One Man Can Do 178
Vigil at Scottish Rite 180
Our Lady of Perpetual Help—A Very Special Place 182
What's It Going to Be . . . Buddy or George? 184
Old Movies 186
Saint Jude—A Man After My Own Heart 188
From Prison in Cuba to Thanksgiving in America 190
At Thanksgiving, Listen to Both Sides of the Record 192
Giving Thanks for Love, Beauty, and Giblet Gravy 193
Rehearsal Pianist for Alliance Theatre—Wow! 195

CHRISTMAS

My Christmas List—With Thanks to Andy Rooney 201
Fernbank Planetarium Lets You Choose a Christmas Star 203
Christmas Comes in One Special, Magical Moment 205
Cabbage Patch Dolls—Only One Part of the Garden 207
Don't Let a Computer Do Your Christmas Shopping 209
Treasured Memories of Christmas Past 211
Raymond—a Christmas Vignette 213
What Ever Happened to Baby Jesus? 216
One More Week 'til Christmas 218
"Did I Miss Christmas this Year?" 220
Grandmother's House 222

AND BEYOND

Miss Jennie: A Loaf of Bread and an Orchid 227
Easter—the Fulfillment of the Christmas Promise 229
Don't Look Now but an Angel is Following You 231
Royal Welcome for a New Little Prince 234
Index of Column Titles 237
Index 239

WINTER

A New Year: Enjoy the Journey

One day last fall I found myself in a predicament.

I had accepted an invitation to speak to a women's group. "Choose your own subject," said the program chairman, "and we can schedule you any month you want to come."

We'd picked a date six months away and I'd looked forward to it. I would enjoy meeting the women and sharing some ideas with them.

But as the time drew closer, I began to worry. Those ideas I'd been so enthusiastic about suddenly seemed trite and boring. One by one I discarded them.

Now here I was—down to the wire. The engagement was a few days away. What could I possibly bring to those women, worth their time and attention? How did I ever get into this situation, anyway? Maybe I could flee to Mexico, or at least get laryngitis. (They say hysteria can bring it on.)

As I flip-flopped and floundered and tossed more crumpled sheets of paper on the piles around me, Patty happened by. One look at her paranoid mother and she knew help was needed in a hurry.

She listened to me babble about my aborted subjects for a speech, assured me my ideas weren't all that bad, chose one she liked best, then said something that's stuck with me ever since, "Mom, why don't you just relax and try to *enjoy* what you're doing? Have a good time getting your speech ready. Just *enjoy the process*."

I don't know how my child stumbled on such a pearl of wisdom (she says it's because she's needed it in her own career, which involves a lot of writing and speaking) but the simple truth went straight to my need.

Of course! Negative fears about my inadequacies could only be counter-productive and mire me down forever. The task was at hand: enjoy it. I felt as calmed and soothed as though baking soda had been spread over a throbbing bee sting.

And it worked. It worked so well that I not only had a good time writing my speech and being with the women that day, but I've tried to remember the advice ever since.

It's my main New Year's Resolution this year: ENJOY THE PROCESS—ENJOY THE JOURNEY.

After all, isn't that what life mostly is? Not a final arrival, but a developing, continual process? School, job, marriage, parenthood, sports, talents—don't we spend most of our time and energy working *toward* goals, instead of arriving *at* them? And if we fret and fume and begrudge the journey, don't we miss out on joy?

How many hours are spent in the classroom, writing term papers, digging in the library—compared to that one moment when we get our diplomas and switch those mortarboard tassles proudly from one side to the other?

How many test tubes does a scientist discard, how many scales does a musician practice, how many contacts does a salesperson cultivate, before that glowing moment of triumph?

Any homemaker would quit on the spot if she compared time spent polishing the house and preparing a holiday feast to the minutes (seconds!) before someone tracks in mud on the carpet, clutter takes over, and the Christmas dinner is reduced to dirty dishes and a turkey carcass. It's the pleasure of anticipating a happy family time that makes all the preparations meaningful.

We writers may be the worst breed of all. We hate to write—what we enjoy is the experience of "having written."

But isn't this completely out of whack? Why miss pleasure 99% of your life, while you're in the process of working toward that 1% of final achievement?

Now that I've begun to understand this truth, I'm discovering it's not exactly a news flash. The ancient philosopher, Seneca, wrote 2000 years ago, "Make haste to live and consider each day a life." The 18th century English writer, Sydney Smith, said, "We know nothing of tomorrow; our business is to be good and happy today." And a long ago teacher of Galilee told his followers, "Take no thought for tomorrow—consider the lilies of the field, how they grow."

By all means, plan your journey and work hard to get there.

But don't forget to enjoy the trip!

JANUARY 5, 1984

Me and the Man of La Mancha

I'm one of those people who make New Year's Resolutions. Some do, some don't. For me they seem to help.

But this year I overdid it.

I think it was because New Year's Eve came on a Sunday and I spent the whole day in church. When I wasn't at First Baptist where I'm a member, I was at St. Joseph's where I play the organ. All those glowing candles and long prayers and homilies sort of got to me. Now here I am—stuck with a list of New Year's Resolutions you wouldn't believe. I have more impossible dreams than the Man Of La Mancha.

I don't know whether to press bravely onward, singing as I go, or chuck the list and forget the whole thing.

For example, one of my resolutions was to Catch Up With The Laundry. Now I haven't been caught up with the laundry since my first baby was born. By the time I had three babies in five years, the pile of unsorted, unironed clothes in our basement was so high we forgot there was a ping-pong table underneath. Only the top of that pile changes. If I ever get to the bottom, I'm sure I'll find tiny little baby shirts and dresses, now yellowed with age.

But for the last three days I've been down there sorting, washing, folding, ironing and stacking. Now and then I come up for air, like a prisoner walking around the prison courtyard. The hardest part is training my family to look in their drawers instead of on the ping-pong table when they want a clean pair of sox.

Another impossible resolution I made was to Go On A Diet. Usually when I do this I make a big thing out of boiling eggs and opening tuna cans, but I'm a closet chocolate and peanut butter eater. This time I'm really trying. It will take a lot of candles up at St. Joseph's.

The worst of all my impossible dreams, though, is one that I blame squarely on my fellow columnist, Rev. Nelson Price.

Nelson wrote a super column the other day about making New Year's Resolutions. I hope you read it. He endorsed the practice—and warned us sternly not to be a "compromiser, goof, or quitter" once we do. Then he added the sentence that got me into trouble: "A forceful resolution bares the teeth of intent."

His choice of words was my downfall. He used the word "teeth." I've been trying to bleep "teeth" from my mind ever since I bit into a piece of caramel candy during Christmas and came down on something hard.

Fearing the worst, I ran my tongue cautiously around the inside of my mouth. Sure enough, I'd lost a filling.

I'd been trying to forget it, but caught up in this surge of idealistic frenzy I made a New Year's Resolution to Go To The Dentist.

Yesterday I called Fritz Hagemann's office. Margaret, his receptionist, said that since it was an emergency, she'd work me in right away. I didn't think Margaret would be so heartless. What's the big hurry?

Now I ask myself: am I a compromiser, goof, or quitter? Don't rush me. I'm trying to decide.

JANUARY 5, 1979

Looking Back with the Bard

When you need to write a New Year's column and say something wise and clever, and you don't know anything wise or clever to say, you can always rely on Shakespeare.

The Bard is like the Bible. Everything's in there. And you can lift it out of context and come up with just what you want!

Looking back over the year just past, I would like to offer the following goodies I've culled from my own copy of "The Works of William Shakespeare" and dedicate them to the following. . . .

PHYLLIS SCHLAFLY: "Thy husband is thy lord, thy life, thy keeper."

PRINCESS DIANA: "Is she not a modest lady?"

MINNIE PEARL: "I hope to see you one day fitted with a husband."

HOWARD COSELL: "Be checked for silence, but never tax'd for speech."

CARL SAGAN: "The earth hath bubbles as the water has, and these are of them."

DOLLY PARTON: "Thy bosom has endeared thee with all hearts."

JOHN DELOREAN: "Wilt thou aspire to guide the heavenly car, and with thy daring folly burn the world?"

BROOKE SHIELDS: "At seventeen years many their fortune seek, but at four score it is too late a week."

TV WEATHERMEN: "Every cloud engenders not a storm."

DAVID STOCKMAN: "Nothing comes amiss, so money comes withal."

JOHNNY CARSON: "I am that merry wanderer of the night."

BARBARA CARTLAND: "Love thoughts lie rich when canopied with bowers."

RONALD REAGAN: "Time, thou shalt not boast that I do change."

MARGARET THATCHER: "There is no English soul more stronger to direct you than yourself."

POLITICAL CANDIDATES: "Will you hear the dialogue that learned men have compiled in praise of the owl and the cuckoo?"

JOHN MCENROE: "Serve always with assured trust."

WALL STREET INVESTORS: "No profit grows where is no pleasure ta'en."

MEMBERS OF CONGRESS: "The little foolery that wise men have makes a great show."

THE EPA: "The first time that we smell the air we waul and cry."

THE IRS: "What's mine is yours and what's yours is mine."

TIGHT ENDS FOR THE NFL: "More are men's ends mark'd than their lives before."

SOUTH GEORGIA RESIDENTS: "When the sun shines let foolish gnats make sport."

As for this New Year's Eve, here's what Shakespeare has to offer . . .

FOR PARTY HOSTS: "Be bright and jovial among your guests tonight."

FOR ME, AS I LOOK FOR SOMETHING TO WEAR: "Thou art not for the fashion of these times."

FOR ME, AS I REMEMBER ALL THE CHRISTMAS CANDY I PUT AWAY: "There's a *divinity* that shapes our ends, rough hew them how we will."

FOR ALL PARENTS OF TEENAGERS: "Some must watch while some must sleep."

AND TO EACH READER IN THE YEAR TO COME: "What is best, that best I wish in thee!"

DECEMBER 30, 1982

New Year's Dieting: A Slim Possibility

The Twelve Days of Christmas are wonderful—but then comes the Thirteenth Day of Christmas. The day you admit that you ate too much during the holidays and have to do something about it.

Different people do it different ways.

Pauline, my cute friend down the street, went on the Grapefruit Diet early in December and lost 12 pounds before the parties even began.

Susan joined Weight Watchers, lost all she needed to, and has kept it off ever since.

Pat, Merrilyn, and Sylvia are self-disciplined stoics. When one extra pound lands on their svelte frames they smile graciously, say no, and stick to it.

Diana runs five miles every day.

Ruth, Nell, and Jeannette work so hard they forget to eat.

Florrie and Barbara were born thin, are thin today, and will remain thin forevermore, amen. Nobody ever said life was fair.

Sarah, Ann, Ginny, Joanne, and a host of others are Tennis Players. Tennis Players ingest only diet drinks grabbed from the sidelines while swapping courts. They may order lunch, but they never eat it. Their French fries get cold while they analyze how they could have foiled Margie's serves by backing up more or Janie's volley by cross-hitting.

Then there's me . . .

Grapefruit three times a day would make me sick.

I don't have the guts (no wisecrack, we're talking emotional guts here) to join Weight Watchers.

I'm not self-disciplined. I'm a slob. If someone offers me goodies, I don't smile graciously and say, "No." I leer, reach for the plate, and say, "Well, just this once."

Diana asked me to meet her at the track, but I couldn't face the embarrassment of walking my four laps while she ran her 20, and *beat me*.

Hard work makes me hungry.

I gave up on any tennis potential long ago. So did my friends. They still ask me to join them sometimes for lunch after they play—I'm the one eating the French fries.

When I get desperate about weight, what I do is get out a little blue book that Henry, my doctor, gave me, and follow its plan. The book is called "Are You Really Serious About Losing Weight?" I knew it was time to be Really Serious About Losing Weight again when the new suit my husband gave me for Christmas was too tight, and when my own mother told me "That dress you're wearing looks nice, dear—it's so *slenderizing*."

Henry's diet plan isn't so bad except for a couple of problems.

First, it allows only one portion daily of what it calls the Fats Group. This means that if I butter my toast (lightly) for breakfast, I can't put mayonnaise (1 tsp) on my sandwich for lunch. What kind of rotten choice is that? Choking down dry toast with your black coffee is a terrible way to start the day. And did you ever try a tuna sandwich without mayonnaise? The tuna can't even stick on there. It just rolls off the bread.

The other problem with this plan is that it completely overlooks one very important food group: the Sweets Group. It has the Milk Group, Vegetables Group, Fruit Group, Meat-Poultry-Fish Group and Fats Group. But no Sweets Group. And since I consider this group absolutely essential to my mental and emotional well-being, I have trouble dealing with this.

Still, I'm trying.

And because motivation is supposed to be highly important, I'm not going to swap my new suit for a larger size. It should inspire me to whittle down in a hurry.

On the other hand—maybe I could try just moving the buttons over . . . ?

JANUARY 12, 1984

Six Flags Auditions (The Grit Behind the Glory)

A cold, rainy day in January is not a good time to visit Six Flags Over Georgia, that delightful, enchanted playground for people of all ages. They're not even open in January.

But last Saturday morning at the crack of dawn Katie and I were there, shivering in the dismal gray coolness of the parking lot, waiting for the guards to open the gates and let us in.

Around us was a thronging mob of young people with dance shoes, hats, plastic bags with leotards, musical instruments—and stardust in their eyes. This was the big day. Today Six Flags was holding auditions for next summer's shows and these kids were hoping for their first big break into show business.

The atmosphere was charged with high tension—nervous chatter, jittery laughter, excited joy—the energetic, love-hate mix that all performers feel before a performance.

As we stood together waiting, I felt a crazy urge to start singing a few bars of "There's No Business like Show Business" . . . I'm convinced that immediately the whole crowd would have joined in, bursting into wonderful 8-part harmony, prancing and kicking in a glorious dance production number all over the parking lot in the rain. It could have been one of those old MGM musicals, come to life.

I sort of wish I had!

These young singers and dancers were here to try out for a rare chance to learn musical theatre from experience. Six Flags presents 35 new shows each season, at their parks in Georgia, Texas, Missouri and New Jersey. If you've ever been to the Crystal Pistol or the Riverboat at Six Flags Over Georgia, you know these are no amateur deals. The young performers are highly talented; the productions polished and professional.

They give five shows a day, seven days a week. Altogether they play to an audience of over two million people each season.

Since Katie is thinking about drama as a career, she decided to work up a song-and-dance routine and audition last Saturday, just for the experience. (We all knew her chance of being selected from many hundreds was slim, but it was important for her to try.)

I went along as her piano accompanist. Harris Wheeler, former choral director at North Cobb High School and the musical director for Six

Flags, was on hand to play for anyone needing a pianist. But as a mom brought up on Shirley Temple-Mickey Rooney-Judy Garland fare, I wanted to get in on the act.

That is, I thought I did 'til we got there!

Stage fright is a terrible malady. I've had it often before playing or speaking, but it's even worse when you feel it for your child. Pounding heart, sweaty hands, trembling knees—I had them all.

They gave Katie her audition number, 22, and told us to take seats in the Crystal Pistol Theatre. When everyone was in, an attractive young woman named Linda Doty, Show Productions Manager for Six Flags, Inc., explained the procedure. The ordeal began.

"Number one!" A young Julie Andrews type went onstage and sang "I Could Have Danced All Night." She was terrific.

I forgot what key Katie's song was in (we didn't have music, had just worked it up by ear). Was it F or G? What if I pitched it wrong? Good grief!

"Number two!" A young Robert Goulet type, handsome and poised, sang "Ol Man River." Fantastic.

I needed to find the rest room.

"Number three!" A young Liza Minelli, in a T shirt that said Atlanta Ballet, did a superb modern jazz dance.

I needed to use the rest room again.

And so it went. One by one, the judges watched and listened to each performer.

Some singers were called back and given a song from next summer's show to test their sight-reading ability. If the judges still liked them, they were called up to learn a dance from the choreographer, a red-haired young woman who moved around like Juliet Prowse, shouting "Truck, two, three, four, dig, dig, dig, dig."

If the judges liked a dancer, they asked to hear a chorus of "Happy Birthday To You" (everyone in a Six Flags show has to sing and dance both).

Finally. . . . "Number 22!"

Somehow I mercifully remembered the right key. Katie sang "Ma, He's Making Eyes At Me," did her soft shoe, twirled her parasol. They called her back for sight-reading. And then she passed the trucking-and-digging test.

Her pianist didn't do so well.

Now Katie has a "call back" in two weeks for the final auditions. If she's smart, she'll use Harris Wheeler this time.

When you see a show at Six Flags next summer, you can be sure the kids in the cast have truly earned their places. As for me, I've decided show biz is a whole lot more fun on the audience side of the footlights!

JANUARY 12, 1979

Oops, Not My Grocery Cart . . . and Where Did I Park My Car?

I lost my shopping cart at the K Mart yesterday.

If you want to feel stupid, try walking every aisle of a discount store in both longitudinal and latitudinal directions, peering into every cart to see if it's yours.

It's worse than losing a child. You can't call it. It doesn't cry. You can't go to the Lost and Found. No one says over the intercom, "We have a little lost shopping cart. It has three tubes of toothpaste, a box of light bulbs, a set of thermal underwear . . ."

After a while clerks began looking at me funny and asking, "May I help you?" That told me how stupid I looked. Clerks never say, "May I help you?" any more.

The reason I lost my cart was I outsmarted myself. I had thought I'd shop by a new method. Since I had so much to buy, I'd leave my cart in one central location and work out from there—the Mountain-to-Mohammed approach. Trouble was, I forgot to spot the place. I should have lined it up carefully: third aisle back from candy, two rows over from Customer Service.

From now on I'll cling to my cart handle and go the distance. A cart in hand is worth two in the bush, or in the hardware or wherever.

Sometimes I lose my cart at the grocery store, too—but when that happens, it's worse. I don't just lose *my* cart, I *find* someone else's.

I'll be rolling merrily along, halfway through, when suddenly I notice strange items in my buggy: chunky peanut butter when we always buy creamy smooth; Rice Krinkles when we get Captain Crunch. I know I'm in trouble. This is *not* my cart.

The person whose cart I got by mistake is usually understanding. Everyone knows grocery shopping is hard these days. If you buy everything you're out of at home, it's impossible to pay for it at the check-out stand. You have to keep weighing needs versus money supply—like buying on the New York Stock Exchange. With such stress and concentration, swapping grocery carts can happen, easy.

It's more embarrassing when you lose the other thing I lose sometimes on shopping trips: my car. Far, far worse than walking the aisles of a K Mart or A&P is walking around a vast, cavernous parking lot at a shopping center, arms loaded with packages, feet killing you, searching in vain for a familiar fender. (I know—they have color-coded signs telling you you're parked in an orange or a purple zone, but I forget to look.)

Feelings of panic set in. You know your car is here somewhere; it *has* to be. If not, how did you get here? But it has completely disappeared. Obviously it has been stolen.

Some driver will start following you, assuming you will soon get into your car, drive away and leave him a parking place. Soon you accrue a whole line of cars rolling slowly behind you, like baby ducklings behind a mama duck. You try to stride purposefully, but you feel like a complete fool since you're only walking around in circles.

It usually starts raining. Your packages get soggy and begin falling apart; so do you.

Meanwhile the policeman, on his third trip around, is watching you with beady eyes. You can't blame him, especially if you identify cars the

way I do. I don't remember my license tag number. I know my car by its color, and by the litter inside it. (Are those paper cups from Burger King? Is my junk mail on the floor?) To do this, I have to peep in the windows. Peeping in car windows makes policemen very nervous.

All in all, I'd do better to stay home and shop by mail or phone.

Anyway you look at it these days, shopping is a losing proposition.

JANUARY 15, 1980

Budding Journalists at West Side Elementary School

When a big fat envelope comes in the mail from West Side Elementary School, I always rush to open it. I know I'm going to have an interesting time.

It's their newspaper, *Inside West Side*, and it's always a treat to read.

To the boys and girls whose articles appeared in this last issue of *Inside West Side*, congratulations on such good work. I have a feeling that one day some of you will be working here at the *Marietta Daily Journal!*

I can tell that your teachers and your principal, Mr. Reid Brown, know how to help children to learn to write, and to enjoy writing.

You get things like grammar and spelling right, and that's important; but they leave you free to say what you want in your own style. This makes your writing fresh, honest and creative—not tired and dull the way we grown-ups write sometimes.

Mr. Brown told me it would be all right to put selections from your latest issue in my column, so that others could enjoy them. It was terribly hard for me to choose which ones! But here are a few excerpts:

From the I–A class:

"We have a new boy. His name is Ryan Messer. He can write good. He sits up straight when he does his handwriting. He sits by Samuel and across from Tyler."

That's good reporting, boys and girls. You told who, what, where and how.

From 4–C:

"In science we are studying nutrition. We made applesauce out of real apples. We cut them and helped cook them, but Mrs. Lyle helped us a little bit."

(Mrs. Lyle's viewpoint would be interesting, too.)

From Ryan Sinclair of 1–C (Obviously a young man who tells it like it is):

"School is fun. We do work and we play, too. When we have visitors come in, we be quiet and when they leave, we start to talk. When it's time for us to go to P.E., we line up. We line up and then we go there. When we come back, we go to lunch. When we come back from lunch we go home."

Amber Moreau of 4–A wrote a story about a little girl named Super Sally which should remove any doubts about female stereotypes in the younger generation:

"Super Sally was the strongest girl who ever lived. She could lift one hundred people with one hand." Amber's story tells how some bad men tried to rob the bank and Super Sally lost her temper. "She took the men by the hand and threw them so far you couldn't see them any more. As a reward the mayor gave her a big badge that said "Super Sally—Sheriff's Sleuth!"

Hello, Super Sally; goodby, Elsie Dinsmore.

From Sidney Parker of 5–A came a story about "A Bath Without Electricity":

"One Saturday night I was enjoying a nice hot bath when suddenly flicker, flicker, the lights went out, right when I was washing my hair. I attempted to get the soap off. An electric water pump is no substitution, nor is grabbing for a towel and drying off with your cat."

Melody Brown's news story about a field trip to the Cobb Civic Center reads

"We'd like to thank the teachers and the bus drivers who put up with us. . . . The reason we went was to learn how the symphony works together and just plain hear the symphony."

An article about Children's Book Week in their paper told me the children came to school dressed as their favorite book characters—and Mr. Brown came as The Cat In The Hat.

Now, a school principal who dresses up as The Cat In The Hat can't be all bad, can he, children?

Thank you for such a great newspaper.

JANUARY 9, 1981

Another Link in the Friendship Chain

Dear Sue,

How long since we've seen one another? At least 15 years, maybe more.

We never get up to New York. And when you come to Georgia to see your mother, we don't make connections.

I've never even met Harvey and you've never met Dallas. I've never seen your four boys though I love reading about them in your Christmas letters.

My own children can't believe we're such good friends. After all I moved away from Gainesville in the sixth grade and we've only visited a few times since then! It *is* hard to believe. They won't know 'til later that those early friendships in life can remain warm and strong.

It may not be that way for them. Times are different now. We were lucky to grow up in such a happy, secure childhood. When I hear that song, "Dear Hearts and Gentle People," I always think of how it was for us back in Gainesville. Do you still remember:

Going to Candler Street School together. . . . riding bikes in summer out Green Street to the swimming pool. . . . exploring the woods behind Brenau College (Remember when we ran over a wasps' nest and they stung us all the way home? I never pedaled so fast in my life.). . . . walking to Town every Saturday to go to the picture show at the Royal Theatre. . . . stopping by Mr. Woodcock's (Harriet's father) drug store afterwards for ice cream. . . . getting uncontrollable, snorting fits of giggles in church when the choir sang. . . . eating dinner at each other's houses? (Dinner was in the middle of the day and our fathers came home and sat at the head of the table.)

We knew each other's parents almost as well as our own. I especially loved yours, Elizabeth and Herbert Marsh.

Elizabeth Marsh (you called her "Munnie") was one of the most charming and gracious women I've ever known. She was our Girl Scout leader and we all adored her.

When I spent the night at your house, she came into the bedroom at bedtime to hear our prayers. You would kneel beside her lap first and say your prayers, then I would.

She made a special dish called Rinktum Diddie. It was a tomato and cheese concoction served on saltine crackers, remember? Now I realize it was a good dish for those Depression days because it was so cheap. Years later I found Mother's recipe for "Elizabeth Marsh's Rinktum Diddie" and copied it.

Herbert Marsh had the brightest brown eyes that always twinkled because he loved to tease. He called my grandmother "The Old Battle Ax." She loved it.

Remember how often our whole families got together? I can remember one night after supper at your house, when we played scary games—all of us. One was called Murder. It involved a secret killer, a victim, and turning out the lights. There we were—my parents, my grandmother, my little brother and I, your parents, your sisters Betty and Roberta, and you—all milling about in the dark waiting to get "murdered." It was wildly exciting.

My favorite place to play was in that wonderful big willow tree in your side yard. We stayed there for hours. That tree became anything we wanted it to—a house, a school, an office building. We used the willow leaves to send secret messages from one branch to another.

And there were the times we went up to the mountains to your family cabin at Sky Valley and your grandparents' home in Sautee-Nacoochee Valley. I loved stories about your great-grandfather. How, when he needed money to pay his taxes once a year, he just went out back and dug up a little gold.

With so many good times together, no wonder we were fast friends for life by age 12.

And no wonder I felt I could write you when our Katie came to New York last fall to study acting. I knew you'd be a friend if she needed one. (Harvey, as a native New Yorker, must think we're nuts down here, Sue, but we have this idea everyone up north is unfriendly, and that the city is a jungle, where danger lurks on every corner.)

Of course, you did more than I ever intended. You called me one night from a phone booth in Manhattan, in the pouring rain, asking directions to Katie's YWCA. You were welcoming her to the city.

You took her with you one evening to the Met. What a thrill for her.

Then it happened . . . her nightmare.

Just before Christmas she called us—a very sick, very scared Katie. With high fever and terrible pain for the last three days, she was frightened stiff. What could she do?

We had only one answer. Call Sue and Harvey. He was a doctor. He could recommend an emergency medical center in Manhattan and a downtown physician.

But that's not what you all did. Instead, both of you left Long Island

and drove all the way, through a heavy snowstorm, to help Katie. Just like the Good Samaritan, you took her with you, put her in your hospital, and looked after her.

In that busy week before Christmas you still found time to visit her, to bring her red roses, magazines and goodies. Harvey and his doctor friends gave her deluxe care and attention. She didn't feel scared or lonesome any more. She felt like a queen.

By Friday she was well enough, though pale and shaky, to check out and fly home for Christmas.

Dallas and I think you and Harvey are the most thoughtful people we know. Our children don't laugh any more about my old friend. They're believers. Katie thinks you're as wonderful as I thought Munnie was—another link in a multi-generation friendship chain.

I've looked for words to express our appreciation. This French proverb I think, is the best way to describe you and Harvey:

"A faithful friend is an image of God."

Thanks, and love always,
Nancy

JANUARY 27, 1983

True Confessions of a Crossword Puzzles Addict

It's time for me to make a confession.

They say when you have an addiction the first step is to confront the problem, admit it openly, and get help. Here goes.

I am a Crossword Puzzles Addict!

There, it's out in the open at last.

It has become a terrible compulsion with me. I don't just work the things now and then. I can't take them or leave them alone. I'm totally obsessed.

When I'm not working on one, I'm thinking about it—counting little squares in my head, sorting letters, muttering under my breath and fighting the urge to go back and try it just one more time.

It's scary how fast I got hooked.

For years I was a teetotaler—never touched the things. Crossword puzzles, I thought, were ridiculous. They are so full of ancient seaports and old Nordic gods, you'd have to be a writer for *Encyclopedia Britannica* to have a chance. Anyone who tried them was a sucker.

But three weeks ago our son Stephen came home from Georgia Tech for the weekend. Usually it's the parents who pass on bad habits to their children; this time it was the other way around.

Stephen began calling out strange questions to me from the den, where he was lounging with the newspaper.

"Mom, who acted in 'Shane'?"

"Alan Ladd," I yelled back from the kitchen, warmed by memories of my old movie idol as I put leftovers in the refrigerator.

"Mom, what's a musical term for 'fast'?"

"Well, there are several," I answered . . . and that's when I made my big mistake. I took that fatal first step; I went into the den and peered over his shoulder to count the squares.

Oh, the challenge of those virginal blocks waiting to be filled in! Those lines taunting you to connect them up and down, back and forth! The teasing pull of a goal just beyond reach, to try . . . just because it's there!

Yep, there was one Nordic god—but there were some sneaky come-ons: easy clues like "Little Orphan. . . ." to lure you with false smugness because you know the answer; more subtle ones like "Ponselle or Bonheur" to make you feel clever because you happen to know it's Rosa. (You forget everyone learns about Rosa Bonheur when they draw horses in the sixth grade.)

By now, I was feeling a Crossword High. They're all the same, these vices—pot, liquor, gambling, crossword puzzles. Take that first step and you're a goner.

Soon dishes were piling up in the sink, encrusted with hardened egg yolks and congealed grease. Beds remained unmade, clothes unwashed, writing assignments unwritten.

I spent more and more time scribbling and erasing and flipping wildly through all the reference books in the house: our atlas, the Bible dictionary, my old college mythology book, *The Birds of North America*.

Stephen said it was cheating to use those books but I didn't care. That shows you how far I've sunk. I never used a Pony back when I took Latin.

I grew crafty and began making deals. Knowing that Stephen worked the same puzzles in the paper every day, I began calling his fraternity house and leaving messages:

"Tell Stephen that Bellini wrote *Norma*," (I knew that because I'd looked it up in *Stories of 100 Operas*), "and ask him, 'What's another big bird with three letters besides an owl?' "

I'm not sure he got all my messages, though. His frat brothers always sounded a little funny when I talked to them.

My secret compulsion began showing in other ways, too.

My friend Virginia called on Sunday School class business—"Can you visit our new members this week?"

"I don't know, Virginia," I told her, "but what's a root for perfumes?"

My friend Sarah called to plan a bride's party we were giving together.

"Don't bother me now with the guest list, Sarah, but do you know an Israeli dance that starts with H?"

No doubt about it; I have a problem.

I'm trying hard to kick the habit. I really am. But as I go about my daily tasks, a little voice keeps whispering inside my head:

"You could finish that lower left hand corner if you just try one more time. Go on! Do it!"

Hey, I just thought of something. Another big bird with three letters is an auk.

Excuse me. There's something I have to go do.

FEBRUARY 16, 1984

Big Band Sounds—Can't Beat 'em

Please, won't you be kind,
And please make up your mind,
I'm gettin' sentimental over you. . . .

That was their theme song.

A gentle smiling man who blew incredibly sweet trombone was their leader. They called him "The Sentimental Gentleman of Swing."

And when they start sending their smooth, pulsing sounds throbbing through the gym of Marietta High on Jan. 28, the Tommy Dorsey Band will make everybody happy!

Our youngsters will finally hear for themselves this Big Band Sound their parents keep yakking about. They'll find out what they've been missing from The Rolling Stones and Earth, Wind, and Fire.

Youngsters who are members of school bands in our area already know. They often study and perform Big Band arrangements. Now they'll get to hear them played by the Big Boys themselves, masters of the trade, legendary musicians.

Music lovers will hear some of the finest instrumentalists in the country, starting with Buddy Morrow himself. Now the leader of Dorsey's group, Morrow was a professional trombonist by the time he was 13. He toured the East coast with The Yale Collegians, playing college campuses, at fifteen. He won a scholarship to Juilliard after high school.

Those are pretty good credentials.

But I know who'll be smiling the most that night, patting our feet and bouncing around in our chairs—we parents who grew up to the sounds of Glenn Miller, Harry James, Woody Herman, and the Dorseys, Jimmy and Tommy.

For a little while we can forget the grim gray world of adult responsibility. We can revel in nostalgia. We might even jitterbug in the aisles if our children will let us.

Gettin' sentimental? You bet. And loving every minute of it.

When I heard about the Dorsey concert, I dug through my old columns and found the first column I ever wrote. It was about radio station WCOB, which specializes in hits from the past. Here's part of that column:

"The more the music pours forth, the more memories rush in and work their magic. I'm not an over-the-hill matron any more. I'm 30 years younger and 30 pounds slimmer, wearing a Sloppy Joe sweater, a full skirt, saddle oxfords, pancake makeup and Tangee lipstick. My hair is long and bouncy like Rita Hayworth's and (can you believe this?) I have a camellia over one ear.

"As old songs fill the air, I dance around the house like one of those idiot women in a tv ad. I glide with Glenn, jive with Jo, swing with Sinatra, dust with Dorsey.

"Never mind that I'm closer to queen of the senior citizens than queen of the senior prom . . . with mellow oldies on my radio matching, decibel for decibel, the shrieking, savage rock sounds of my children's radio, we're all happy!"

Columnist Ellen Goodman says, "I have always been suspicious of nostalgia. It distorts the past all out of proportion."

But Ellen Goodman only graduated in the '60s, for heaven's sake. What does she know about nostalgia? Wait a while, Ellen baby.

It will be wonderful to hear the Dorsey Band. I'll see you there. You'll know me by the flower in my hair.

January 16, 1981

(Note: WCOB is now WJYA AM and FM, playing "The Music Of Your Life." It's still going strong—and I'm still jivin'.)

I'm a National Public Radio Freak

Can you answer the following questions?

1. Describe Lake Wobegon, Michigan.
2. What do you know about Powdermilk Biscuits?
3. Who is Garrison Keillor?

Now for the answers . . .

1. Lake Wobegon, Michigan is a little town that time forgot and the decades failed to improve. In Lake Wobegon all the women are strong, all the men are good-looking, and all the children are above average.

2. Powdermilk Biscuits are made from whole wheat flour grown by Minnesota bachelors. They give shy people the strength to do what has to be done. As the jingle says, "If your family's tried 'em, then you know you've satisfied 'em, they're a real hot item—Powdermilk."

3. Garrison Keillor is the creative, witty genius who dreamed up Lake Wobegon, Powdermilk Biscuits, and all the other funny ideas heard on a weekly program for public radio called "Prairie Home Companion."

If you made 100 on that quiz, it's a cinch you do what we do each Saturday night: tune in Atlanta's WABE, 90.1 FM, for this wonderful radio show from 6:00 to 8:00 P.M. If you failed the quiz, you just don't know what you're missing. Radio hasn't been so much fun since the old Hit Parade days when you were a real drip in high school if you didn't know songs one through ten each week, not to mention the Lucky Strike Extras.

The program is broadcast before a live audience in St. Paul, Minn., and heard across the nation on public radio affiliates. A variety of music is performed by guest artists—folk, blues, spirituals, bluegrass—and the studio band, the Butch Thompson Trio, always brings some great ragtime music.

The magic is not in the format of this show, however. It's in the charm and wit of one man—Garrison Keillor—originator and emcee of "Prairie Home Companion."

He combines down home folksiness with hip humor (hip enough to have been a writer for *New Yorker* magazine), and spins his yarns so easily he seems to improvise them as he goes. We laugh at the people of Lake Wobegon and we laugh with them, for if we are Every Man, then Lake Wobegon is Everyman's Home Town . . . we know them all, very well!

There are no commercials (one of the best reasons to listen to public broadcasting) but the pseudo "commercials" for Powdermilk Biscuits, Ah Hoo Ah Sauce (the hot pepper named for the sound you make when you taste it), the Kitty Boutique, and other "sponsors" are a hilarious part of the entertainment.

Keillor's humor is decidedly offbeat. He claims he's a shy person, and devotes much of his humor to shy people. ("Christmas is a hard time for shy people. People keep telling us to have a good time—we ARE having a good time. We just smile on the inside.") To his Jewish listeners: "Happy Hanukkah. It must be tough being a Jew in America at Christmas—sort of like living downstairs from noisy neighbors."

One wonderful feature of the program is the dedications from listeners to friends or relatives. I've jotted down a few:

"To Carol from her marimba teacher" . . . "To John in Apartment 211, from Sally in Apartment 109" . . ."To Dad in Boston from your children in California, 'Happy Birthday and may all your gifts be car repair tools or chocolate,'" . . ."To Mom and Dad on their anniversary—we're glad two such shy people got together."

It's nice to think that such genuine, special communication is taking place. In fact, this Saturday night there should be a special greeting "to Buddy in Austin, Texas, from his folks in Marietta, Georgia,"—for our son turns 25 this week and he listens to "Prairie Home Companion," too!

This show is one reason I'm hooked on public broadcasting.

Ernie Kovacs (remember how he lit up the early days of television?) once said "Television is a medium, so called because it's hardly ever rare or well-done." Public television is the exception. You may already watch some of our favorites—"Masterpiece Theatre," "The MacNeil-Lehrer News Hour," "Mystery Theatre," "Live from Lincoln Center," "All Creatures Great and Small," "Washington Week in Review."

It seems a lot fewer people know about public radio. Did you know WABE has a Sherlock Holmes drama each week—and a Lord Peter Wimsey? The daily news shows, "Morning Edition" and "All Things Considered," are the best way I know to get in-depth news plus interesting features. (MacNeil and Lehrer themselves call "All Things Considered" the best news program on the air today.) A wonderful man called Dr. Karl Haas brings a program at 11 each morning on classical music. And I'm hooked on "My Word," a BBC program on which British experts discuss poetry, language, and words—as cleverly and articulately as only the British can do.

We've accidentally discovered on some of our trips that public radio stations are usually on the same frequency. Just keep your car radio turned to 90 FM, and you'll find similar stations in cities like Raleigh, N.C., Greenville, S.C., Savannah, Ga., or Orlando, Fl.

Of course, eventually you'll feel guilty at fund drive time and start sending your own donations—but it's still cheap at the price.

The good news: I've been a housewife for 30 years and I still don't watch any soaps. The bad news: I'm hooked on national public radio—and I don't even care.

JANUARY 13, 1983

Side Effects—A House by the Side of the Road

"To live in a house by the side of the road and be a friend to man" is a noble calling. There's a poem that says so.

But to live in a house by the side of the road can get you into a lot of trouble—especially in icy winter weather.

Our house sits on a curve. At the same time the road curves, it also goes downhill. Many drivers have discovered to their dismay and ours, that the hill is much steeper than they thought it was when they started down.

In front of our house beside the road are a weeping cherry tree, a mailbox, and a magnolia.

The cherry tree used to be lovely with long swooping branches that brushed the ground and feathery pink blossoms in spring. The magnolia was a thick glistening green, shaped in perfect symmetry. The mailbox was nice, too. Dallas made it of gray shingles to match our house.

Now the cherry tree has a reason to weep. Its branches don't swoop down any more. They just stick out in short stumpy spikes. The magnolia is full of open spaces where green leaves used to be and its shape is sadly lop-sided. The gray-shingled mailbox was replaced long ago with a plain black metal one from the hardware store.

We've lost count of the cars that have skidded into our yard at one time or another due to rain, sleet, or snow. The television Action News Team would be smart to station a crew in front of our house in bad weather. They'd always have something to report.

The gray mailbox got totalled by a teenaged boy who slid on the ice, knocked on our door, and apologized. He asked us please not to report the accident as he was already in trouble with his dad over the car. He promised to send us a check for a new mailbox. We said, "Fine." We never heard from him again.

Most of the drivers who slide into our yard are much nicer. We serve them hot tea or cocoa and get to be good friends while we wait for the police and the wrecker to come.

We felt really sorry for the guy who woke us up one rainy night two weeks ago to sounds of crunching metal and splintering glass. He had met another car on our curve, overreacted, skidded on wet leaves, and taken the inevitable path into our yard. His hands were shaking so hard he spilled his cocoa, but he said it tasted good and left the mug in the mailbox.

Last Tuesday, when the raindrops began to thicken and freeze on the bare tree branches, we thought "Oh-oh, here we go again."

Sure enough! About five o'clock that afternoon, our neighbor, Roy Duncan—a kind, thoroughly sober man, good doctor, and fine driver—suddenly left the street and sashayed and dosey-doed right around our cherry tree, mailbox, and magnolia. He left an interesting pattern of tire tracks and his own fresh nicks in the trees.

An hour later, a young woman delivering pizzas wasn't as lucky as Roy. She slammed into the cherry tree so hard she ruined her car.

The policeman who wrote up the accident said they sure did get a lot of calls to our front yard. We said they sure did.

If we ever move again, it won't be to a house on a curve down a hill.

We want to "be a friend to man" . . . but surely there's a better way.

FEBRUARY 1982

Twisted Words and Teen Talk

Theoretically we all speak the same language in America, English, but that doesn't mean we always communicate.

My friend, Elsie Baker, has worked many years in a government agency in Marietta. Many of the folks she serves have their roots in the north Georgia hill country. The words used in medical and welfare programs are as foreign to them as Chinese.

Elsie sympathizes with them but some of their sayings have been so funny she's jotted them down. Here's her list:

Sign a relief	(release)
Doctor's receptacle	(receptionist)
Utensil bill	(utilities bill)

An emasculine house	(immaculate)
Night suppository	(depository)
Workman's conversation	(compensation)
Acceptable to infection	(susceptible)
Candle lobsters	(candelabra)
My-gram headache	(migraine)
Profile language	(profane)
Dis-aided husband	(disabled)

Another kind of speech that calls for special translation is slang expressions of teens. Their "in" words change as fast as the top 40 records. Parents need a continuing education course in teen talk to keep up.

From My Daughter the Cheerleader I've gleaned the following definitions for other parents struggling to understand what their teen is saying:

A cute boy is a "fox." (Katie's older sisters would have called him "tough.")

When she likes something, she "gets off on it." (Her sisters would have "gotten into it.")

Here are others:

chow down	(eat a snack)
pig out	(eat lots of snacks at once)
the pits	(awful, terrible)
eyeball	(to give an insult or perfect squelch)
burned or busted	(get eyeballed)
off the wall	flaky, crazy (her sisters said "spaced out")
decked out	dressed up

(I'm surprised at that last one, since we used to say the same thing. Ditto for other words in their jargon now: "threads" (clothes) and "wheels" (car).

Two words used most by teens right now are extremely important for parents to understand. These words are their one-word answers to any question, any time.

They are "whatever" and "really."

There's a subtle difference.

"Whatever" is a laid back sort of answer, fairly agreeable and nonchalant. If your teenager answers with "whatever," he doesn't care one way or another.

"Really" can mean "whatever" . . . but it can also mean more. It sometimes is a passionate, fervent endorsement. As in "right on!" The clue to the meaning is the loudness with which "really" is spoken.

I'm fascinated with "really" and "whatever" myself. I'd like to use them but I don't dare.

Cardinal rule: parents should never, never use teen jargon themselves, just understand it. For a parent to speak teen jargon would be terribly embarrassing to their children. It would be the absolute pits. Really.

FEBRUARY 10, 1978

Why Mothers Should Never Have the Flu

I had the flu last week. What a ghastly experience.

The worst part wasn't how I felt—though that was bad enough. When your bones ache, your stomach's a hard knot, and you try to keep staring in one spot because it hurts to move your eyeballs, you're in a bad way.

But the worst part of having the flu was my family.

When you're a wife and a mother you can't do anything by yourself. You can't even be sick and miserable by yourself. You have these other people in your life, who won't go away if you close your eyes—no matter how hard you wish they would.

Even when you start coming down with the bug, instead of nursing your scratchy throat and trying to rest, you have to get on the phone and swap car pools, scrabble in the freezer looking for something to keep them from starvation, write notes reminding them to feed the cat, go to soccer practice at 5, and get the band uniform from the cleaners.

Then, succumbing to your feverish, aching body, you crawl in bed, pull the covers over your head, and try to die. But what happens?

They come at you, angels of mercy. They plump up your pillows, bring juice and hot soup, show sweet concern and say "Just rest, now, and don't worry about us, we'll be fine."

If you had any sense, you'd think, "Why *shouldn't* they be fine? They're not the ones with the flu." But instead, you start feeling guilty. (Moms are very good at feeling guilty.) Poor dears. Look at all the trouble you've made for them by getting sick.

But hold on. They won't be angels of mercy long.

As your flu worsens and you're zonked out unable to defend yourself, they go into another phase: their martyrdom phase.

They don't talk about it. They do it with body language. Long, gusty sighs. Pitiful drooping shoulders. That big-eyed, hangdog look that Tony Randall mastered to perfection in "The Odd Couple."

When they bring your tray in, they walk in heavy measured tread like a prisoner in a chain gang—as if a glass of juice and a bowl of soup is a terrible burden for one person to carry.

If you weren't so weak and helpless, you'd confront them, tell them how selfish and heartless they are. But before you feel up to it, they move on to yet another reaction.

They're disgusted. It's clear they think this sickly, neurotic woman has been lolling around long enough. "How are you feeling now?" means "Aren't you better *yet*, for Pete's sake?" They don't bring trays any more. You totter into the kitchen for your own stale crust of bread.

Through this entire flu experience, there's one bright spot for a woman: your family is beginning to appreciate you. They're understanding new truths: dirty sox don't leap from floor to washer to drier to drawer on their own; groceries don't automatically replenish themselves in cupboard and refrigerator; car pools don't operate by magic carpet. Good old Mom has her uses after all.

This morning I finally feel better. I stuck my head outside and breathed in the sweet fresh air. No one had told me the dogwood is blooming—my weak eyes are dazzled by the white brilliance and the sunshine.

Back in the kitchen I prop up on my shaky legs and start frying bacon, just as my husband comes into the kitchen and says his throat hurts. He thinks he's coming down with the flu.

Oh, no! Surely he's not going to be a baby and go to bed.

If there's one thing I can't stand, it's a sickly, neurotic husband.

JANUARY 18, 1978

How Can You Judge a Little Girl's Doll?

The call came from Volunteer Cobb: would I please help judge a doll contest?

The Cobb Parks and Recreation Department was going to have a Dolls and Models event. Little girls would bring their favorite doll, little boys their best model. It would be held at the Cobb Civic Center.

On the night of the event the children were to bring their dolls and models at 6:30. Judging would begin at 7:00. The winners would be announced and ribbons awarded at 7:30.

At least, that was the plan.

It didn't work out that way.

Folks at the Parks and Recreation Dept. were worried that there might not be much interest. They'd never held such an event before. What would the turn-out be?

They needn't have worried. Judging from the number of entries, it was a smashing success. But before it was all over, the judges wished they were smashed, too. Barbara Bowden, Ann Hildreth, and I—the judges of the doll contest—never had such an ordeal.

To begin with, I'm as bad about dolls as a lot of grown men are about model trains. I absolutely *love* dolls. My girls outgrew them years ago but I still visit the doll department every Christmas to enjoy the latest crop. And so I said, "Yes, I'd be a judge."

The first quiver of impending doom hit me when I couldn't even find a parking place at the Civic Center. Grim reality hit when I entered the gym and saw the massed array of children, dolls, models, mothers and dads. The place was packed.

I am not a person who makes up her mind easily. I go crazy at Baskin-Robbins deciding ice cream flavor.

Here I was facing 400 dolls!

There were 10 categories for us to judge—and to award 6 places in each category. This meant there would be 60 winners; but it also meant there would be 340 losers.

How can you tell a little girl her doll is a loser? Especially when it isn't true? Any doll is a winner when some little girl loves her. (The department had thought of this and they issued a certificate to each child—but any dummy knows the difference between a blue ribbon and a certificate.)

Donna Orford, the young woman in charge of the event, mercifully formed a flying wedge of her co-workers from the department and conducted us judges back to our private room, away from the big, solemn, wistful eyes of the dolls' owners.

It took us longer than 30 minutes to make our decisions . . . it took us 2½ hours!

We ignored all the voices (especially fathers') drifting through our closed door: "How much longer is it going to take, for crying out loud?"

Trying to choose winners from what must have been the world's most perfect doll collection, we went from bewilderment to frustration to hopeless despair.

For example—"*Which doll best represented a nationality*?" The authentically dressed Oriental doll, or the ones from India, South America, Scotland, Norway, or dozens of other nations—all just perfect?

"*Which doll had the best homemade outfit*?" The ones wearing outfits which were obviously beautifully made, but on a sewing machine . . . or the ones which were hand-stitched in struggling little stitches that you knew meant pricked fingers and painful effort?

Worst category of all: "*Which doll was the Best Loved Doll*?" The dolls whose features were dimmed and hair half gone from fondling, or the dolls whose little owners treated them so carefully you could tell they were greatly cherished?

Obviously it was impossible. You can't rank a child's love on a scale of 1 to 10. Yet beyond our closed door the gym was full of people waiting for our decisions. Donna was poised at the mike, hoping we'd tell her something soon!

Somehow we muddled through and did what we had to do.

Next year the department already has different plans . . . allowing a full day for the dolls to be displayed and admired by the public. At least every little girl will know her doll has value and is appreciated.

In the wonderful children's book, *The Velveteen Rabbit* by Williams, a toy rabbit talks to a stuffed horse:

"Being Real isn't how you're made, it's a thing that happens to you. When a child loves you for a long time, not just to play with, but REALLY loves you, then you become Real."

I want to tell every little girl who entered the contest, "Thank you very much for showing us your beautiful doll. We loved her. And we *knew* she was Real."

FEBRUARY 6, 1976

Memories of Lilian Sullivan

When a house has been home for a long time, it takes on its owner's personality. That's how it was with the home of Mrs. Lilian Bennett Sullivan.

The big, rambling house with its wide front porch seemed to say, "Come in and welcome." Even the tangled growth of its grounds heightened the charm of the place. Though it sat squarely between Marietta High School and the downtown square, its tall boxwoods, shady towering oaks, and old garden paths gave sheltering seclusion. It was a perfect setting for the beauty and music inside.

Now Lilian is gone, but it's good to know of plans to continue her influence and honor her memory.

Her personal musical library—a lifetime collection of a master musician—has been donated to the music department of Kennesaw College. The Lilian Bennett Sullivan Memorial Scholarship Fund has been established at the college, too. Ruth Delmar Sullivan, widow of Lilian's only son John, hopes that the fund, by assisting advanced voice students, will promote musical excellence as Lilian would have wished.

She was a remarkable woman. Bill Kinney has already written of her outstanding career as a singer and a teacher. She established the voice department at Georgia State University. Her teaching career there is a story in itself—Lilian taught long past the customary retirement age; no one really knew how old she was; and anyway, because of her outstanding ability, no one even cared!

Finally Lilian admitted to her age herself, when she decided to "retire." She was 77!

Even then, she only shifted her place of work from campus to home, continuing a full load of teaching 'til her death at 88.

My own delightful friendship with Lilian began eleven years ago. One night my daughter called me to the phone, whispering that a man wanted to talk to me. I heard a deep, resonant voice of someone, explaining that she—not he—needed a piano accompanist for a special voice student being prepared for a concert with the Atlanta Symphony. Would I like the job? I accepted, and began one of the most enjoyable experiences of my life.

For more than a year, I went once a week to Lilian's house on Polk Street. The three of us made an unlikely trio. Charlotte, the gifted young black soprano, was half my age. I, a housebound mother of young children, was in awe of the legendary Mrs. Sullivan.

Soon, however, we were having a ball. We spent several hours together each time, taking a lunch break (Lilian loved to cook and usually prepared a treat for us, serving in her stately old dining room) and sharing ideas and laughs.

I discovered what many others did: that Lilian was not only an incredible voice teacher, but an incredible human being.

She demanded top performance, using her flashing eyes and booming voice to correct a mispronounced German word, a tone sung off-pitch. She could mimic a student in perfect parody, or discuss seriously a passage.

But the disciplined musician was also the tolerant lover of life and of people. To everyone she was Lilian, not Mrs. Sullivan—contemporary, ageless, our friend.

Jean Somerlot, another accompanist who worked with her for nine years, has helped me put this vivid, complex, gallant lady into words. Jean says she was "a spontaneous fountain of new ideas, with a steady flow of wisdom."

Peggy Benson, who began studying voice with her at age 17, admired Lilian's enthusiasm whether it was for a book, recipe, or pattern. Her interests were keen and wide-spread.

Peggy, Dr. Jim Manning, and other voice pupils of Lilian's are planning a concert to benefit the Sullivan Memorial Scholarship Fund.

The pupils who loved her ranged from high school young people to college department heads, from a gospel singer in Mableton to a New York City Opera star. Each was special to her. Each returned her love.

One who knew her perhaps the longest and the best first met her as an eleven-year-old schoolgirl in New York City, when she went home from school with a schoolmate named John Sullivan to meet his singer-mother. The little girl began a lifelong friendship then with Lilian—and became her daughter-in-law.

Now Ruth Sullivan is a professional voice coach herself in Corpus Christi, Texas. She has spent many weeks here recently putting Lilian's affairs in order and making thoughtful arrangements to honor this remarkable lady.

The college memorial gifts are a fitting way to remember Lilian. Those of us who knew her have many other ways to remember her, too, all of them happy ones.

FEBRUARY, 1977

(Note: Since 1977, The Cobb Arts Council has named its annual award to an individual contributing significantly to the arts in our community, The Lilian Bennett Sullivan Award.)

Strictly for the Birds

If you have the winter blahs, here's a prescription: fill up the bird feeder, sit near the window with binoculars and a cup of tea close at hand, and get ready for the show!

Before you can say "tufted titmouse," little fellows will be zooming in from all directions to brighten up the bleak gray landscape with their lovely colors and fascinating antics.

First thing you know, you'll be a Bird Watcher! Bird Watchers aren't the weird, wimpy characters they're cracked up to be. A lot of nice people are Bird Watchers.

Georgia is a great place for this hobby. We have many kinds of birds here in Georgia year round, and many other varieties migrate just this far in winter. Right now with trees and earth bare and exposed, it's easy to see their bright blobs of color against black trees and gray sky.

The reason birds fly south in winter—besides that old vaudeville bit of "being too far to walk"—is not to get out of the cold weather, but to get food. Worms, seeds, and other food sources are more available here and easier to get to than in the frozen north.

Even so, when we have a spell of ice or snow, they could use a handout. Make sure your bird feeder is placed near bushes or trees. Birds like to eat near cover. Remember to scatter some seed on the ground for the birds who are ground feeders. (Plus extra for those pushy little squirrels who always horn in.) And if you're extra generous, tack up some suet in nylon net on a tree trunk.

It won't take long for word to spread that you're throwing an al fresco party. You'll have a style show to watch with your guests in their colorful duds: goldfinches in burnished yellow-gold, rosey-pink purple finches, sassy little chickadees wearing jaunty black berets, cardinals who seem to know they're the most beautiful of all in their brilliant designer-red.

"Eating like a bird" is a crazy expression, according to our environmentalist daughter, Patty. Birds eat several times their weight in food each day! It takes that much to replace the heat they lose, due to their high rate of metabolism.

They also heat their bodies out in that cold winter air by trapping air under their ruffled up feathers. It's a natural down insulation which works as well as those down jackets the kids order from L. L. Bean, and it's a whole lot cheaper.

Their feathers are the first known "zippers." Each quill has tiny barbs or teeth. When pulled apart they "unzip"; when closed they lock together again. When a bird preens himself, he's not slicking down his feathers to impress a lady friend, like "The Fonz" of the aviary world. He's redistributing oil to protect his feathers from moisture—an instant rain coat.

One more fascinating fact I've learned from Patty: birds are such territorial creatures, they even follow a territorial path each time they go to the bird feeder! Watch and see. They come and go from the same twig, same branch, same tree, to the same side of the feeder, over and over.

Bird watching is a hobby our whole family enjoys together. We keep a big bird book (*Birds of North America*) and the binoculars (out of the case, easy to grab if we see something interesting) on the kitchen table. In the front of the book is our list we keep of each bird variety spotted in our yard and the date we first saw them. So far we have 25 varieties, beginning with "slate-colored junco" and ending with "rose-breasted grosbeak."

By one of the entries we jotted down the actual moment when we saw the bird . . . it was a hummingbird, spotted at 8:30 a.m.! Reading that

entry brings back the thrill of a very magical moment when we saw that rare tiny miracle in motion.

Take a bird out to dinner this week. You'll both enjoy it.

FEBRUARY 1, 1980

A Valentine for Garfield

Dear Garfield,

Happy Valentine's Day!

As the world's most famous cat you must get a lot of fan mail. I hope you read this—it's a special valentine letter to you . . . and it could change your life.

We want to bring you love! It doesn't seem right that the world's most eligible bachelor cat, the Tom Selleck of tomcats, should have no sweetheart of your own. And we have just the girl for you.

Her name is Liza. Remember that name—Liza. One day the world will speak both your names in but a single breath if we can bring you together, just as they name the other truly great lovers of history.

Romeo and Juliet . . . Tristan and Isolde . . . Prince Charles and Princess Diana . . . Garfield and Liza!

You may think you have no time for love. Your superstar life is so full posing for cartoons, dictating Garfield books, endorsing Garfield buttons and notebooks and posters.

But admit it, Garfield. Isn't it lonely at the top? When you have wrapped up your latest "Kibbles and Bits" commercial, done your last take of "Chow-Chow-Chow," and gone home to your own little basket—don't you miss a soft, purring female in your life?

We know it's hard for a macho guy to admit he needs anyone. Frankly though, Garfield, that's your problem. You're overdoing this macho bit. If you keep on swiping goldfish, beating up on dogs, and tormenting that nice man who feeds you—pretty soon it won't be funny any more.

You may be a tiger in the ratings now, but next year you could be a has-been alley cat, skulking around in back alleys looking for old tuna fish cans.

You may not have noticed, but tough males are going out. Tender is in. Alan Alda-type sensitivity is what sells these days. You need Liza to cure you of your redneck fighting ways.

Why do we think Liza is the cat for you?

First, she is gorgeous. Beautiful, soft gray fur that has such a silvery sheen it makes an aureole around her, like a Silver Cloud Rolls Royce. Very classy. And eyes that are a cool, clear jewel green.

She does have one flaw: a tail that is shorter than it used to be. It happened when she got caught between two bachelors fighting for her affection. We think her short tail keeps her from being vain.

Another reason Liza is right for you is that she has a background in show business. Our daughter found her backstage at the theatre at Six Flags Over Georgia. She's named for Liza Minelli, because she sings, dances, and even plays piano (like Victor Borge, using various parts of her body on the keyboard).

You'll be glad to know she enjoys sports, too. She's a runner, doing laps through the house each morning. She climbs well. I think she rappels. How else could she get to the places she does? And she hunts. You would enjoy her trophies more than we do. We keep begging her not to bring moles and chipmunks up on our back porch. She even plays football—defensive tackle. She can stop any human, when she's hungry, by circling his feet at every step.

Liza's personality is just what you need in a woman. She is assertive and liberated. Any other kind of female would bring out the worst in you. She'd end up in a shelter for abused cat wives, and you'd be under indictment by the Humane Society.

There's one thing you should know: due to a certain surgical procedure, Liza can never have little kittens. But that's probably best. The world is not ready for any offspring you and Liza together could produce. We need to solve the nuclear arms problem first.

If you want Liza for your Valentine, tell your agent to put a want ad in the *Marietta Daily Journal*.

Frankly we think it could be the love affair of the century—un-categorically.

Sincerely,
Liza's Mistress

FEBRUARY 10, 1982

A Formula for Love

Ever notice how some of the worst family hassles can lead to some of the best understandings?

On our small kitchen chalkboard is a reminder of such a time for us. It's a special note from our daughter, Katie—so special we haven't wanted to erase it. We don't use the blackboard for phone messages and shopping lists any more. We keep Katie's note on it; and when the chalk gets smudged, we fill it in again.

It's a family classic and now hangs over our breakfast table.

What does it say?

Nothing we didn't already know. Yet something we badly needed to hear. It makes a nice story to tell you for Valentine's Day.

One night last year Katie came to her dad for help with her algebra homework. As an engineer, he's the one that can help with math (not me!); he finds it as natural as breathing and can usually show them what they need to know. Unless, that is, they're using "new math" techniques and terms he doesn't understand.

That was the case this time. Dallas knew how to solve Katie's algebra, of course, but not in the way she was being taught. The more he tried to help, the less Katie understood. The less she understood, the more anxious and defensive she grew.

Patience waned as tempers rose. Of course, as mothers will, I had to jump into the fray, only making it worse.

The algebra problem by now had escalated into a family problem, a scene of hostility, hurt feelings and tears. By bedtime only a halfhearted truce had been negotiated.

The next morning, feeling down about the whole thing and dreading the day, I went into the kitchen to start breakfast.

Instantly my gloom turned to joy!

Propped against the coffeepot where I couldn't miss it was the kitchen blackboard with Katie's note. She must have written it late the night before, after we had gone to bed.

It was one of the most creative ideas I've ever seen and it lifted my heart in thanksgiving. Our daughter was telling us she loved us and forgave us. I knew she still might not understand the math principle her dad was trying to get across. But far more important was the life principle she did understand, expressed in her note. Not new math—but old truth.

She had summed up a verse from the "Love Chapter" of the Bible, the 13th chapter of First Corinthians: "And now abideth faith, hope, and love, these three, but the greatest of these is love." Somehow she got the idea to do it with math!

She had drawn the math symbol for greater than: >. And her note was like this. . . .

Good Morning!
Love > Faith & Hope
(I Cor. 13:13)
Have a nice day!

FEBRUARY 10, 1982

Jury Duty

Help! I'm a prisoner in the Richard B. Russell Building in downtown Atlanta!

I've been held captive here for two weeks and the end of my sentence is nowhere in sight.

I have eleven cellmates. You know us by the badges we wear. They say "United States District Court Juror."

We wear it at all times, as lepers used to wear a sign, "Unclean." It separates us from the rest of humanity. We're not supposed to fraternize with anyone else.

Two weeks ago this group of people were strangers to one another. Now we know each other very well—better than we ever wanted to! We sit together in two straight rows in the courtroom all day. We take breaks together in our special Jurors' Waiting Room. We eat lunch together in our special Jurors' Dining Room. The only thing we don't do is walk together in lock step down the halls.

They don't keep us overnight. We get to go home each afternoon—just in time for the rush hour traffic. We drive in each morning—in rush hour traffic. All in all I'd much prefer being locked up overnight.

Actually I'm kidding. If you read this, Judge Shoob, Your Honor, sir, please know this is just a joke. I realize you could pronounce those three little words any time . . . *contempt of court*. I sure don't want you and me to have any misunderstanding, please Your Honor.

The truth is that, except for developing prison pallor and shattered nerves from driving bumper to bumper from Marietta to Atlanta and back each day, I am finding this entire experience interesting and educational.

This is the first time I've ever served on a jury. I've been a registered voter in Georgia almost 30 years but I've never been called to any jury duty before—not county or district, civil or criminal, petit or grand. (Pardon me for throwing these terms around but I'm fascinated with my newly acquired knowledge.)

On my first day, excited and apprehensive, I reported as instructed to the Jury Lounge of the Richard Russell Building to begin my two weeks' duty. (It *can* last longer than two weeks, if you're put on a complicated case . . . which in my case, pardon the pun, has happened.)

Here are my impressions of the juror experience, first time around:

The court prepares us well for our duties. We were first shown a good movie and given follow-up instructions. I learned that all violations of federal law are handled in the U.S. District Court. In our North Georgia

District 46 counties are covered! There are eleven judges and eleven courtrooms.

I've been very impressed with the efficient method by which we're told if we are needed each day. Each juror is given a number. Each night after court closes in the afternoon, we are expected to telephone the code-a-phone and hear instructions for the next day. If my individual number is called out to report, I go; if not, I'm excused. This eliminates a lot of wasted time.

For each jury trial, the lawyers involved are allowed to question three times the number of jurors needed, and then make their selections by eliminating ("striking") those they don't want.

To me it's a dramatic, mystical, fascinating procedure. Some of the questions the lawyers ask are predictable (age, spouse, children, occupation, etc.) Some are totally off-the-wall! They're trying to find out how your mind works, what your emotional/intellectual make-up is, whether you're a maverick or will be pliable in a group—anything they can squeeze out of you!

Their final choices are based on reasons known only to them . . . except that they want you to be good to their clients if they're defense attorneys and to uphold law and order if they're prosecutors.

If you are selected for a case, your job is to listen to all the testimony, observe and weigh the evidence, and decide—based on facts, not feelings—if the law has been violated.

Judge Shoob cautioned us carefully not to receive any information outside the courtroom and not to discuss the case with anyone else (not even our fellow jurors) until we go into our final deliberation.

In our system, of course, every single defendant is assumed innocent until proved guilty "beyond reasonable doubt." Jurors take their solemn oath "to well and truly try to render a true verdict."

They tell us we don't have to be experts on the law. The judge serves that role. He is called "the judge of the law" and we are called "the judge of the fact."

Throughout our trial Judge Shoob, like a benevolent father, turns to us and explains patiently every step of the procedure and any legal implications. When we're through hearing testimony (it seems to be going on and on in this particular case), he will finally go over with us the charges and laws we are to apply to them.

But . . . the buck stops with us.

When we go behind our closed door, it's all up to us.

This is why, when a jury enters the jury box in the courtroom each morning, everyone else rises in respect. This is why, at the end of each day, I find myself exhausted, as do my eleven "cellmates."

We are trying to give our total concentration to everything said and shown to us. We are responsible for what will happen in these people's lives. We are responsible for this aspect of justice or injustice in our society.

"Man's capacity for justice makes democracy possible," Reinhold Niebuhr said.

You and I, together, make it happen. I'm glad I've had the opportunity.

FEBRUARY 3, 1983

Old Friends

Last week Dallas and I packed, told the children goodby, and took off for a week's vacation.

A vacation in February, unless you go skiing in Colorado or cruising in the Caribbean, is crazy. But there we were on our way to Hilton Head Island, usually a beautiful place, but deserted, windy, and cold at this time of year.

We had the best reason in the world for going: we were meeting old friends. The weather wouldn't matter as much as just being there together.

Poets and sages agree on the value of old friends. "Make new friends but keep the old . . ." And when good friends come in pairs, so that both members of a couple are congenial with another couple, it's a double blessing.

Our reunion last week was with three couples whose friendships have spanned more than 20 years of our lives. While the sea gulls swooped over the lonely beach and empty boats creaked at the docks at Harbor Town, we had a wonderful time.

All of us had married and moved to Marietta in the 1950s. Lockheed Georgia had opened, bringing Dallas and Ralph. Bob was playing ball for the Atlanta Crackers. And John had just come home to Marietta from the Army.

Marietta was booming then and housing was scarce. We rented tiny houses just across "The Four-Lane"—all there was then to East Marietta.

The baby boom was on, too, and we did our share. Among us, we had 13 children.

Our social life revolved around children's birthday parties and evenings of bridge, when we'd practice "Gracious Living" by serving pie on our wedding china.

On Saturdays our husbands, desperate to escape our little houses filled with playpens, drying diapers on folding racks, and zwieback crumbs, played golf. Never mind what the weather was. Never mind none of us could afford to join the country club, and the nearest public golf course was all the way to Canton.

Small wonder that when one of our group had the bright idea, in the summer of '58, of taking a weekend trip somewhere together—without the children—we jumped at the chance!

Baby sitters were booked, grandparents appealed to, and we descended en masse in July on the grand old Highlands Country Club in North Carolina—famous for its quiet elegance and style, its velvety green golf course and sumptuous food.

Gracious Living at last! We tried to quiet down our noisy exuberance but it was hard. After all, it was our first real vacation since our honeymoons. We slept late, dined leisurely, were served impeccably. It was a dream come true.

By Sunday we were ready to get back to our children—but resolved to do it again next year.

And so we did. Not just for one year, but for ten. One trip each summer. Sapphire Valley, Hendersonville, Asheville—but most often, back to Highlands Country Club, our first love and our favorite. Thanks to healthy children and patient grandmothers and plenty of calendar and budget juggling, we managed somehow every year.

Then in 1968 Alice and Bob Boring moved to California. And the next year John and Ella Jo Shell moved, too . . . to their very own mountain inn. They bought Hemlock Inn in Bryson City, N.C. We shouldn't have been as surprised as we were. Every time we'd go on a trip John would say in his soft drawl, "Some day I'm going to have me a place like this."

Sarah and Ralph Farrar were the only ones left in Marietta to keep us company.

After ten years without our "Four Seasons Club" trips (Alan Alda's movie reminded us of ourselves!), last week we had a lot of catching up to do. We looked at wedding pictures of our children—those babies we used to leave behind. We heard tapes of the Shells' little granddaughters. We listened to Alice's stories about her new career directing a retirement center. And they made hilariously impossible suggestions for my columns.

We laughed long and hard at memories of mishaps . . . the time a waiter at Grove Park Inn in Asheville turned an entire pitcher of water over on Ralph's head . . . the terrible time we teased Ella Jo too much and she fled from the room crying and we felt awful . . . our first breakfast at Highlands, when the waitress asked Dallas "Do you want peaches, blueberries, raspberries or honeydew melon?" and he answered "YES"—and ate them all.

We laughed too at our new bifocals and gray hair (Sarah was the only one with neither) and pill bottles.

But I thought everyone looked young and handsome, and that there was something as solid and lasting in our friendships as the sea and sand and skies of Hilton Head.

Music I heard with you was more than music,
And bread I broke with you was more than bread.*

I don't know who Conrad Aiken was thinking of when he wrote those lines but I'd like to tell these friends they're the tune in the music, the substance to the bread, of all our celebrations together. They'd come up with a joke, but I'd still like to tell them.

Make new friends, but keep the old. Especially when they're as dear as these.

*Credit: from *Bread and Music* by Conrad Aiken

MARCH 10, 1978

The General's Lady

"There, on that sofa, sit two ladies whose husbands probably did more for the growth of this county than any other men."

The two ladies were Mrs. Lucius D. Clay and Mrs. L. M. Blair. The one paying them tribute was Bill Kinney of *The Marietta Daily Journal*. We were in the office of Cobb solicitor, Herb Rivers, where Mrs. Clay had dropped by to visit her grandson Chuck, an assistant solicitor.

Bill's remark referred especially to the key roles played by "Rip" Blair and Gen. Clay—along with County Attorney Jimmy Carmichael and Cobb County Commissioner George McMillan—in bringing Dobbins Air Force Base to Marietta.

Dobbins made it possible for Bell Aircraft to open a plant here, which in turn led to Lockheed Georgia—Cobb County's largest single industry.

Their joint effort was just one more chapter in a longstanding association of the two men, begun when their fathers were law partners in Marietta, and continuing in the friendship today of their widows.

Mrs. Clay, the former Marjorie McKeown of Newark, N.J., met her future husband when he was a West Point cadet (top ten, Class of 1918.)

Chuck: "Is it true, grandmother, that he proposed to you after only three dates?"

Mrs. Clay: "Yes, but they were spread out over a period of time."

(Even then the young West Pointer showed he was an excellent decision maker; their marriage lasted 60 years until the general's death last spring.)

His long, illustrious military career took them to many places but they came home to Marietta often to visit his mother, and when they were here, they enjoyed good times with the Blairs.

"People thought of the general as dignified and stern," says Mrs. Blair, "but he certainly wasn't when he and Rip got together!"

She recalls that the general liked to do one-handed handstands. After watching one of these performances (Gen. Clay was 70 at the time), Mrs. Blair's young grandson, John Renshaw, declared "Gen. Clay is my very favorite general!"

When you visit with Mrs. Clay, you have a rare opportunity to get a personal glance at some of the most significant events of this century. Her husband and his associates were the movers and shakers of the free world before, during, and after World War II.

The friends she speaks of ring with the sound of history: MacArthur, Eisenhower, Patton, Bradley, LeMay.

"MacArthur could be completely charming when he liked you." A pause and a twinkle—"He liked me."

Eisenhower and Clay served together on Gen. MacArthur's staff in the Philippines.

"We lived right across the hall from one another. Mamie and I are still good friends. I saw her only last week in Washington."

Clay—always the army engineer—was personally chosen by Ike to be his top deputy, after successfully unsnarling traffic supply problems in France.

Mrs. Clay's memories of living in Berlin during the tri-partite years after World War II are especially poignant. Clay was Commander-In-Chief of the U.S. European Command and Military Governor of the U.S. Zone in Germany.

She recalls that Berlin was a devastated, flattened city where the people coped with desperate poverty. Army regulations forbade U.S. personnel from fraternizing with the Germans. But that didn't stop the compassionate General's Lady. Each week she would fill her large knitting bag with her personal rations and her husband's (coffee, chocolate, chewing gum), and share them with the Germans.

Finally she felt guilty enough to tell her husband what she was doing. "You can't go wrong doing right," he told her.

Mrs. Clay led a successful drive to bring hospital supplies, food and clothing to the children of Germany. "Mary Margaret McBride, well-known journalist and radio personality of the day, helped us by telling about it on her program, and Pan-Am flew them overseas free."

Did the general ever fear that the famous Airlift (the free world's way of thwarting the Soviet blockade) would fail?

"No, he never gave up—for a minute!"

Says Bill Kinney, "Clay was on a spot where too much temper or too little toughness might bring matters to the shooting stage." He showed neither. He came home a hero.

His lovely wife must have been a large part of this man's success. She is a kind, intelligent, beautiful lady. True, she's the only four-star general's wife I've ever met, but I'll have to echo young John Renshaw:

She's my very favorite general's wife!

FEBRUARY 23, 1979

Did Anything Exciting Happen While I Was Away?

I was just breading the pork chops for dinner and considering cooked apples to go with them when I heard the banging of the back door. Dallas was home from his business trip.

"Hi, honey. How's everybody? Did anything exciting happen while I was away?"

He asks that question every time. And I always wonder what on earth he expects to hear. Car pools, committee meetings, and laundry sorting are not the stuff of high adventure.

I'd like to rock him with an off-the-wall answer . . ."Oh yes! So much I hardly know where to begin. The White House called. The President wants my advice on Mideastern policies. *Reader's Digest* phoned, begging me for an article. And Edna Lee called from high school to say our children are so brilliant and well-adjusted, it's a privilege to have them at Marietta High."

But I resist the sarcasm. The question is really his way of plugging in to our lives while he's been away—because he loves us.

I bring our cups of tea to the kitchen table and start recapping the week.

"Monday I took Wendy to the vet. He kept her overnight, but thinks she'll be o.k."

Did you ever drive alone with a frightened cat? Wendy had scrambled from the back seat to my shoulder, dug in her claws, gouged her way across my chest and lap, and finally lodged firmly on top of my feet. Our trip across town was one of wild stops and starts and frantic grabs to remove her from the gas pedal.

But the wicked looking bite in her soft fur would heal, and her soothing purr would continue to calm our rambunctious household.

"Tuesday we took the baby for your folks to see."

My husband's parents, no longer able to drive, hadn't yet seen two-month-old Gary. Tuesday was the red-letter day. Dixie dressed him in his spiffiest little blue suit, loaded all his gear in the car (I had forgotten—so much for one so small!) and we made the 100 mile trip down to Perry.

It was one of those special times I'll always remember:

Daddy Ryle coming out to meet us in the driveway, a broad grin on his kindly face. Mother Ryle waving from the big window in the kitchen. And a moment later, both of them gazing down at the miracle staring up from his plastic infant seat—their first great-grandchild! Soft red hair, solemn blue eyes, perfect little hands, and right on cue—a heart melting, million dollar smile!

What else had happened this week?

Buddy had phoned from college. Physics was giving him trouble. (How I miss his tall, gangly exuberance, the bear hugs, our rap sessions now that he's through adolescent rejection and considers me a real person again.)

Patty, our career daughter, came out from Atlanta for dinner. She directs an outdoor activity center for inner city children, and her enthusiasm for the program, the youngsters, and their parents convinces me she's found her niche in life. (But surely it was only yesterday she and Dixie were playing with their Chatty Cathy and Tiny Tears.)

We speak of Katie and Stephen, the two youngest still at home—their problems with juggling school-band-soccer-cheerleader schedules, "going steady" decisions (or whatever today's jargon calls it) and other worries. Our older kids tell us we're too lenient with them! Somehow rules about curfew and phone call limits and other teen-age hassles don't seem so important when we remember how soon they, too, will be gone.

We discuss Ken's new job at Lockheed. (How great to have a son-in-law we love so easily.) I fill him in on the illness of a friend in the Sunday School class Dallas teaches, and a neighbor hurting from a broken marriage.

Did anything exciting happen while he was away?

No, not really.

Yes—if life itself is exciting. Old people and young, their joys and pains and struggles, the many ways each finds to grow, relate, and celebrate the lives God gave us.

And that's about as much excitement as one woman can handle.

SPRING

Spring Will Be a Little Late This Year

Will spring ever come this year?

It seems forever since the crocus first popped through the hard earth in late January. It's always so early, so cold when they appear. I want to push their little heads back down, tell them, "Not yet, too soon, go back to sleep." But they insist.

They unfurl their tiny purple trumpets in the morning sunshine each day and form a solid bugle corps in our front yard. I wish I could hear their trumpet fanfare.

"Hail to the Chief" announces our president. "God Save the Queen" heralds the British ruler. The fanfare announcing spring's approach must surely be impressive. Maybe it's one of the mockingbird's 16 songs—but who knows which one?

The jonquils usually bloom too soon, also. Their bright golden banners flash through dreary rains of February and bitter winds of March. Bundled up in warm coats, we look at them with despair. They must be kidding; surely spring is not here yet.

And sure enough, it's not.

A week ago today we woke up, looked outside, and—as the kids say—flipped out. *Snow*!

March was almost over, and in Georgia it was snowing.

Will you ever forget that unbelievable sight—snow sifting down its powdered sugar topping over the pink cherry blossoms, yellow forsythia sprays, starry white pear blooms?

As I looked out the window at our weeping cherry tree by the street, its delicate pink blossoms covered with fluffy white rosettes like a fancy wedding cake, that line from A.E. Housman's beautiful poem came to mind about "the cherry hung with snow."

Of course he was using poetic imagery to describe snowy white cherry blossoms. But it's literally true in Marietta this year. The cherry tree is hung with snow!

One of my good friends, who loves literature and knows it far better than I do, tells me she doesn't know that Housman poem. Neither do my children. I guess they skip it in school nowadays. I'm going to correct that oversight right now.

It's one of the most sensitive, lovely poems I know. It captures so well the yearning springtime induces in every heart, the desire to hold fast to its elusive, fleeting beauty. Looking through the house for it, I found a copy in a great paperback book, *Immortal Poems of the English Language*, (Washington Square Press) that sold for—can you believe it—ninety-five cents when it came out in 1952!

Loveliest of trees, the cherry now
Is hung with bloom along the bough,
And stands about the woodland ride
Wearing white for Eastertide.

Now, of my threescore years and ten,
Twenty will not come again,
And take from seventy springs a score,
It only leaves me fifty more.

And since to look at things in bloom
Fifty springs are little room,
About the woodlands I will go
To see the cherry hung with snow.

Housman's poem reminds me of Edna St. Vincent Millay's "O World, I cannot hold thee close enough." It touches the same chord of aching sadness.

The Germans have a word for it: *angst*. It's deeper than nostalgia. Nostalgia means we wish for something that used to be. Angst means we wish for something that never was—and never can be.

It's the feeling I get from a Strauss waltz. And from John Denver's singing—and Pavarotti's. And from a beautiful poem.

And from springtime.

Especially when the cherry tree is hung with snow.

MARCH 31, 1983

Don't Crack No Acorns for No Chickens!

"Good for you, Mama. You said, 'No!'—I can't *believe* it!"

I couldn't blame Dixie for being surprised. I was surprised myself. I had just turned down a request to help with an organization I belong to. Learning to say "No" isn't easy after a lifetime of saying "Yes." But I'm learning.

I'm trying to remember a wonderful family story my mother once told me about the chickens and the acorns.

It seems that when my mother's Granddaddy Copeland (my great-grandfather) lost his first wife, Martha Adair, in childbirth, it left him with five small children to raise and his South Carolina plantation to run. He needed help.

Martha's mother, a dear old lady they called "Mud," came to live with them and help raise the children. Granddaddy Copeland appreciated it, but he told Mud that when the children were grown up and gone, he wanted to look for another wife and marry again.

And that's what he did. After they were all grown—Uncle Johnny, Aunt Janie, Aunt Sally Hamp, Isaac (my grandfather) and the youngest, Uncle Billy—Granddaddy found another wife: a nice spinster lady named Miss Hattie.

Miss Hattie had never lived on a farm and knew nothing at all about life in the country.

One night at the supper table Miss Hattie told her husband:

"Mr. Copeland, I noticed today what a fine crop of acorns we have in the yard. It seems to me if you would crack those acorns and shell them, they would make nice food for the chickens."

They always said Granddaddy was an easy-going man.

He didn't blink an eye at Miss Hattie's innocent but appalling suggestion. He just put down his napkin, leaned back in his chair and quietly told her,

"I never cracked *no* acorns for *no* chickens."

That settled that.

I'm afraid I've cracked a lot of acorns in my time.

I cringe now to remember how often my children, when they were small, put up with a tired, cross mother who got her spirit of altruism mixed with false guilt and tried too much.

Today's young women seem to have their act together better than my generation did. Dixie and Patty have fulltime jobs and they *know* to limit the options on their precious free time. But my generation wanted to be good homemakers and mothers, active P.T.A. members, Junior Leaguers and garden clubbers, serve in our church women's groups, teach Sunday School—the whole works. The Super Women.

And many times what we did was crack acorns . . . spending our time in jobs that could have been done another way, or by someone else, or left undone.

(One of my worst memories is the year I served as chairman for residential United Way solicitations in my part of town—which was from the Marietta square to the north city limits. When some of the neighborhood chairmen didn't come through, who knocked on doors up one street and down another, block after block? You got it. United Way is a worthy cause . . . but the entire outcome wasn't my personal responsibility!)

Now in these middle years of life I'm understanding how important it is to make my *own* choices, based on my *own* priorities. I'm the only person who really knows how much time, energy, and commitment I can give to whatever I do.

I'm learning that some activities are fine for others, but not for me. (I have my own list of "acorn-shelling"—you have yours.) I will probably always *want* to do more than I'm *able* to do, and I have to make choices whether I like it or not. Some activities are such a drag no one should do them at all!

Only when I choose freely, without feeling manipulated or setting false standards, can I do my best and be happy about what I'm doing.

Don't get me wrong: we all have to crack a few acorns now and then. Everything worth doing in life has a certain tedious routine connected with it. A parent has to change diapers, a teacher grade homework, a business person comply with boring and time-consuming government regulations. (Right now I'm into my sixth straight week of jury duty. It's amazing, in the due process of law, how much "acorn-shelling" goes on in a courtroom!)

But we need to learn all we can about goal-setting, time management, and assertiveness.

Someone has said, "Before a man can do certain things, there must be other things he will not do."

I like Granddaddy's version better. . . . "Don't crack *no* acorns for *no* chickens!"

MARCH 3, 1983

Beginning Drivers, Hysterical Parents

Stephen just had his fifteenth birthday.

If you've ever had a teenage child, you can read between the lines and know that our traumatic nightmare is about to begin: The Year of the Beginning Driver.

If he were our first child, I'd probably be sentimental about this Rite of Passage. After all, there's something quite touching in a child's eagerness to grow up. His pride in each new sign that he's getting older—the birthday cakes and candles, the new shoes a size bigger, the loose tooth. Always pressing on to be old enough for school, old enough for Boy Scouts, for something else special.

Getting old enough for a Beginner's Driving permit is the modern version of grandpa's first long pants, grandma pinning up her hair. It's Christopher Robin leaving his friends in the Enchanted Forest. Jackie Paper saying goodby to Puff, the Magic Dragon. (I don't pay attention to the double-talk about drugs in this song. My children and I took it as a sad, sweet fairy tale, and we've always loved it.)

I'm not sentimental about having a Beginning Driver. Stephen is not our first child, but our fifth. I know what we're in for. I'm paranoid.

Being the parent of a Beginning Driver is one of the most excruciating experiences of parenthood.

Dixie, our oldest, managed to have her first wreck before she ever drove a car! Right in the driveway one evening, showing a spend-the-night friend what she knew about the car, she turned on the engine and zap! It took off. She had remembered how to start it. What she forgot was how to stop it. The car zoomed across the street and into the neighbor's driveway. The neighbor's mailbox put an end to her driving . . . and her driving put an end to the neighbor's mailbox.

We thought having a wreck in the driveway was some sort of record. But no. Another child of ours did it, too—not once but twice.

The second time it was absolutely spectacular. The car catapulted down the bank and through the trees. The man from Crain's Wrecker Service never did figure out how it got there because the space between the trees was smaller than the car.

We stalled Stephen off as long as we could. Saturday, we couldn't get his birth certificate because it's in the vault and the bank was closed. Monday, the State Patrol office wasn't open. But Tuesday was the day. He passed the written test and come out with permit, smile, and a definite swagger. Once more, into the fray!

Having a Beginning Driver is like owning your own personal Scream Machine—who needs Six Flags? Just get in the car with your young driver at the wheel, and scream away.

Actually, screaming is a bad thing to do. Your neophyte driver is already nervous, so hyped-up that your screaming makes him overreact and everything gets worse.

You should speak calmly. But have you ever tried saying, "Look out, we're going to crash!" in a calm voice?

You can begin each remark quietly, under tight control. But then you lose your cool and each remark ends in hysteria.

"That's fine," (spoken quietly) ". . . now stay over on our side of the . . . LOOK OUT! (scream) CAN'T YOU SEE THAT CAR COMING?" (You're overreacting, too, as the approaching car is still two blocks away, but you're in shock and can't help it.)

Meanwhile your Beginning Driver is frantically trying to do his thing. His only goal is to somehow keep the car in the road. He does this by wobbling around in fascinating configurations. He underestimates. Then he overcorrects. Power steering adds an extra thrill.

He steers in zig-zags, curves, angles, and loops. The only way he doesn't steer is straight.

Speed at first is no consideration. Who cares? Your child is too busy steering to think of anything else, like brakes or gas pedal. And you're on a suicide course anyway, fast or slow.

Slow Beginning Drivers pick up a whole Conga line of impatient drivers creeping slowly behind them, like a funeral procession, anxious to pass. You learn not to look back in the rear view mirror. The rude gestures they're making, you wouldn't believe.

Speed will fluctuate regardless, as erratically as everything else with a Beginning Driver. Fast, slow, fast, slow, fast, slow. The fits and starts jerk you back and forth so much it's a wonder parents don't get whiplash. I think the reason is that at the same time you're jerking back and forth, you're also zig-zagging from side to side. The two motions counteract one another.

I won't go into the other catastrophic details of a Year Of The Beginning Driver: like learning to shift gears, to pass a car, to parallel park.

This weekend Stephen's father plans to take him to St. Catherine's Court, a quiet little street around the corner, for his first driving lesson. Batten down the hatches, neighbors, here we come.

March 17, 1978

Kaleidoscope: The Ides and Arts of March

March is a terrible time. The Ides are only the beginning. Taxes, of course, and miserable wind and rain that crush the daffodils 'til they droop on their stalks and wipe out all hopes of an early spring.

On a wet, gusty day last Monday I stopped by the Cobb Civic Center to check out preparations for Kaleidoscope, the county schools' art festival. Splashing through great puddles in the parking lot, I made my way to Hudgens Hall.

All around me strange figures were hobbling through the rain—teachers loaded down with boxes of children's art, trying to protect them from the rain by crouching over their valuable cargo and juggling umbrellas.

At the door Dr. Barbara Shaw, visual art coordinator for the Cobb Schools, had a bright smile on her pretty face. (I wondered if, inside, she was humming to herself "Rainy Days and Mondays Always Get Me Down.") Barbara is chairman of Kaleidoscope.

Inside the place was in chaos. It looked like an advance crew setting up for Barnum and Bailey.

Boyd McKeown and John Lawhorn were rigging up the p.a. system, placing pianos, stages, and risers for various performing groups. Boyd is Instrumental Music Supervisor and John is Choral Supervisor for the Cobb Schools. Stella Ross, Drama Supervisor, was running around doing a dozen things at once. Jim Bruner, Cultural Affairs Supervisor for Cobb Parks and Recreation, was making a terrible racket hammering scenery for his Cobb Teen Theatre production. Marilyn Greider, President of the Cobb Arts Council, was checking out schedules with Liz Fields, the Civic Center Manager.

Barbara told me many of her fellow members of the Georgia Council for the Arts plan to come to Kaleidoscope—they visited it last year and were greatly impressed.

I nodded my head at Barbara—but I had my doubts. The whole scene was organized confusion. At least one hoped it was organized. We'd soon find out.

We did. Tuesday morning it all came together. The gym glowed with color, from yellow mums lining the entrance and stairs, from bright colors that swirled and splashed over posters, canvases, montages on myriad surfaces throughout the gym. Our boys and girls had enjoyed one of the greatest pleasures human beings can know—the act of expressing and creating something from their imagination.

On the gym floor, round tables and chairs were ready near the stages for folks to enjoy a snack while they heard musical and drama groups.

Then the children began coming—busload after busload from our city and county schools. At 3:30 in the afternoon the Kincaid School Chorus appeared as the opening act of the performing groups—a new group every 20 minutes 'til 9 each evening, three days in a row. That's a *lot* of performing arts!

In addition, other groups strolled over the floor, such as Sprayberry High School's mime players, the Mossketeers (named for director Mike Moss).

Adults came in after work, many admitting it was the first art exhibit they'd ever seen—including some of the school principals.

By closing time Tuesday 3,000 people had visited Kaleidoscope. At the end of the three days it was clear that the struggle to launch Kaleidoscope last year and to keep it going has been worth it.

Those of us who live here know we have excellent quality of art in many forms—by professionals and amateurs. But it's a well-kept secret.

Now Kaleidoscope is shouting it out loud.

The crowds have been great. Channel 8 and Channel 11 took pictures for their newscasts. Volunteers from the Junior League, Cobb Symphony Guild, and other art support groups are enthusiastic about the potential for Kaleidoscope.

Phil Blackwell, school administrator, says, "I don't see how it can get any better!"

Next year don't miss Kaleidoscope. It can make you smile in the rain. It can even help you make it through March.

MARCH 21, 1980

(Note: Kaleidoscope is a good example of what seed-planting can do. From this nucleus, Cobb County held its first full scale arts festival on Labor Day Weekend, 1984, drawing thousands to enjoy the Cobb Community Symphony; local theatre, ballet, and choral groups; artists and craftsmen. The arts are alive, well, and here to stay.)

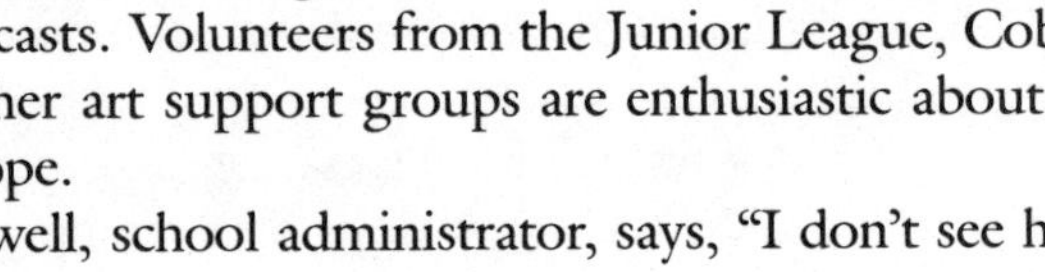

Spring Celebrations

Spring fever comes in many forms.

Right now all creatures great and small seem infected with it, just glad to be alive.

Caroline, our bird dog, can hardly contain her excitement at the end of winter. She's been doing her spring cleaning, dragging her old blanket from the dog house to air in the sun.

Now she's having spring soccer practice with the old cake pan that's her food dish, kicking and tossing it through the air and making a great commotion.

We think she's also trying to build a Par Three Golf Course. She's dug dozens of new holes all over her dog yard, attacking each one with joyous fervor and scattering dirt madly in all directions.

Wendy is much more dignified (a cat would never celebrate spring as overtly as Caroline does), but in her own way she, too, responds to this wonderful season. She's just too cool to show it.

She doesn't hang around the pantry all day waiting for Meow Mix now. She's willing to sit outside, her tawny fur blending with the dappled sun and shade, warming her bones and blinking sleepily as she looks around.

Early in the morning when her bio-rhythms are up, she chases squirrels. This is fine with us because the squirrels keep muscling in on the bird feeder.

One morning recently, while we were eating breakfast, Dallas pointed out the window. "Look!" He directed my gaze to an old black gum tree in our back yard. It is a huge tree and grows at a peculiar slant, so that the tree trunk is almost at a 45 degree angle to the ground. (One of these days it will probably fall over into the Newtons' yard.)

There, carefully walking right up the tree trunk as though it were a gangplank, was Wendy. Higher and higher she climbed, until she was at least 50 feet above the ground.

We held our breath. She looked so tiny up there. A little toy cat, helpless and innocent, framed by leaves and sky.

Only her twitching tail betrayed her heinous intentions. She was stalking a squirrel.

The squirrel, of course, had already gone up there twice as fast, was twice as high, and was not about to be dumb enough to come down while Wendy was around.

After a while she gave it up and started back. Her descent was even more hairy to watch than her climb had been. Slipping, sliding, catching hold with her claws, scrabbling down further, sliding again—'til finally she made it safely to the ground!

We sighed with relief and poured a second cup of coffee.

Now Wendy's caper is a daily habit. When she can't be found on the ground, she's up in the black gum tree.

The birds at our feeder now really put on a show, flashing so many gorgeous rainbow colors (blue, red, gold, purple), it's obvious their creator has a flair for color and beauty.

And after this unusually harsh winter, the dogwoods seem unusually full of blossoms. Our woods sparkle with their snowy white, brilliant blooms against a background of tender pale green.

Maybe Nature's trying to tell us her war with the earth is over for another winter, she's unfurled the white banners of peace, and we're invited to the celebration.

APRIL 14, 1978

Leo Aikman

"Did you read Leo today?"

That was a question we asked one another often in Georgia, in the 1950's and '60s.

Leo Aikman's daily column in the *Atlanta Constitution* was always good for a story you wanted to pass on to someone else. The problem was it was sort of like the *Reader's Digest*—they'd probably read it, too. It was a very popular newspaper feature, in a day when we read the papers more.

Each year at the University of Georgia, the Journalism School and the Georgia Press Association name someone to the Georgia Newspaper Hall of Fame.

This year, five years after Leo's death (the minimum time required for this honor), they named Leo. I'm so glad that his widow Ira and daughter Susan could be on hand for the ceremonies recently in Athens.

When you want to know what a man was *really* like, you ask his family. When you talk with Ira ("The Lady Who Reads Over My Shoulder," Leo called her) and Susan (The Redhead), it's clear their love and admiration for Leo was a bright and shining light in their lives.

Ira says, "Leo was my life—and Susan was our bonus."

She met Leo in Mrs. Abbott's Tearoom (now the Brickworks) at the historic Kennesaw House in Marietta. She was a young school teacher from South Carolina and had come to teach Latin at Marietta High School. He was the new Park Historian at Kennesaw Mountain National Battlefield Park.

Theirs was an unusually close, happy marriage for 37 years.

Susan says, "I never minded being the daughter of someone famous because he was so wonderful." You may remember the moving column Susan wrote in our newspaper after Leo died. I kept it because it was such a beautiful tribute—and because he and my own father were friends.

In it Susan said, "I may be biased but I don't think there's ever been a better person than Leo Aikman and I know the world is a better place for the threescore years and ten he spent here."

Leo didn't start out as a writer. He majored in history at DePauw U. in his native Indiana (Phi Beta Kappa), got his master's in history at the U. of Michigan, and joined the U.S. National Park Service, which sent him down south to Kennesaw Park.

He joined Marietta Rotary Club, began writing their weekly newsletter, the RotaLight, and that's how he came to Otis Brumby, Sr.'s attention. Mr. Brumby knew talent when he saw it. He invited Leo to become editor of the weekly *Cobb County Times*. Leo took the job for several years. In 1949 he moved on to the *Atlanta Constitution* and began the columns that made him so beloved throughout Georgia.

Leo wrote humor without a sting, inspiration without being preachy, folksy, homespun stories that succeeded with city and country readers because his own genuineness shone through.

He often said, "A stranger is just a friend you haven't met yet."

He knew every small town editor in the state and often quoted them. His own writing is still quoted frequently in the *Reader's Digest*.

He became a popular speaker too—speaking in every state in the union except Hawaii and Alaska.

But he always belonged uniquely to Marietta. He was an elder in First Presbyterian Church here and for many years taught the young couples' class. To everyone he was just plain "Leo," hometown booster and friend.

The summer after Susan's freshman year at Agnes Scott ("when the folks seemed to think I should get a job") she asked Otis Brumby, Jr., for a place at the *Marietta Daily Journal*.

Today she's our capable news editor, carrying the Aikman-Brumby association into the second generation. Says Otis, Jr., "Susan is very valuable to us with her knowledge of the pulse of the community. She's also my

'In-House Grammarian,' since she has that expertise with words her mother had. *She's* 'The One Who Reads Over My Shoulder!'"

Ira graciously loaned me Leo's columns, so I could choose a few quotes to share with you today:

"The candidate called his wife and exclaimed, 'Honey, I've been elected!' 'Honestly?' asked his wife. 'Now, let's not get into that . . .'"

"How to cure a cold: Sit in a tub of high octane gas and strike two matches. The trick is striking the second match."

"Fewer women have ulcers than men because women don't have wives."

"A man who lives on a one-horse farm these days probably has a daughter who rides."

"Good advice for everyone: 'Shut up and listen.'"

"Hospitality meets its greatest test when a new idea drops by uninvited."

Leo closed every speech he gave with the same poem, which was the model for his own life (author anonymous):

'Build a better world,' God said.
I answered, 'How? The world's so large and vast,
And I so small and useless am.
What is there I can do?'
And God, in all his wisdom, said,
'Just build a better you.'

MARCH 22, 1984

Being Middle-aged Means Always Needing Your Glasses

Life after 40 is basically a process of losing things that matter—like hair, teeth, skin, eyesight, figure, and memory.

They all go, or they change their original texture, color or shape so you don't look like yourself anymore. You look like someone vaguely familiar, maybe a distant relative. It's hard when inside you know you're the same vibrant, youthful self you always were.

Having coped with these vicissitudes of aging for quite a while now, I've decided the worst part of being middle-aged is the steadily dimming vision. After seeing fine all your life, suddenly you need your glasses to see anything, do anything, or go anywhere.

Your entire well-being depends on a small folding object made of plastic, so small it's—alas—easily forgotten or misplaced.

This morning I went to the post office without my glasses.

The stamps I bought were so tiny I couldn't tell which way was right side up and which was upside down. When I was young, if you got a letter with a stamp on it upside down, it was terribly exciting. It meant, "I love you." (I don't think young people do that any more. They make expensive long distance calls and charge them to their parents.) Now if I get a letter with an upside down stamp, it just means someone else can't see any better than I can.

I had another problem at the post office: which slot to put these letters in. Were they "Local" or were they "Out Of Town"? I hated to stop a stranger and ask him. Finally I found that by holding them out in front of me far enough and squinting my left eye, I could barely make out the capital M in Marietta. If any of them were going to Milwaukee or Montezuma, I'm in trouble.

Such predicaments occur to middle-aged people every day. You used to laugh at Mr. Magoo. Now you *are* Mr. Magoo.

Have you ever noticed how menus in fancy restaurants seem to be parchment imitations? They're not. It's where middle-aged women hold them too close to the candle and singe them around the edges.

When you're young, a dimly lit restaurant is romantic. When you're older, it's a nuisance. When you're young, you lean over the table to gaze into your sweetheart's eyes. When you're older, it's the only way you can see one another.

Fortunately, this vision problem comes in stages.

First, shortly after you turn 40, you discover publishers today are using much smaller print; except for the telephone company—they're using ancient Egyptian hieroglyphics.

So you get your first reading glasses.

The next stage comes a few years later when you can read the hymns in church with your glasses on—but you can't see the choir any more. Someone waves whom you don't recognize, and when they get closer they say, "Hi, Mom." The TV picture is fuzzy and there's nothing wrong with the TV.

It's bifocals time.

Bifocals are tough. I still don't have the hang of it. They require holding your head at a very precise, rigid angle, and they tend to make you seasick. The good news is that they reveal a whole new world you didn't know was there. The bad news is you now see the dirt on the carpet and the spots on the walls. (Luckily your friends never knew because they're as bad off as you are.)

If you try to play the piano or organ with bifocals, you have a special problem. To see the music you must tilt your head back as though you're gargling, and sight the notes down the side of your nose. This leads to a crick in the neck and looks really weird.

Thanks to a tip from Annette Brown, our church organist, I asked Bob Taylor, our family eye doctor, to prescribe special "music glasses" for me. Now I don't look like a giraffe with a stiff neck at the piano. (I know—I should call Bob an "ophthalmologist" but I can't see to look up the spelling.)

Now I have one more problem to solve: keeping up with where my glasses are. Dallas keeps his in one place, on his chest of drawers. Where I leave mine is anyone's guess. I try to stroll nonchalantly around, looking for them covertly, but I get ridiculed, "Mom's lost her glasses again."

The eyesight, the memory . . . tough when they both go at once.

April 28, 1984

What, Exactly, Does a School Principal Do?

When I taught kindergarten, one of my cutest little boys was Rodney Sanders—a shy, sweet child with big brown eyes and light blond hair. Rodney's parents were Jane and Charles Sanders. Jane teaches school at West Side and Charles, at that time, was a principal in one of the Cobb schools, before he went to the central administration office.

We had a unit on fathers and each child was asked to tell what his father's job was and what he did.

Rodney told us:

"My daddy is the school principal. He mops the floor."

I knew they'd just had a P.T.A. spaghetti supper . . . and I could well believe that Charles had been the one to mop the floor.

School principals do it all.

Each year the South Cobb P.T.A. Council, which represents 18 schools, gives an annual "roast" for their principals. From what I hear, the Friars Club and Dean Martin aren't the only ones who can really burn with a "roast." According to Nick Pedro of Cobb Schools, the South Cobb P.T.A. always has a hilarious program for this event and everyone looks forward to it each year.

This past Wednesday was the day.

I ran into Bill Dennard, principal of Harmony Leland, at Kaleidoscope on Wednesday around noon, and he was all smiles. He pulled something from his pocket to show me.

It was a medal . . . sort of. Anyway, it was something put together with a medallion and fancy ribbons. He got it for coming in third place in the contest to see which principal had the best jogging outfit at the "roast" that morning.

What was Bill's outfit?

His P.T.A. president had designed it for him, to match the Z-28 car he drives: gold lamé jogging shorts and a matching gold lamé cape! Oh yes, and it was fireproof. It seems Bill is trying to live down a speeding ticket he got. His P.T.A. Members call him "Flash."

Joyce Corn, President of the South Cobb Council, says each P.T.A. honors its individual principal annually. "Without our principals, we couldn't even have a P.T.A.," says Joyce, "and we're so grateful to them. But we think it's nice to have a little fun, too. I always say you have to put the F-U-N into FUNDS if you want a good P.T.A."

This year the program theme for the council meetings has been "Jogging Through the '80s." They called the principal's roast, "Now It's Your Turn To Sweat."

Each of the 18 school P.T.A. presidents presented her principal with some special gift for jogging—"chosen to blend with his or her style and personality!"

Johnny Coleman, secretary of the council, told me about some of them.

Millard Jones of Riverside School received a long pair of sweat pants, which every child in the school had autographed for him . . . and on the seat of the pants was a pair of rolling eyes so he could see all the students behind him.

Frank Hair of Clay Elementary School received an umbrella that fits on his head like a hat "because he's always so neat with never a hair out of place."

Since Dr. Frank Croker, of Garrett Middle School, is under consideration for county superintendent, his gag gift was a shirt that said "Frank Who?"

"The Principal of Floyd Middle School, Mr. Harmon, is the 'Great American Hero' type," says Ms. Coleman. "You know—curly hair, good-looking. His outfit was a cute little outfit because he's cute—a Nike box with a tiny pair of baby shoes inside, a tiny little pair of shorts, etc."

Mr. Barber of Tapp Middle School was given a tote bag with his get-away necessities, including a fishing pole and—in case he didn't catch anything—a fish.

The first place winner was the jogging outfit Hollydale P.T.A. President B. J. Malone gave to principal Kenneth Moore: it included all the accessories—Ban Roll On, an Alligator shirt, the whole bit. Oh yes, since their P.T.A. treasurer is tight, they substituted an old shirt with "LIZARD" printed across the back.

Being a school principal isn't exactly a barrel of laughs. It's good the South Cobb P.T.A. Council helps them manage this good time at least once a year.

MARCH 20, 1981

Parents Need Their Freedom, Too

Orlando, Fla.

I'm standing at the foot of a tall ladder holding it steady for my father. He's up in a grapefruit tree.

I've spent this pre-Easter week visiting my parents. During spring holidays at home who needs me? Better I stock the kitchen with plenty of milk and Captain Crunch and leave them to their own loud music and phone calls and late nights in uncensored bliss.

My father is picking fruit for me to take home to Marietta on the plane tonight.

He has hung his plastic bucket over the end prongs of the ladder. He stands with one foot on the top rung, the other spraddled over the tree trunk. The foliage is almost too thick to part it, so I act as the grapefruit spotter on the ground.

"There's a nice one just to your left. . . . Now reach over your head . . . A little higher—that's it!"

My father is 78 years old. He doesn't see as well as he used to. He's a good 20 feet up in the air. I really don't want to look.

I half close my eyes and gaze beyond him, where the sun's rays are deflected by the thick leaves into sparkling angles of light, splintering out in radiant lines in all directions.

Over and behind these light sparkles, dark green leaves and gnarled branches of the old grapefruit tree, and the green-shirted, small figure of my father arches a perfect, cloudless, bright blue, Florida-Chamber-Of-Commerce sky.

A wonderful light breeze brings delicious smells: my father's roses (several dozen varieties he knows lovingly by name, and picks for daily bouquets for Mother and their friends), Mother's Confederate jasmine (it's the South Carolina state flower and she's had one everywhere we've ever lived), Ann Jones' sweet hedge next door, Daddy's Don Juan red climbing rose at the back door.

A pair of cardinals feed at one bird feeder. An unknown bird that Mother has named "The Great Speckled Bird" flaps his wings and scares off sparrows at the other.

A tiny chameleon, like a miniature alligator, is poised against the screen of the back porch taking a sun bath.

I savor this moment, knowing I'll remember it. Each time I cut a piece of grapefruit, I'll remember my father up in the tree and this jade-and-turquoise-and-sapphire-jeweled morning.

Someone has said, "The best legacy you can give your children is first, roots, then wings."

Each time I come back here where my roots are, where I was myself first—Nancy Dendy—before I became Nancy Ryle, wife and mother, I squirrel away souvenirs. They are symbols of my parents and their friends, who gave me roots of security and love.

This time in my suitcase I'm taking home a little box with a seed inside. It's the size of an English pea. Ruth Cooper gave it to me. (A sign of my maturity: I now call my parents' friends by their first names!) Ruth told me it's a winged-bean. She had read about it in *Time* magazine and being Ruth, wrote a scientist at the U. of Fla. Now she has winged-beans in her garden. They're supposed to have the potential for easing world hunger because almost every part of the plant is edible. "The Presbyterian women in Florida," Ruth says, "are sending them to Haiti."

Ruth has that secret of perpetual youth Ponce de Leon looked for in Florida. It's not the water. It's the quest for continual growth, through new ideas. Ruth is a honey.

One day I went to New Smyrna Beach with my parents' Supper Club. It was our first visit to the Porters' since Buck Porter died. I had dreaded it. I should have known better. Dorothy Porter is gallant, smiling, serene. And the Supper Club Gang—once six couples, now three couples and three widows, are as frisky and upbeat as ever.

I'm taking home more souvenirs of my "roots":

Family photos. My mother and her sister as little girls in dainty dresses and big hair bows; my father's home in Seneca, South Carolina.

A handmade apron from Catherine, Mother's dear friend. Last time I came, Catherine and Dick Cain drove me back to the airport. Dick died last year. Catherine's eyes are still soft and shiny and glowing. "Nancy, you can't feel sorry for yourself. You have to keep going."

A list of books recommended by Louise MacDowall. We had lunch and played bridge with Louise in her beautiful high rise apartment. She's over 80. She tapes one eyelid open, because surgery couldn't correct the "droop"—a gay, ingenious way of coping with a problem. And she still reads avidly. It was "Louise Mac" who shared a priceless treasure with me and my children: many of the autographed books of Jesse Stuart, whom she had known back in Kentucky.

On Maundy Thursday we went to the service at church, with Mary and Clarence Peterson and Mary's sister, Diana. (How patient they were with our children the summer they taught them to water ski!) The First Presbyterian Church suddenly seemed peopled with Mary and Di's parents and so many others who belonged there when I was young, now "a cloud of witnesses" around us.

Now my dad is lowering the bucket and coming down from the tree.

I want to call out to him to be careful! I want to protect him. For the first time, I see him as vulnerable, older, needing me.

But I say nothing.

He and Mother gave me my roots and my wings.

The least I can do is allow him to keep his.

April 24, 1981

I Love New York!

Last fall our daughter, Katie, went to New York to study acting. Her letters have bubbled over with enthusiasm about The Big Apple. She loves it. On the back of each envelope she draws the letter "I," a heart and an apple. *I Love New York.*

But we worried.

She was only 21 years old. She had stars in her eyes and blind trust in her heart. Would she be o.k.?

We worried about her apartment. (The American Academy of Dramatic Arts where she studies is a wonderful school, part of the university system of New York and one of the finest drama schools in the nation—but has no campus.) Even though that apartment cost her an arm and a leg, we worried that it was probably a miserable hole in the wall infested with rats and roaches.

We worried that Katie and Maureen, her roommate, would forget to lock their door.

We worried: that criminals and villains lurked on every corner; that every person in the city of New York was cold-hearted and ruthless; and that Katie would never eat any vegetables.

You name it. We worried about it.

Finally, I decided it was time to go up and check out the place for myself. (Besides, I've always wanted an excuse to go to New York.)

I discovered that all of us listen to too many horror stories. New York is not the city of bleak filth and rampant crime it's cracked up to be. It's a delightful, exciting, wonderful city and if I were a budding actress of 21, that's right where I'd be.

The seamy side is there, all right.

I saw the bag ladies. Katie says the same ones sleep in front of Woolworth's every day.

Times Square is terrible—porn shops, X-rated movies, hookers lining the streets at night; although by day it's where tourists (including me) and thrifty New Yorkers go to buy tickets cheap. There's a large ticket booth in the center of the street, selling tickets to most of the Broadway shows at half price for that day . . . definitely worth the hour's wait in line.

But there is a new spirit of pride in New York. The city is now on a sound financial footing and I was impressed with the many civic beautification and historic preservation projects I saw.

For example, many vacant lots downtown have been converted into community gardens. Anyone can ask for a plot, get a key to the gate, and have his own flower, fruit, or vegetable garden. Last Saturday, we saw folks there happily working at their roses and blueberry bushes in the sunshine, while two blocks away was the tower of the Empire State Building.

"Little Old New York," the world of Edith Wharton, Damon Runyon, and O. Henry, lives again in the many historic restorations. The brand new Helmsley Palace Hotel was formed from a prestigious old apartment building and a cathedral put together. You can take tea there and imagine you're an Astor. The gilt and marble splendor is gorgeous.

The New York Life Insurance Building is a marble fortress with bronze doors and a gold-covered tower. It's the old location for Madison Square Gardens. (The doorman proudly told me about the gold on their tower, and I told him about our Georgia gold-domed capitol.) Such buildings tell you a story of a proud and unique city.

Once you learn certain facts New York with its noisy rush-rush pace, multi-ethnic culture, and blend of old and new, is a fascinating place to visit.

Just remember . . .

1) No one understands a Southern accent. They understand Chinese, Greek, Italian, African, Mideastern, and Lower Slobbovian words but not Southern. You must point and do pantomime to make yourself understood.

2) You can't get biscuits and gravy—just bagels and cream cheese.

3) Don't cross the street according to traffic lights. Cross whenever a clump of other people cross. Lodge yourself right in the center of them and let them be a flying wedge. And walk very, very fast.

4) When you see people standing by the street with their hands lifted high in the air, they're not feeling the Spirit. They're calling a cab.

Katie's apartment is perfect—shiny clean and new, no roaches, triple locks on the door, more locks on the outside door, and an intercom to let guests in.

She and Maureen eat right. They took me to their corner grocery store. It's a tiny doll-sized store right in the heart of Manhattan, with the most beautiful fresh produce I ever saw. People walk around bins of salad fixings and put their take-out salads into plastic containers on their way home from work.

About those cold-hearted New Yorkers . . . right across from the girls' apartment building is an old Moravian church, built almost 200 years ago. It offers a shelter for the homeless, staffed partly by volunteers. All day long they come there for help with food, lodging and jobs—or just to rest and get a friendly cup of coffee.

"New York, New York—it's a wonderful town!" I hope my child stays long enough for me to visit again. I'm just now getting the hang of it.

MAY 12, 1983

Spring Means the Cobb County Symposium

It happens every spring. As sure as the dogwood blooms in Georgia, Cobb County has its annual symposium.

It's the only one like it anywhere.

At least that's what experts like Charles Kuralt say. Kuralt has traveled all 50 states for the CBS series "On The Road" and earned the nickname "Everyone's Friendly Neighbor." When he accepted the invitation to be the dinner speaker for the 1983 Cobb County Symposium, he told leaders this is a unique event. He knows of no other place in America that has one like it.

Of course, symposiums are nothing new. Every college, professional group, and large company has them, borrowing the idea from the ancient Greeks of gathering together to discuss new ideas.

What makes ours special is that it's a cooperative effort of the entire community. Once a year everyone puts his special interest aside—or more accurately, puts it *together*—to hear leaders in the fields of education, medicine, law, religion, business and industry, social studies, the arts.

Look at the roll call of past speakers to the Cobb Symposium: Margaret Meade, Elizabeth Kubler-Ross, Norman Cousins, William Buckley, Robert Schuller, Mary Calderone, Eliot Wigginton, William Pinson, Joyce Brothers. Next year Eugenia Price, best-selling author, and Dr. Jonas Salk are already scheduled to come. Today's leading thinkers and doers . . . one by one they've found their way to our little "Harvard-in-the-Pines," Kennesaw College, to address the "town meeting" we call the Cobb Symposium.

The symposium began one year when the Cobb Medical Society and the Cobb Ministerial Association decided to hold a joint meeting and invite a speaker concerned with people's total needs: spiritual, physical and mental.

The next year the Cobb Bar Association wanted to be included. Then the local colleges (Southern Tech, as well as Kennesaw College), dental and pharmaceutical organizations, the Junior League, and many others joined. Now the event is held for two evenings and one day. It draws diverse audiences from college students getting extra credit to housewives like me who look upon it as our "continuing education" program and one of the most exciting opportunities we have for learning and growing.

This year the symposium theme is "The American Story." I asked Margaret Ann and Dr. McCoy Rose, co-chairmen for Symposium '83, why they chose this theme. Said Margaret Ann, "Well, we've had many different programs through the years, but we've never had a symposium on America before. We thought it was time to remind ourselves and our children that we live in the most fabulous, wonderful country in the world. We're going through a terrible time now economically but we have the intelligence to solve the problems. We have the best economic system in the world, the natural resources, the top leadership in medicine, in the arts, in moral and religious principles—and we don't say it often enough!"

Mac McCoy added, "The American story is changing so fast. The book *Megatrends* reminds us that soon 65% to 85% of our employment will be in informational services rather than manufacturing industries. We need to take a good look at America today."

Outstanding speakers this year, besides Kuralt, include Dr. Robert Good, former director of the Sloan-Kettering Institute for Cancer Research, now director of Oklahoma Medical Research Foundation, and Mike Bowers, the Georgia Attorney-General.

If you have time, attend the symposium next Thursday night and Friday (check the paper for times and places). See for yourself how fortunate we are to have this event. As a spring tonic to wake up new thoughts and ideas, it even beats sassafras tea!

April 8, 1983

My Three Fathers

An open letter to a former Marietta resident:

Rev. John Moore
Pacific Regional Seminary
Box 1200
Suva, Fiji

Dear Father Moore,

We're missing you around here. I hope your trip to the Fiji Islands was pleasant and that you'll enjoy your new assignment.

My son Stephen and I found the islands in our atlas and then we were sorry we did. They look so tiny and so far away.

Furthermore, with all that ocean around them, we wonder: can you hit a golf ball without sending it splashing into the Pacific? And that near the Equator, is it too hot to play golf at all? Somehow, I don't think the Lord would ever send you where you couldn't play golf!

It still doesn't seem possible that five years have gone by since you and I came at the same time to St. Joseph's. I don't know which of us felt greener—you, suddenly finding yourself a parish priest after teaching in seminaries for 30 years, or me, a Baptist, trying to play the organ for Catholic mass!

Until then the only Catholic priests I knew were Bing Crosby and Barry Fitzgerald in "Going My Way." I had never attended a Catholic service before and had vague impressions of Latin, candles, and chants. I thought of a priest as someone secluded from the real world, telling his beads and meditating behind sheltered walls.

I quickly found out how wrong I was.

I learned that many positive, wide-sweeping changes had occurred in the Catholic Church, thanks to Vatican II, the historic church council convened by Pope John in 1962. Catholics were using English in their services, and were even singing many of the same hymns Protestants sing—including "Amazing Grace." I felt at home. The worship at St. Joseph's, though different from my church, was relevant and meaningful, as well as beautiful. (I especially like exchanging "The sign of peace." Someone in the balcony always comes over to shake my hand. It is a ritual which insures that families—father and son, husband and wife, whoever—will tell each other at least once a week, that they forgive and love one another. Not a bad idea at all.)

You, Father Cummings, and Father Kellermann showed me patient understanding while I learned the ropes—and every time I made goofs (which was often). You became my friends. I learned to call each of you "Father" as your people do—and I nicknamed you "My Three Fathers."

There have been so many times when you showed kindness.

Remember the Christmas Eve midnight mass when we got our signals crossed?

The choir was going to give a one hour program of Christmas music starting at 11:00 p.m. Then at midnight sharp, I would go into "O Come, All Ye Faithful"—the signal for the procession to begin for the mass.

Of course, the church was packed, as it always is, for Christmas Eve midnight mass. The last song of the choir's preliminary program was a contemporary carol. It had a rhythm that was—well, to be honest, a definite rock beat! I worried about that song a lot! I had modified the organ part, so it would sound less jazzy, more churchy, but let's face it. It was not your basic Gregorian chant.

Remember what happened?

The choir program had evidently gone over the allotted time. They were singing that final modern carol, belting it out for all they were worth, and I had the pedals going on that semi-rock beat, when suddenly Bob Bishop, the choir director, pointed wildly. I looked down from the choir loft and froze in horror . . . the midnight mass procession had begun!

It was 12 o'clock midnight and in you were coming! You, Father Cummings, Father Kellermann, some visiting priests, what looked like 100 altar boys—all bearing candles and incense and the figure of the Christ Child to place in the manger at the altar.

All of you were moving slowly and relentlessly down the aisles from the back of the church, swaying back and forth in perfect unison to our rock beat!

Someone has defined "class" as "grace under pressure." When we apologized later for the fiasco, you just smiled, Father Moore, and said, "I thought the processional had a certain style to it!"

Thank you for running up the hill to the rectory the time I forgot my organ key, to get your extra one. (Early mass sometimes was too early for me to think straight!) I wouldn't have blamed the lector for saying, "Welcome to the 8:00 o'clock mass. Well, actually, it's the 8:10 mass. It would have been sooner but the organist forgot her key."

When I apologized later to you for that, you said you didn't remember. (I don't believe you!)

Many of us can forgive—but to forgive and forget is the stuff saints are made of, along with other qualities we saw in you, Father Moore . . . like humility and kindness and love.

One by one you, "My Three Fathers," have gone. Father Cummings first, to be chaplain at St. Joseph's Hospital in Atlanta; then Father Kellermann all the way to Rome, Italy; and now you.

Your flock is in good hands now with Fathers Zolota, Schmuhl and McShane—but I hope the Lord will see fit one day to return you to our fold.

Bishop Dozier of Memphis recently said the church should be "a fellowship pouring the oil of mercy and love on our fellow man." I immediately thought of you. You seem to be always filled to overflowing with the mercy and love you're entrusted to pour. I'm glad to have been a stray Protestant sheep in your flock!

APRIL 8, 1977

Windows Aren't the Only Things I Don't Do

I'm all tuckered out. I've been doing my spring cleaning.

You think I'm late with spring cleaning? You don't know *how* late! I'm not talking about the cleaning I haven't done *this* spring. I'm talking about the cleaning I never did last spring. Or the spring before that.

To be honest, I can't remember the last time I really dug in and tried to clean out, organize and polish up this messy house.

There comes a time, though, when you can't put it off any longer. You know you need to clean house when . . .

• Every morning looks foggy and cloudy when you wake up—and you finally realize it's not the weather, it's your windows.

• You decide it's time to get out the summer clothes. Then you discover you don't have to. You never put them away.

• You can't stuff one more thing under the bed without tripping over it when you make the bed up.

• You can't find anything in the kitchen cabinets—not only little flat things like onion soup mix, but tall things like ketchup and Crisco. They're hidden behind instant tea that has petrified into never-never tea, marinated artichokes that nobody likes but you can't throw out because they're too expensive, and yeast packages that say, "Expiration date: Aug. '67."

• You can't hang guests' coats in the hall closet. You take them into the front bedroom instead. If guests innocently start toward the closet, you lunge in front of them and throw yourself, a human barricade, against the closet door. Behind that door lies Fibber McGee country: two card tables, four folding chairs, a carton of popcorn the cheerleaders sold but your daughter never sold hers, stadium seats, hockey sticks, the vacuum cleaner, and six cans of dead tennis balls—one of which has the top off and will empty its contents on your head.

Despite all of these conditions, I might never have done spring cleaning this year if my friend, Helen, hadn't laughed so hard at my kitchen drawer.

We were having a Sunday School party at our house and Helen was helping out in the kitchen. She pulled out a drawer looking for a big spoon, let out a scream and clutched her sides laughing.

"John, John!" she yelled for her husband. "Come look!" Both of them nearly had hysterics.

I didn't see anything funny. All that drawer had in it were a hammer, pliers, icepick, Mason jar lids, cookie cutters, a whetstone, the pressure cooker rack, the waffle iron cord, birthday candles, pot holders, spatulas, knives, spoons, and a margarine container full of pennies. So what's the big deal?

Helen said it was because John has always wanted them to keep a "junk drawer" like that in their kitchen. I didn't tell her that wasn't my junk drawer.

Anyway, philosophically, I'm totally against cleaning house. It's an exercise in futility.

For one thing, all you do is move stuff from one place to another. I cleaned out the hall closet. Now we hang coats there without any trouble—but you should see our basement, where we put all that junk from the closet.

You can have clean closets or you can have a clean basement but you can't have both at once.

For another thing, how long will it stay that way?

I organized my kitchen cabinets. I even lined up all the spices in alphabetical order like they do in the stores. (It's amazing how many duplicates I found. We now have a lifetime supply of garlic salt, dry mustard, and poultry seasoning.)

But when someone makes cinnamon toast and fails to put the cinnamon back in its proper place, between celery seed and curry powder, what will I do? Slap their hands?

Yesterday I mopped and waxed the kitchen floor. Now the fellows are planning to go blackberry picking this afternoon. They'll come home with dirty boots. Great hunks of clay will drop from them, clump by clump, and be crunched into powdery red dust in a trail across the kitchen. So much for my shiny floor.

A clean house only leads to an uptight housewife.

I like the motto I saw framed in a little shop at the Galleria. It said, "Good Housewives Are Boring Women."

Boy, if that's true, I must really be an exciting person to know.

JUNE 28, 1984

Allergy Sufferers: Here's Looking Atchoo!

This is the time of year I dread.

Pine pollen has drifted down 'til it covers our corner of the world like gold dust—causing noses to quiver and eyes to weep.

I knew, sooner or later, I'd be in for it. Sure enough, Tuesday was my hay fever day.

It was cool and rainy. Whether the change in the weather did it, or the rain flushed out the last pollen and sent its wet fall-out showering down, I woke up sneezing 20 times and knew it would be a really rotten day.

When you get hay fever, you have two choices: you can keep going and tough it out, hoping it will get better (it doesn't); or you can give up, take an antihistamine and hope it won't make you sleepy (it does).

I managed to cook breakfast by keeping the Kleenex box tucked under my arm and holding my head in a carefully up-tilted position to reverse the flow. After that was done, I decided to stay in for the rest of the day and spare my garden club members the sight of my red-nosed, miserable self.

According to our family allergy specialist, Dr. Vanderpool, 20% of the population suffers from allergies today. It has something to do with the body's immunization system, which has five parts—G, M, D, A, and E. It's the "E" part that spells trouble for those of us with allergies. Sneezers, wheezers, and coughers evidently have more Gamma E than we should have.

Wonderful strides have been made in this field. By taking immunization shots for de-sensitizing, and by taking new medicines (that don't all make you sleepy), we don't need to suffer as much as we used to.

Dallas and Katie have both been on the immunization program with great results; and we've decided it's time for me to get started, too.

Meanwhile, according to Dr. Vanderpool, there are many other practical helps allergic people should know:

1. Work hard to keep your *bedroom* dust-free. It's hopeless to make the entire house allergy-proof, but we spend a good third of our time in the bedroom, and a school-age child gets 75% to 95% of his exposure to house allergens in his bedroom. (An "allergen," naturally, is the villainous substance causing an allergy.)

2. Make the bedroom off-limits to pets. (They are bad news! You wouldn't believe how much trouble they bring to you, invisibly, by their fur or hair.)

3. Have only one bed in a room if possible. Cover mattress and box springs with a zip-on plastic cover, and the zipper with plastic tape. Mold (one of the worst allergens of all) thrives in mattresses.

4. Wash hair at night.

5. Use only comforters, pillows, etc. with synthetic fibers—not cotton, feather, or kapok.

6. Use a humidifier (the colder the weather, the drier the house, and the more dust.)

7. Change furnace filters once a month; also install filters on vents in each room.

8. Close the windows at night (grass pollen rises with dew). Of course, air conditioning is ideal.

9. When you're having special allergy problems—as I am today—avoid foods with high mold content. You won't believe this, but it's possible to avoid a whole lot of hay fever when you're on the brink of an attack—just cut out such foods: cheese, smoked meats (sausage, hot dogs), yeast breads, melons (especially cantaloupes), mushrooms, soy sauce, dried fruits, and canned or frozen juice.

10. Stick to cosmetic products free from Orris root—look for labels that say "non-allergenic" or "hypo-allergenic."

Did you know:

The number one cause of days missed from school is upper respiratory problems?

16 million people suffer from hay fever or asthma, making these aller-

gies the fourth most common disorder in the nation—twice as common as diabetes?

Misery loves company. It helps my feelings to know that, on one of my sneezy days, I'm not alone. I plan to do something about it. Taking the allergy shots and watching the "do's" and "don'ts" ought to help a lot. If you're coping with allergies, too,—here's looking atchoo, baby. Take care.

MAY 28, 1980

Sidewalks

Do you know one thing I miss about the Good Old Days? I miss the sidewalks.

My children have never lived on a street with sidewalks. They've been deprived of a lot of pleasure.

When I grew up in Gainesville, sidewalks were perfect for things like hopscotch and jump rope. Sometimes our chalk hopscotch squares would stay there for weeks, getting smudged a little but easily touched up when we wanted to play again.

The sidewalk was just right for "Mother, May I?" and "Red Light." We would start at the front steps at our house, go past the Bensons next door, clear down to the corner of the block where George Harrison lived. That was room enough to really travel if you ran fast enough when the one who was "It" closed his eyes.

We skated on the sidewalks, too. As I remember, they weren't great for skating. They were so bumpy-textured your teeth rattled, and the cracks between the pavement squares were a hazard. If you weren't going fast enough, a crack would get you every time.

But we'd never heard of a skating rink back then, so who knew the difference?

We'd sit on the steps, buckle the straps and tighten the sides with our skate keys (kept on strings around our necks), yelling for Mother to come help if we couldn't get them tight enough. Then we'd take off.

The boys would race to see who was fastest. The girls tried to sway gracefully from side to side like Sonja Henie.

The best sidewalk games of all took place after supper in the summertime. My little brother, Billy Benson next door, Jean and Margie Meeks across the street, and sometimes their big brother, "Lit," would play. We'd have ferocious contests and battles of will such as Kick-The-Can and Snake-In-The-Gutter—in which the snake stayed on the sidewalk and had to catch the others as they ran across. The fun came from taunting the snake by walking as slowly as possible and making derisive gestures. We had a singing game—"Ain't No Booger Bears Out Tonight" (Daddy killed them all last night . . .) I didn't know what a Booger Bear was but it sounded chilling, evil, and deliciously scary.

When it got too dark to see any more, we'd get jars and catch lightning bugs 'til our mothers made us go in.

Children don't have such places to play any more. We have big yards but we don't want them to mess up the lawn.

Driveways aren't the same as sidewalks. Driveways are isolated. Sidewalks are friendlier.

Sidewalks belonged to everyone. They ran through the town like ribbons, tying neighborhoods together in closeness and community.

Of course, in Gainesville we knew all the sidewalks in town. We walked everywhere. We walked to school, to our piano lessons at Miss Whitson's, to the movies, to friends' houses.

We liked the sidewalks made of octagon-shaped pieces. We fit our feet inside the pieces, because "if you step on a crack you break your mother's back." Now and then a piece would have inscribed letters or numbers (the paving contractor's name or something). That would be good luck. We could stand inside it, make a wish and believe it would come true.

We knew people better in our town because of sidewalks. When you pass houses every day, in all seasons, you learn about the folks who live in them.

We knew who swept their front porches and sidewalks neatly each morning; who grew a nice garden; whose house always had good baking smells coming from inside; who took time to speak to a little child.

Today all we know about neighbors sometimes is what kind of car they drive.

Sidewalks phased out as dependence on automobiles phased in. They're a thing of the past—like dime movies on Saturday (Flash Gordon serial, Roy Rogers feature, plus cartoons—now, *that* was real value for your money!) and nickel ice cream cones you ate slowly inside the drug store under the cool ceiling fans, so the ice cream wouldn't melt too fast.

Nothing happened too fast back then.

Today I like driving through the older streets of Marietta which still have sidewalks and seeing young mothers with babies in strollers, children at play, joggers enjoying a safe place to run, older couples strolling in the sunshine.

Sidewalks are nice.

If this energy crisis lasts, who knows? Sidewalks may come in again.

One day our children may recall how it was in the Good Old Days—when they rode around the streets in something called an automobile.

MAY 18, 1979.

Motherhood: Openings For Challenging Career

WANTED:

Women for highly demanding but rewarding career.

POSITION:

Motherhood.

JOB DESCRIPTION:

Nurse-babysitter-cook-maid-laundress-chauffeur-playground supervisor-seamstress-arts and crafts instructor-hostess-teacher-counselor-chaplain-friend.

QUALIFICATIONS:

No previous experience required. On-the-job training provided.

PHYSICAL REQUIREMENTS:

Strong back, long arms, level head, keen eyes, quick ears, available lap, thick hide, warm heart.

EMOTIONAL REQUIREMENTS:

Adaptability (no Standard Method of Operation—each child varies and the unexpected is the rule).

High stress tolerance (i.e. ability to remove cat from cream pitcher, blow child's nose, pull baby from cupboard, turn hamburger patties at stove, and plan Girl Scout meeting on phone simultaneously).

Courage under fire (walk into room for conference with teacher, wearing a confident smile).

Coping skills (Murphy's Law for Mothers: everything that *can* go wrong *will*, when (1) guests are expected momentarily, (2) it's your pediatrician's day off, or (3) your husband is out of town).

HOURS:

Non-stop 24 hour duty. (No holidays or weekends. Shifts may be arranged with co-worker [see "Fatherhood"]. Extra night duty in early years feeding, burping, changing, and rocking; in teen years listening to thumping record player, listening for car in driveway, listening for imaginary phone calls from hospital or police.)

SALARY:

This is a volunteer job. (You will never be rich. Solvency depends on whether your child wears braces, what band instrument he plays, and if he gets a Guaranteed Student Loan for college. The best you can hope for is the kid becoming independent before you retire.)

OCCUPATIONAL HAZARDS:

1) Inconvenience (i.e., looking for a Market Basket at midnight that sells notebook paper, for a composition due next day).

2) Extreme embarrassment. (your child will act his worst before your best friend, mother-in-law, or minister).

3) Insomnia. (See "Hours." Remember babies have colic, teens stay up all night and sleep all day.)

4) Cultural deprivation. (Goodby to French movies, symphony concerts, gourmet food, Michener novels. Hello to Sesame Street and Disney, Mother Goose and The Cat In The Hat, French fries with ketchup).

5) Dwindling friendships. (See "Cultural deprivation," and don't blame your friends.)

6) Fatigue. (Escalates in proportion to number of children and age of mother. Total burnout when child leaves for college. [Note: many recuperate in time to enjoy grandchildren.])

RETIREMENT PLAN:

No retirement. ("The Empty Nest" is strictly a myth. Active continuing duty depends on high cost of apartments for young singles in the area and mother's willingness to do laundry.)

FRINGE BENEFITS:

Breakfast in bed second Sunday of May.

Constant companionship. (You'll never be lonely again. [You may *want* to be lonely sometimes but you never will.])

ENTRY LEVEL:

Apply at maternity wing of local hospital.

EDUCATION:

Read Spock and Dodson, attend Lamaze class.

JOB OBJECTIVE:

To make yourself finally dispensable. (The more you succeed as a mother the less your child will need you. Goal: to help child become fully developed, happy, loving human being.)

However, as writer and mother Marjorie Holmes writes, "No child ever really grows beyond the reach of a mother's heart."

RECOMMENDATION:

Most women who are mothers report love, joy, and fulfillment beyond all expectations and all other professions.

"Love alone is capable of uniting living beings in such a way as to complete and fulfill them, for it alone takes them and joins them by what is deepest in themselves."

MAY 10, 1984

School Bands Earn Excellence the Hard Way

To a stranger, the Band Banquet would seem just another typical end-of-the-year affair: chicken and mashed potatoes, honors, awards, ho hum.

But none of us at the Marietta High Band Banquet were strangers. We were parents, teachers, and members of the band, and we knew—ah, how well we knew—the meaning behind each announcement on the program.

Anyone who has had a child in a school band knows that band awards, like sports awards, stand for untold hours of sacrifice. Tough physical training, practice, and determination go into each one. No one had to make flowery speeches. We knew.

We knew what they were saying, when they talked about . . .

Marching Band. . . . Early rehearsals before sunrise. Late rehearsals in the cold twilight. Drilling the half-time show routine over and over and over, to get it perfect. Friday suppers at 4 o'clock in the afternoon or no supper at all. Marching in soggy rain and mud. Marching when you're sick and should be home in bed. Marching because you have a place to fill in the formation, so you must be there.

Marching Festival. . . . Giving up fun for an entire weekend. Cooped up for hours on a bumpy bus. Facing Monday morning with no sleep. (Proud note: the M.H.S. Band made all "superiors" in every marching festival they entered this year.)

Concert Band. . . . Switching from jazz music to marches and difficult symphonic music, which is comparable to college level standards. Counting measures and measures—waiting for the one where you come in. Dreading the thought that beeping your clarinet or tooting your flute one beat too soon will turn you into an instant idiot before the world. Or, if you're the first chair player, agonizing that you'll fluff a note in your solo passages.

Feeling the pressure that comes when your school band has made "su-

perior" every year of its existence, and who wants to be the first to—pardon the expression,—blow it? (Another proud note: M.H.S. Concert Band has made "superior" for 25 years in a row!)

Solo and Ensemble Festival. . . . The time when you're judged for your own solo performance or duets and trios with a group. Mastering your number, working with your private teacher at times wedged in between soccer games, school golf team matches, decorating for Junior-Senior, S.A.T. tests, and term papers.

Getting to the place (usually Marietta's First Methodist Church) on a Saturday morning in April with butterflies in your stomach. Waiting in the hall for your turn, fingers so stiff and mouth so dry you know you'll mess up the runs and maybe can't even make a sound at all. Playing your heart out—to a judge who looks over his glass with a dour expression and never says a word. ("Please Lord, don't let me squeak, don't let me crack, why did I ever get into this, what is the judge writing down about me?") (Proud note: 36 M.H.S. band students took part in this year's Solo Festival, and not one drew lower than "excellent" rating.)

All-State Band. . . . Still more competitions. More butterflies and prayers and clammy hands. Competing against the cream of the crop from the entire state of Georgia. (M.H.S. had seven band members chosen this year for Georgia's All-State Band, more than any other high school in Cobb.)

"Next year's drum majors, field and squad leaders, flag corps, and majorrettes will be the following:. . . ." The crowning moment after hours of spring practice. Excited winners. Disappointed losers, who accept gracefully (tears come later, in private.) Susan Pickering and Kim Satterfield hand over the baton, as last year's drum majors, to Chip Bowden and Sarah Speed—talented kids passing on a tradition to other talented kids.

This column isn't really meant to brag on the M.H.S. Band alone (though as a little David-sized school amid the Goliaths in the county, we have to brag some!), but to praise every school band in our area. They are some of the finest musicians you can find anywhere. The youngsters, their band teachers, and supporters contribute so much to our community. And the character-building principles demanded from these youngsters will benefit them always.

That's why Dallas and I don't find a band banquet boring, ever. (We've sat through such a banquet eight years now). We watch girls with shining hair and shy smiles, gangly boys suddenly dignified in their coats and ties, and we know the real-life drama behind the scenes. They deserve all the applause—and then some.

MAY 23, 1980

Help Someone Into A New Life Through Reading

Tom is a young man in his mid-20's, bright and a hard worker. He works in food service in one of the hospitals in Cobb County. His boss gradually discovered that Tom has a problem: he can't read.

Mary is a good, caring mother. She feels frustrated, though, by the constant bafflement of one who can't read: not knowing what sort of Campbell's Soup is in a can, because it doesn't have a picture on it; not being able to read her mail or recipes in a cookbook; most of all, not being able to read stories to her children.

Paul had a chance for a very good job at Lockheed. To qualify Paul had to take a test. He doesn't know how to read. He's still working his old job as a janitor.

These are not their real names—but they are real people. And thanks to a wonderful volunteer program called Cobb Literacy Action, they are being helped to a new life.

The other day I dropped by the Main Library in Marietta, where the Cobb Literacy Action office is located, and talked with the director, Jeani Kessler.

Jeani began volunteering as a tutor with Literacy Action after seeing a TV ad, "Teach Someone To Read." The ad grabbed her attention.

"I'm one of those people who really love to read! I'm not a scholar—I got through high school almost 'on a wing and a prayer,'" she said. "But I can't imagine life without the pleasure of reading. So I called the Atlanta Literacy Action number in the ad and volunteered. Since I live in Cobb, they referred me to the program here."

She and her husband, Tim, a nuclear engineer, who moved here from their native Connecticut four years ago, both began tutoring in the Cobb program. This year, when the director, Marge Johnson, and her successor, Norwood Rachels, had to give up their involvement with the project, Jeani agreed to take over as director.

It's a labor of love. She receives no salary for the job though she gives two full afternoons a week (Tuesdays and Thursdays). She fits it into her life somehow, despite commuting to a job in Tucker each day, because she believes passionately in the worth of Literacy Action.

"We see people completely change. When you give them the tools for living, there's no stopping them. It's a domino effect. Where else can you spend two hours a week and do so much good? It's a life-changing process—they become whole new people."

Today in America, according to the U.S. Department of Education, there are 23 to 27 million adults who are functionally illiterate, one out of five in our population. Some dropped out of school early. Some had learning disabilities which went unnoticed or for other reasons "fell through the cracks" in the system.

Adults in Cobb who want to learn to read can get help free of charge, just by calling Jeani at 429-3042.

Of course . . . they won't read this announcement!

If you know someone, tell them. Jeani hopes employers, church pastors, social workers, anyone dealing with the public, will tell them about the program. They can meet with a tutor twice a week, at any time convenient to both, in a quiet place in one of the Cobb libraries.

"The library staff people are extremely sensitive to the needs of the students, and have been very cooperative in giving us privacy," Jeani said. She tries to match students and teachers by finding common interests. "The young man I taught last year enjoyed gardening, so I got my Burpee's seed catalogues and we made our flash cards from them. Some of the sentences were crazy, like 'I ate blue corn . . . ' but he was learning the words, and it was exciting and wonderful."

Before Jeani gets more students, however, she is more concerned about getting more teachers.

"We need a lot more men and women to volunteer. You don't have to be a teacher. You don't need a college degree. You just have to be committed to giving one hour a session, two sessions a week, to help someone."

As if to underscore the need, while we are talking, her phone rings. A young woman named Kim wants help learning to read. She lives near the Merchant's Walk Library. Jeani agrees to meet her there on Saturday morning. It's not during her regular hours—but Jeani cares.

I hope some of you care, too.

AUGUST 16, 1984

SUMMER

June's Sweet Girl Graduates— Then and Now

What is so rare as a day in June—without another graduation invitation coming in the mail?

Our own Patty came home two days ago, with the symbol of her proud new status as a college grad upstairs on display—her diploma from Eckerd College.

The rest of the evidence is piled in the basement downstairs: books, clothes, record albums and cooking pots, weaving loom and knitting bag, posters and macrame hangings, 40 houseplants and a faded old rug her dad couldn't persuade her to leave behind when we packed the trailer ("It only cost me $10, Daddy, and it's *so* beautiful").

The night before her Graduation Day, we set the alarm for 5:00 A.M. It's a long drive from Marietta to St. Petersburg pulling a U-Haul. I should have gone to bed early but I got hooked on the condensed novel in the June *Redbook,* and sat up 'til dawn finishing it.

It was written by a marvelously talented Atlanta woman, Anne Rivers Siddons. Anne is from Marietta author, Nell Abbott's, hometown and told me once that her girlhood ambition was to write as well as Nell.

Her story is called "The Last Quiet Summer," condensed from her novel *Heartbreak Hotel* (to be published by Simon and Schuster). It depicts a typical Southern college girl, Maggie DeLoach, in the 1950's.

Maggie is so real and believable that I, class of '49—with a few changes such as being rich and beautiful, which I was not—could have been Maggie.

Don't start this story late at night. You can't put it down. And don't read it if you're only looking for nostalgic pleasure. Siddons probes beneath the fads and mindset of that era, to reveal inner concerns (or *lack* of concern) in that quiet decade before our world erupted into the tumultuous '60s.

I was still half-trapped in that fictional world of Maggie Deloach the next day, when I watched our daughter, Patty, file into the Eckerd Gym in her academic gown. Scenes from Maggie's day—*my* day—were superimposed on the present day. It was an emotional collage of "then" and "now."

Maggie and Patty: both were young, Southern, beautiful, and intelligent—but poles apart.

Girls like Maggie were flowers carefully grown, displayed at age 18 (debutante age), then "cut and pressed and dried," preserved in marriage.

Tradition and conventions were strictly followed. Maggie (and I) chose our angora sweaters and pleated skirts with care, slept uncomfortably on snail-like pin curls, girdled and padded our inadequate figures, and worried all the time about looking our best.

We considered brief careers teaching or nursing . . . but only 'til the right boy came along. A boy who would be rich, we hoped, as well as nice. Marriage was the ultimate security and fulfillment.

We had never known anyone but Southerners. We had never been outside the South. We were vaguely uncomfortable about racial injustice and other wrongs in society—when we were confronted with them—but that didn't happen often.

And our Patty?

She would never understand Maggie. She is natural and unaffected, totally herself from her slim, almost boyish figure to her long, straight, shining hair. Not a hothouse flower, but one naturally grown—and not to be picked so quickly! "It's not what a person is on the *outside*, but what he is *inside* that matters," she tells her parents over and over. It's the creed of her generation—no artifice, no masks.

She's now willing to wear a dress once in a while as well as her beloved jeans—pretty, romantic dresses that look like her great-grandmother's, quaint, demure and lacy.

She introduces us to boy friends with beards, boyfriends with afro hair-dos, boyfriends with pony-tails. We don't know if they're rich. They do seem to be nice . . . now that we're learning "it's what's on the inside that matters most."

She's studied in England, worked a summer in Colorado, another summer in New England. She's had friends at college from Japan, Saudi Arabia, South America.

Her material desires are simple: she wants to own a pick-up truck and to live in a log cabin.

Marriage? Maybe sometime in the future. But she is totally dedicated to her career, planning to use her Bachelor of Science degree in Environmental Science to try to clean up the whole world.

Maggie and Patty. My generation and hers. I guess the big difference is this:

We Maggies weren't quite ready for the Real World.

And I wonder . . . is the Real World quite ready for Patty?

JUNE 28, 1976

Father's Day

Ogden Nash wrote a wonderful line about fatherhood:

Being a father is quite a bother.

But Nash went on to write of the joys of fatherhood, too, ending with these thoughts:

> But after you've raised them and educated them and gowned them
> They just take their little fingers and wrap you around them.
> Being a father is quite a bother—
> But I like it rather.

Every father would probably agree with him on both counts.

Being a father *is* a bother. I hope that on Dad's day this Sunday we can let him know he's loved enough to "like it, rather."

Being a father, for one thing, is costly.

A recent study from Florida State University says it costs an average, middle income American family $64,000 to rear one child including his education at a state-supported college. (No wonder our family stays broke. I hope Dallas doesn't stop to think how rich he'd be without the kids.)

Being a father costs in much higher ways than money.

It costs freedom. A man accepts responsibility for those young lives in his care physically, mentally, and morally. Parenthood brings awesome loss of freedom.

It costs peace of mind. Fathers worry about things men without children never dream of—from how they'll pay the next orthodontist bill, to whether or not a child's fever will come down in the middle of the night, to a child's entire future and how to guide him.

Fathers usually believe their kid is definitely above average in every way, so being a father costs loss of false pride and adjustment to reality. To help Dads with such inevitable disappointments (we parents forget our children "take after us" sometimes!), let me quote from one father's letter to his son:

"Never have I received a really good report of your conduct in your work from any master or tutor you had . . . I am certain that if you cannot prevent yourself from leading the idle, useless, unprofitable life you have had during your schooldays and later months, you will become a mere social wastrel, and degenerate into a shabby, unhappy, and futile existence."

The letter was signed "Your Affcte. Father, Randolph S.C." The no-good, wastrel son headed for a futile existence was Sir Winston Churchill.

No matter how rewarding parenthood ultimately is, a good father must feel stretched to the limits of his capacity sometimes—trying to be wise enough, strong enough, good enough.

One of the hardest things a loving father must do is hand out punishment. His child will never understand until he or she is grown and a parent, too, how true it is when we say, "This hurts me more than it hurts you."

Sometimes I run into writing by a man named Tagore, a poet, story teller, a philosopher from India (some of his children's stories are in the "Book House" collection), and I always love the way he says things. This is what he wrote about punishing his child:

"When I must punish him, he becomes all the more a part of my being. When I cause his tears to come, my heart weeps with him."

These are some of the reasons we honor our fathers on Father's Day.

We thank him by wrapping up a shirt or tie. We even look for a card that's not too "mushy"—it might embarrass him. But what we want to thank him for is the very fabric of our lives.

I want to thank my father: for polishing my shoes when I was a little girl—while I put my foot up on his homemade wooden shoe stand and he flipped the rag for a final shine and touch of pizzazz . . . for taking us on a family picnic on the river banks of the Chattahoochee where it's a small stream near Gainesville; and for reading to my little brother and me those beautiful lines of Sidney Lanier about the river, so that I will remember them always ("Out of the hills of Habersham, down the valleys of Hall"), having first heard them in a valley of Hall, watching the water "Split at the rock and together again . . ." for his endless jokes and funny songs . . . for teaching me to play baseball ("Keep your eye on the ball, follow through, *follow through!*") . . . for loving Chopin so much it brought tears to his eyes . . . for living, not just preaching, God's love.

These are some of the things I thank him for in my heart, every Father's Day.

Henry Van Dyke wrote a tribute to his own father, that may seem extravagant—but if you're lucky enough to have the kind of fathers my husband and I do, still going strong at 75 and 80 (and the kind I think my children do), the words are true:

"What do I owe my father? Everything. He was my best friend: a parent who knew how to be patient with an unruly child, a good companion in the woods and the library, a Christian without pretense or bigotry, a fearless man with a kind heart. Every day I give thanks for him."

JUNE 17, 1977.

You Know You're a Parent When. . . .

Charles Lloyd is a special person in my life.

In the two years he's been our pastor at First Baptist Church in Marietta, we've come to love this dynamic young man whose broad shoulders rammed football opponents in high school and college in Mississippi, and now carry the burdens of others as a dedicated minister.

We love Carolyn Sue too—his pretty little wife whose pint size belies her enormous talents and energy.

Recently Charles called a special meeting of his staff.

As they gathered in his office at the church wondering what this was all about, in walked Charles and Carolyn Sue with a surprise—their new adopted infant son, Andrew Philip Lloyd.

Carolyn Sue is one preacher's wife who knows how to keep a secret! For ten days little "Drew" had been in their home on Colston Road, his presence unsuspected until the legalities of his adoption were complete—and until they had time to enjoy him *all to themselves*.

Two weeks ago our congregation held a "Welcome, Little Drew" party.

Patty Hames Hilderbrand, whose murals grace the halls of most of the

Marietta schools, decorated the church fellowship hall with paintings of Mother Goose and Disney creatures to give to Drew.

Iris Hensley, founder of the Cobb-Marietta Ballet Company, taught several men in the audience choreography to "Rock-a-Bye Baby" so they could demonstrate for Charles how to do it.

Several people gave their advice for the new parents.

One, Larry Hutcheson—a father of two—had such a hilarious lecture for the Lloyds that I asked his permission to share it with you. Here it is.

"You know you're a parent when:

• You wonder what you did with all the time you had before the little darling arrived.

• You can get up at all times of the night and not care.

• You smell like baby burp.

• Your clothes have baby burp spots all over them.

• You realize changing little boys' diapers is dangerous.

• You believe the greatest thing in life has to be when your child is potty-trained.

• You wake up one morning and realize you slept all night.

• Your biggest expense is Olan Mills followed closely by Judson Trippe (the Lloyds' pediatrician).

• Those places you used to go and things you used to do seem so distant now.

• As far as you're concerned, "Sesame Street" is the best show on television.

• Your precious darling comes home with a new word learned and you have to explain what it means.

• You tell your oldest not to do what you let your youngest do.

• You want to spank and hug them at the same time.

• Eating takes twice as long as preparing the meal.

• You make promises only *they* remember.

• The local child's clothier and shoe salesperson become close personal friends.

• You start feeling sad as soon as they can wear your shoes.

• You don't mind any of the above."

OCTOBER 20, 1980

My Perfect Father-in-law

He was a perfect father-in-law.

He was always glad to see us. When we went for a visit, he would be looking for us in the side yard under the pecan trees. A wide smile would crease his face, the face my husband said "had the map of Ireland on it," and he would come to our car with outstretched arms to give each of us a hug. He was a man not embarrassed to show physical affection, to say, "I love you," often and mean it.

Gradually through the years, as our children grew older, we went less and less—but he never complained. Now we realize we didn't see him often enough—grown-up children hardly ever do until it's too late.

He saved pennies for his grandchildren in a big Mason jar. He would always have a big box of pecans ready for us to take home, or some Georgia cane syrup, or a jar of honey. He cut his best camellia blooms and wrapped them in wet newspapers for us as we started back.

His Sunday breakfasts were a specialty. We would lie in bed (the children scattered through the house on cots) and smell the bacon. He liked bacon so much he always cooked three pieces for everyone. His scrambled eggs and biscuits made from scratch were delicious.

He had a wonderful rapport with each child at any age. He took them fishing at Big Indian Creek. He let the boys help dig up small cedar seedlings to bring home and plant in our yard in Marietta. Now they are flourishing and green.

He told them about the woods and swamps, the animals and birds, and the flowers he grew so well. Grandmother planned the color coordinated iris beds, he put his green thumb to work, and each spring everyone in Perry drove by to see them in bloom.

When the children were older, he did a far better thing than talk to them—he listened to them. They felt no generation gap, for they sensed his acceptance of them and his belief in them (I'm sure he never read a child psychology book, but he didn't need to.)

When they went through their teenaged rebels phase, he not only didn't show any disapproval of their old tattered jeans and long hair—he didn't even seem to notice them.

Though his own two sons were the apple of his eye, he never made his daughters-in-law feel that we were anything but real daughters to him.

There were paradoxes to this man. He had no college education, but for many years he was chairman of the local school board. He didn't like the laws that ended segregation (after all, he was born only 30 years after the Civil War, in the deep South), but he treated his many black friends with kindness and respect. He was a World War I veteran and a member of the American Legion, but he had his own ideas about world peace, placing it above national pride.

He was patient and humble—the true humility which is not self-deprecating, but selfless, but he was a respected leader: the foreman of the large company where he worked, the chairman of the deacons in his church, the teacher of his men's Sunday School class.

His favorite reading was the Bible and *The National Geographic*.

He was miserable when the Atlanta Braves lost a game. He spent every night all summer watching them on TV, in that special love-hate concern of a true fan.

The only fault he had, as far as I know, was that he didn't want to ever leave home. We couldn't get him to travel the 120 miles to visit us. Oh, maybe for a child's graduation or a wedding, he'd come for one day, but he couldn't wait to start out for home the next morning.

He did leave home finally, to come here to Kennestone Hospital. Even in his pain he remembered to thank us for nursing him all we could, and to apologize for "being so much trouble."

"Blessed is the man," read his minister at his memorial service last week, "that walketh not in the counsel of the ungodly. He shall be like a tree planted by the rivers of water." And so he was.

Beneath our sadness is a deep joy for his life with us, and the knowledge that his new home can't seem very strange to him.

He's been on his way there for a long time.

JUNE 28, 1981

Summertime—and the Livin' Ain't Easy

"Summertime, and the livin' is easy," the song says.
Obviously a man wrote it.

Women know better. Ask any mother. Summertime livin' is *not* easy. It's the supreme challenge to family life: three long months of mother-and-child togetherness.

Summertime is prickly heat and pricklier dispositions . . . dirty bare feet, itchy chigger bites, and poison ivy . . slamming screen doors that seem to let two children inside the house for every one that goes outside.

Summertime is a kitchen where the action never stops. One mealtime merges indefinably into another. The counters are never clean, someone's always eating a meal when no one else is, and the bacon intended for a sleepyhead's late breakfast becomes someone else's BLT.

Summertime is going to get out ice and discovering some sickening purple stuff in the ice tray—homemade popsicles.

Summertime is peach pits and soft drink bottle tops dropped into the disposal, shattering your nerves with an ungodly clatter when you turn it on.

Summertime is trying not to use the air conditioner to save on the power bill, finding out how cross and cranky the heat makes everyone, and discovering a new axiom: "the family that sweats together frets together." The air conditioner is cheap at any price.

Summertime is taking your child to swimming lessons every morning for two weeks, and encouraging a goose-bumped, shivering, miserable little beginner into the water. Why is it always the coldest and cloudiest weeks of the summer that you sign up for swimming lessons?

Summertime is trying to coax your other children, prune wrinkled and lobster red, that they've been in swimming long enough—and worrying because your teenager's new bikini covers so very little of her and she'll have to get another suit before she visits Grandmother.

Summertime is sending your child off to camp for the first time, having a lump in your throat all week because you know he's homesick . . . but he's having a blast and doesn't want to come home.

Summertime is your college boy coming home for vacation with a big grin and a pile of dirty laundry as high as Stone Mountain. It's listening to his records for three months and never once to the Music Of Your Life.

Summertime is not ever having a schedule for anything. Between the baseball games and the other kids' summer jobs, it's a major achievement if you can answer the question, "Do you know where your children are?" Usually you don't.

Summertime is knowing that kids' summer jobs not only don't *pay* much, they might *cost* you. Figure the black work pants and work shoes they have to buy, the lunches they have to eat out, and the gas taking them back and forth (because if they had their own car they wouldn't need a summer job) and all a job does is to keep them off the streets.

Summertime is three months of arbitration and peace-keeping. No one can fuss like brothers and sisters at home in the summer. "They seem to be born with only one object in mind," says Carol Bartholomew (mother of six and author of *Most Of Us Are Mainly Mothers*): "to make each other's lives as miserable as possible." You have to mentally paraphrase every charge and counter-charge. Bartholomew points out, "He won't let go of me" should read "Gary will not let go of John for the obvious reason that John is going to club him with the flashlight the instant he does."

Don't try to say "share," or "take turns," or "don't fuss." Just say, "Shut up." And pray that September will hurry and get here.

JUNE 10, 1977

How We Gave the World's Worst Cook-Out

One of my new magazines has an article on "How To Give a Perfect Summer Cook-Out."

They've got to be kidding.

Everyone knows there's no such thing as a perfect summer cook-out. There are just too many ways to foul up.

Either you run out of lighter fluid and everyone's starving but the charcoal is just lying there, cold and gray . . . or you drop some meat through a crack in the grill when you flip it over . . . or you forget to make extra ice . . . or your husband takes up the meat before you finish making the salad so the meat gets cold. Something will always go wrong.

Maybe I'm a bit touchy on the subject. Two years ago Dallas and I gave a cook-out that was a total disaster. It was so bad it was funny—once we had lived through the first painful memories. Now we laugh about how we gave The World's Worst Cook-Out. I don't know if the friends who came to it laugh, though. I don't know if we're even friends any more.

Let me tell you how it was.

We invited couples who didn't know each other. That's supposed to be a great way to spark up a party. Those magazine articles always say it develops lively conversation and refreshing new friendships.

Then we planned our menu.

We decided on shish kabobs. Looking back, that was our first mistake.

Shish kabobs are delicious, a favorite of ours. But shish kabobs for a crowd are impossible. You need a hotel-sized kitchen and a staff of ten. Each person wants at least one skewer, maybe two. And on each skewer you need 8 or 10 good chunks of meat, onions, tomatoes, and bell pepper. We'd invited seven couples—plus us. Now, multiply the number of skewers needed times the number of items to be placed on each skewer, and you begin to understand the problem! It was enough cutting, dicing, chopping, and skewering for an army.

Lesson 1: *Never plan shish kabobs for more than two people, tops.*

On the morning of the party, I pulled out the drawer where our skewers stay, ready to go to work. It was empty! Then, and only then, did I remember I'd loaned our skewers to the College Sunday School Class at our church for a party—and never gotten them back. A hurried telephone survey revealed that very few of our friends own skewers. Fortunately, my next-door neighbor Joanne did, and loaned me hers.

Lesson 2: *It's hard to cook shish kabobs without skewers.*

I then attacked the mountain of raw meat and produce piled in the kitchen. And I might have made it . . . if Patty and David hadn't dropped by. Our daughter and her boy friend said they wanted to "have a talk" with Dallas and me. I had a sinking sensation. Patty had stars in her eyes, David looked scared, and they were holding hands. Obviously this would not be a quick conversation.

But how can you tell your daughter and her sweetheart you can't talk to them—because you have to chop up onions? I wiped off my greasy hands, the four of us filed into the den, and they told us they wanted to get married, and could they have a church wedding on Labor Day weekend?

It took us two hours to convince them that, though we were thrilled they had found one another and enthusiastic about their future together, no way could we pull off a big church wedding in six weeks.

Lesson 3: *Don't let your daughter become engaged on the day you're giving a party.*

Well, all those articles say—"Be flexible. Be innovative. Enjoy your own party and so will your guests."

I gave up on being ready in time. I decided to use subterfuge. We would make a big deal out of drinks and appetizers served outside by the grill. If we could keep the guests there chatting for a *long* time, Dallas could get the fire going. I could do my Kung Fu act privately in the kitchen, and no one would notice how late dinner was.

We set up a table on the lawn, laid out glasses, napkins, drinks and crackers; and just as we finished, two things happened: our first guests, Jim and Flora, arrived—and it started raining!

Lesson 4: *When you plan a party out-of-doors, it's a good idea to look up at the sky now and then.*

Lesson 5: *Just because you invite a preacher (Jim is the local Presbyterian minister,) don't think the Lord won't let it rain on your party.*

This is when everything started falling completely apart.

Everyone tried to be helpful. They grabbed up the table and moved it to the porch, turning over glasses and spilling crackers which were too soggy by now to eat anyway. Dallas ran hysterically back to the kitchen, yelling for me to hurry up and give him the shish kabobs before the rain put out the fire.

I got nervous and cut my hand; not just a little cut, but an awful gash that bled profusely through the paper towels I had around it. One of our guests, Nell, was a nurse. She wrapped my hand in a bandage and I tried to serve dinner, while dripping this bright red trail of blood in my wake. "It's nothing, ha ha," I said as our guests stared at the gushing red flow and lost their appetites.

It was no good. By then I was dizzy from loss of blood. One of the

men drove me to the emergency room at the hospital where, two hours later, they sewed up my hand.

As I lay waiting in a cubicle, wondering dismally how the party was faring, our daughter Katie came to sit with me. "Mom, it's awful quiet out there on the screened porch. Nobody is talking much." Then I remembered. They don't even know one another. I was going to develop sparkling new friendships.

Lesson 6: *When you give a party, stick around.*

Later I learned they did get to know each other—very well indeed. Disasters always draw the victims closer together. They even pitched in to clean up my kitchen together. That's when they found all the dirty bowls and knives and pans I'd hidden in the cabinets.

Lesson 7: *Your sins will find you out.*

These are the things that magazine articles never tell you. Maybe it's just as well. Who'd ever give a party? Anyway, reading about my fiasco may help you give your own cook-out this summer. Whatever happens, it can't compare with the World's Worst Cook-Out Ever. I already did that.

JUNE 23, 1983

Mother of the Bride

It's all over now.

A week ago I was out on "special assignment," as my editor called it. Not one he gave me, but one taken on many years ago when my first baby was born.

Last Saturday was her wedding day, and my special assignment was learning what it's like to be the Mother Of The Bride.

Now there's nothing left of the wedding cake but one small stale wedge which no one wants to throw away. The bride's bouquet has turned from a creamy pale yellow to an ugly yellow. And in Dixie's room hangs her wedding dress, a shimmering reminder of the daughter who shed it for pants and a shirt, ran giggling through a shower of birdseed (church custodians frown on rice), and sped off for a Florida honeymoon. Sped, that is, after finally escaping from the devilish groomsmen who decorated their car with shaving cream graffiti.

Those same groomsmen would never let Ken, my new son-in-law, forget it if I wrote a gooey, sentimental column about his wedding! Moreover, the marriage of my first born, like most life experiences, is too much to comprehend at once. Falling in love, giving birth, graduations, weddings—who can appreciate them fully when they happen?

As Thornton Wilder wrote, maybe the saints and the poets. The rest of us merely cope with the demands of the moment, and know that life is moving steadily on regardless of what we say or do.

So, as Mother Of The Bride, these are just some of my impressions coming spontaneously from the top of my head and the bottom of my heart.

First—I had trouble realizing this was not my little girl "playing wedding." Just as, when she began teaching school two years ago, I had trouble realizing she was no longer "playing school" with a chalk board, teaching her baby sister when they were small.

But it *was* her wedding and I tried to let her make all the decisions. My closed-mouth policy was good practice for becoming a mother-in-law, and I was rewarded by the light in her eyes.

Next, for every small crisis that popped up in the busy pre-wedding weeks, we tried to keep a "don't worry" attitude. It became a game we played—Dixie, her father, and I. Like whistling in the dark, you don't really kid yourself but it helps you over the bumps.

The magic words were: 1) "It doesn't matter," 2) "It's not really important," and 3) "Don't worry about it."

When I almost panicked over drawing up the invitations list, (will they be hurt if I leave them out? Will they wonder, why? if I invite them?) . . . when one of the bridesmaid's dresses didn't come, had to be re-ordered, and still wasn't here three days before the wedding . . . when Dixie chose a song I didn't think was appropriate . . . I kept muttering, "It doesn't matter, it's not really important, don't worry about it."

And you know what? The solo, "Evergreen," was beautiful, the bridesmaid's dress got here, and anyone omitted from our invitations list can surely be included in one of our next four children's weddings!

Finally, I felt more joy flooding our lives than we could ever imagine. Friends and relatives of ours and of Ken's family showed their love, not just in gifts but in giving parties, writing us notes, phoning—even by long distance, to add their blessings as our children began their new life together.

My biggest fear had been of crying at the wedding and making a disgraceful spectacle of myself. I always cry at weddings. It's a disease. Some people are free bleeders; I'm a free weeper. But this time, to everyone's astonishment, I didn't. Each time tears welled up, a larger joy rose to put them down.

Everyone special in our lives was here in this place. And everyone looked so happy—my daughters in their bridesmaids' blue, my sons and their dad in splendid black tuxes, my minister father in his clerical robe.

The last tinge of bittersweet regret faded away when I saw the radiant smiles that went from Ken to Dixie and back again. It was enough to melt the heart of the toughest groomsman.

Which is probably why they didn't use anything more than shaving cream on that get-away car.

AUGUST 12, 1977

A Modern Good Samaritan

A certain woman went down from Marietta to Powder Springs, even at the dawning of the day, because her son had a construction job and no car to call his own.

And it came to pass that as she returned, her Volkswagen fell into grievous trouble which stripped it of its gears, leaving it half dead on the Powder Springs Highway.

And the woman pulled to the side of the road. And there she sat in great despair, for she knew not what to do.

Now it was the hour known as Morning Rush. And great throngs of people and traffic hurried hither and yon.

Many cars whizzed by her—but when they saw the little sick car, they passed by on the other side.

In like manner, campers and vans and big, strong trailers appeared. But without slowing down one jot or tittle, they, too, passed by on the other side.

Then a tremendous 18-wheeler did loom into sight. And the poor woman took heart. "Oh, surely he will help me. It is said that truckers are always kind to drivers in distress," she thought.

But alas! With a roar of his engine and a honk of his horn, the big truck also passed by on the other side. And in the wake of his diesel, the little car did tremble on its four little wheels.

Just as the poor woman was considering sackcloth and ashes—thinking that even on Powder Springs Road in the hour of Morning Rush, sackcloth and ashes should get attention—there came into view a beautiful lady in a sedan. And when she saw the little sick Volkswagen, she was moved with compassion. And she did stop and offer help . . . even before she recognized the driver of the sick little car as a friend whom she knew, for she saw her through a glass darkly.

She drove her poor friend to a far country, even unto the Dallas Highway, to find a mechanic who could go to the little car and anoint it with oil, 30 weight, and bind up its wounds.

Then, having done so, she made sure the poor woman had two silver coins: one to call her husband at work to break to him the bad tidings of car trouble, the other for a cab to take her home. And only then did the beautiful lady depart for her job at Cobb General Hospital.

Verily I say unto you—for I am that poor, unfortunate woman—there is no greater kindness than this: to rescue a stranded motorist who is far from home.

I will tell you the beautiful lady's name, for though she is a modest lady, her light should not be hid under a bushel. She was Lillian Kirkpatrick. But now I call her "Sam"—for truly she is a Good Samaritan.

JUNE 23, 1978

The Varsity: "Three MKO Dogs and a Large PC"

I'm sorry I never told Mr. Frank Gordy what the Varsity means to me.

Everyone has his own special Varsity memories. Mine cover half a lifetime.

First Varsity experiences: long ago Saturdays in the fall . . . dates with Tech boys for the football games (heady excitement for an Agnes Scott girl) . . . dressed up in my brand new off-to-college wool suit and yellow mum corsage . . . curb boys scrambling to jump on the running board (that tells you how long ago it was) and take your order . . . sometimes splurging, paying an extra tip so one of the "showmen" like Flossie would chant out the list of food and drinks in a catchy rhythm, tap dance to the beat, and even turn hand flips.

Several years later: moving to Atlanta from Texas and heading for our favorite place (the Scottie had married the Tech man) . . . making a shocking discovery—women were now going *inside* The Varsity! (it used to be an all male hangout) . . . feeling like a loose woman the first time *I* went inside, as though the Agnes Scott Dean of Women were frowning over my shoulder.

My husband's order at The Varsity, always, never changing: "Three MKO dogs and a large PC" . . . the first time I heard him say that, after we were married and went inside, I gave him a hard time: "What in the world is THAT? Nobody will know what you want. They won't know what you mean by MKO dogs or a PC." He just gave a smirk. They knew. Varsity lingo had not changed since his old days at Tech.

An MKO dog was a hot dog with mustard, ketchup and onions, of course. A PC was a plain chocolate milk. The lingo was a talisman of youth, a token of his younger, carefree years. I think he liked that fact as much as he liked those juicy hot dogs and the carton of cold chocolate milk he poured over ice in a paper cup.

For 30 years now Dallas has this great moment, each time we go to

the Varsity, when he can forget he's a care-ridden husband and father, saunter up to the counter and say in his best macho manner:

"Give me three MKO dogs and a large PC."

Family trips to the Varsity with five little Ryles, our favorite tradition . . . any happening was a good excuse to go there—before a movie at the Fox, after a trip to Rich's, on the way to visit grandparents, returning from a vacation trip . . . The Varsity has been a dear, familiar landmark and the fragrant smell of those delicious onions told us all was well . . . Endless hassles compiling our orders in the car before we marched inside. . . . I would get the onion rings, Dallas the hot dogs, the oldest child the drinks . . . Special memory: Mr. Gordy coming over to take my arm and courteously lead me past the men in line; ladies did not wait with Mr. Gordy around! . . . the kids loved looking at tv while they slopped their French fries around in ketchup; we loved not having to watch our sloppy kids.

Now: fun times with our young adult children at the Varsity . . . meeting friends there . . . stopping by after a play or late Braves game for fried pies.

Our son, Stephen, is a Tech student now. Whenever we can, Dallas and I meet him at the Varsity. He's not far from home, it's true. But he's our youngest. You know how it is.

I hope, now that Mr. Gordy has gone, they don't change the Varsity in any way. The hot dogs are, of course, the most delicious anywhere in the world. And I'm not ready for life without going there now and then.

JUNE 30, 1983

Getting in Shape for the Peachtree Road Race

Man, the Peachtree Road Race sure takes a lot out of you. It's as tough as they say it is. This was my first year for it, and it's a real physical challenge.

Today it's Thursday. The race was last Monday morning and I still haven't recovered. My hands are red and raw from applauding so hard, and I'm still hoarse from yelling, "Go, runners!" for a solid hour.

I'll have to train and get in better shape before the race next year.

We've never been too eager to watch the race, but Patty kept insisting. "Mom and Dad, you really ought to go. You can't get the same impact on television—it's wonderful. We'll pick you up at 6:30 next Monday morning."

Our hearts weren't in it. What's the 4th of July holiday for if not for sleeping late?

But we tagged along with her and David and discovered it's an unforgettable experience.

If you've avoided going to the race because of the crowds, you don't have an excuse. We parked only a few yards from Peachtree on Peachtree Battle, and found curbside places to stand with no problem.

Watching the spectators was almost as much fun as watching the racers.

I stood beside a beautiful older lady who lived in that neighborhood—aristocratic, impeccably dressed even that time of day in a dark navy Izod dress, every white hair in place. Her husband sat behind us on a wall.

They come each year to watch their son, Bill, she tells me. Her husband is 81. He can't really see Bill from the wall—but he's so comfortable there.

The old gentleman motions her to him and whispers in her ear. She rejoins me at the curb. "He told me my slip is showing. Hell, he's lucky I even put on a slip this time of day!"

Now the motorcycle cops come down the street, herding the crowds back on the sidewalk.

Suddenly a few runners appear! David explains, though, they're not officially in the race. "They probably came from out of state someplace, planning to run, and didn't know they had to sign up ahead of time."

David knows about the race because he ran and earned his Peachtree Road Race T-shirt three years ago. That same night he had his first date with Patty. (The date wasn't a total success—David kept falling asleep.)

A skater comes zooming along, curving from one side of the street to the other in graceful loops, one arm tucked behind him. I guess he figures this is a great time to have a long, empty stretch of pavement all to himself.

"Here come the wheelchair racers!"

I look to the left at a sight I'll always remember—those beautiful young men and women, so strong and healthy within their limits, so very brave in their wheelchairs, racing by us with concentration and courage. Suddenly I know who is handicapped here . . . not them, but me. Slovenly, undisciplined me.

Now the press van passes, photographers sitting backwards as they shoot their pictures up Peachtree.

And here come the runners!

The first batch are the serious contenders. As light as gazelles, feet barely touching the pavement, whipping by us in a whoosh of movement so swift you see only a blur of arms and legs. Can they be humans, part of the same species as I?

We wait a few minutes for the other runners. Then they come. Almost as fast, almost as beautiful. Shirts drenched with sweat. Young women, young men, older men and women, children, until the street is a solid mass of striving humanity.

No costumes are allowed in the race—but one guy wears a small flag on top of his head, another a laurel wreath of green leaves.

"Yeah, runners! Go, runners!" Patty and I yell non-stop.

We see a few friends from Marietta, all looking great as they fly by: Judge Dorothy Robinson, Emily Read, Cheryl Dotson, Allyson Ray Murphy and her husband Jim, Rex Kaney, Wayne Waldrip, Chuck Misiaveg and his daughter Theresa.

And we yell our heads off as our curbside neighbor's son, Bill, streaks past us.

Twice we see runners on crutches. One, who has only one leg, bows gallantly to the crowd as we applaud, and motions to the other runners so we'll acknowledge them, too.

One handsome fellow flashes us a grin as he runs past and yells, "Which way to Piedmont Park?"

The last runners of the whole race are a darling little boy about three years old and his young mother, holding hands and jogging together.

Afterwards, it took three peach pancakes and two strips of bacon at The IHOP for me to forget my own lousy physical condition and enjoy the rest of my holiday. All that physical energy yelling and clapping was debilitating. It's not easy to be in the Peachtree Road Race, you know.

JULY 7, 1983

Under the Spell of Georgia's Golden Isles

Last week I didn't write a column, nor cook a meal, nor wash a dish, nor lift an iron.

For five wonderful days I enjoyed a glorious, lazy vacation at St. Simons Island. I've come back sounding like a travel agent, but so be it. No wonder this area is called "The Golden Isles." What a treasure trove of beauty.

I hadn't visited St. Simons since childhood (with grandparents in Florida we usually go there), but now I hope I can come back at least once a year for the rest of my life.

On our trip down I slept most of the way. (Is there a woman anywhere who can get the family off on vacation without staying up all night doing just one more load of wash?)

I woke as we entered Brunswick and were driving across the causeway to the island. A waving sea of salty marsh grasses was rippling in the breeze . . . freeing you from tension just by seeing such tranquil, open flatness . . . yet exciting you, too, with the mysterious sense of rich, secret life sheltered beneath the surface.

You breathe in the tangy air and resolve to look up Sidney Lanier's "Marshes of Glynn" and read it again, first chance you get.

Before you've had your fill of the marshes, you're into still another world: the oasis of beauty called St. Simons Island.

Wide curving roads take you through graceful Spanish moss (it's disappearing in Orlando and it breaks my heart), sun-dappled leaves and vines, and enormous live oaks whose branches form cathedral arches overhead.

The first time I saw the redwood trees in California I knew they were the most beautiful, majestic trees on earth. Now I don't know. These live-oaks have the same impact. Silent but oh, so eloquent. Their gnarled, twisted old limbs say age can be beautiful. Such majestic grandeur suddenly makes man's everyday hassles seem unnecessary and his problems rather puny after all.

We were staying at the King and Prince Hotel so we followed their blue and white signs past the lighthouse to the end of the island. While Dallas checked in, Katie, Stephen and I hurried to the beach.

What a contrast to other beaches—no cars, drink stands, boardwalk or snack bars; just a quiet, lovely stretch of sand, sea and sky.

The hotel was built in 1941 and has charm not found in chain motels. High ceilings, period furniture, and hurricane lamps not only add to the romantic ambiance but are extremely practical in a place where storms come often. It's named for King George, the ruler under whom Oglethorpe secured the island for the British in 1743 by defeating the Spanish at the Battle of Bloody Marsh.

A special feature of the hotel is the dining room, famous not only for its cuisine but for its gorgeous stained glass windows. Yes, stained glass. The windows have clear panes to a height of six feet, affording a view of the ocean on one side and the landscaped courtyard on the other. But high above the clear glass are arched panels of stained glass, depicting various scenes of the island.

Can you imagine a nicer way to start the day than to see soft, rich colors filtered through the ruby and royal blue glass, above a glittering, sparkling ocean? Especially while enjoying a late breakfast of melon, ham and cheese omelet, grits, and biscuits?

It's just as nice in the evening, with the rosy sunset glow—as you sip your coffee and eat key lime pie!

Of course, you can't spend all your time sunning, swimming and stuffing. There are too many interesting landmarks to visit:

Lovely little Christ Church, where you feel you're coming home to a friend after reading Eugenia Price's *Beloved Invader*. There are the tombstones, telling their story . . . which no one had the perception to put together 'til Miss Price read between the mossy, often almost obliterated lines and recognized the human drama right under her eyes.

Fort Frederica, site of a model town planned by Oglethorpe (each settler was chosen because of his trade or craft to fill a specific place) as well as the fort. The National Park Service is doing a great job of preserving and restoring this fascinating site.

Cumberland Island, a day's journey by boat from St. Mary's to a place that, for once in our lives, we've done the right thing by: preserving its rare beauty and ecology so that you feel like Robinson Crusoe when you put your footprints into the pristine sand.

And marvelous seafood places on St. Simons and all around. Umm, what eatin'! I'd like to tell you more—but I have to go exercise and drink my Sego. And start figuring out when I can go back.

JULY 1, 1977

Friendship Force Comes to Cobb

In Orlando High School in 1945 I sat in Señora Dyer's Spanish class and practiced my Spanish conversation:

"¿Dónde estamos? Estamos en la sala de clase. ¿Es pequeña la sala? No, señorita, es grande."

As I remember it, that meant:

"Where are we? We are in the classroom. Is it a small room? No, miss, it is big."

Last Wednesday night I stood in the lobby of the Cobb Civic Center theatre with 152 Costa Ricans milling around me, and wished fervently I could say something to them besides "Where are we . . . we are in the classroom . . ."

Mute with bilingual deficiency, I smiled broadly, gestured often, and fell into the trap everyone does—speaking pigeon English in a slow, loud voice, as though the problem were not my words but the other person's hearing.

Fortunately I learned something this week. I learned that feelings of good will do not depend on language.

The Friendship Force—the program that brought these visitors to Cobb County—is indeed a "force," a power to overcome many barriers and help people make friends with one another.

A steering committee of the Cobb Chamber of Commerce headed by Marilyn Greider, president of the Cobb Arts Council, is planning special activities for the Costa Ricans. Nancy Bickley and Sam Rothermel are co-chairmen of the local Friendship Force trip.

The program on Wednesday night got their visit off to a fine start. The visitors enjoyed a presentation by the Cobb-Marietta Ballet, a Menotti aria sung by Cobb soprano Linda Tucker, and piano music by Bill Maples—some Scott Joplin ragtime music and Dave Brubeck jazz.

But the ones who stole the show were the Li'l Generals! The young cloggers, girls flipping their short skirts, boys vying with each other to tap toes fastest and click heels the highest, brought rhythmic handclaps from the Costa Ricans in time to the fiddling music—just as audiences do at the Grand Ole Opry.

Then it was the Costa Ricans' turn. And although The Li'l Generals were a hard act to follow, the visitors did with flying colors—the flying colors of long skirts of bright blue, red and yellow as their girls twirled with barefoot "gaucho" partners in their native dances.

Interpreter Carlos Aguilar, a Cobb resident and a native of Costa Rica, explained they were not professional dancers but typical youngsters who had practiced only a month before coming to the States. They performed with a happy, natural grace and charm.

I felt I had a real glimpse into life in a village of Costa Rica on a Saturday night in the village square. (If they have disco fever there, like we do, don't disillusion me; I don't want to know.)

The attractive Sylvia Flores, also an interpreter for the program, announced each act in Spanish first, then switched to a "Hi, y'all" for the rest of us.

Mayor Dana Eastham welcomed the group and reminded us Marietta has a sister city in Costa Rica, where he and others from Marietta have visited. The Costa Rican Consul, Rose Cunningham, read a proclamation from Gov. Busbee welcoming the group.

A reception after the program was hosted by the Cobb-Marietta Junior League. The star attraction was a mammoth cake with flags of both nations and a replica of the world in sugar icing. How do you bake such a cake? Said its creator, Jo Ann Crimm . . ."One layer at a time!"

In case you want to try it some time, you make five 8-inch layers, one 16-inch layer, a 3-inch divider, a 12-inch layer, and more 8-inch ones. A labor of love, for sure.

Jimmy Freeman finally came to my rescue with my language problem. He rounded up a young Spanish exchange student from Barcelona, and thanks to him, I interviewed a few of the Friendship Force Visitors.

They all said the same thing in different words—that a program like the Friendship Force is the best way to develop understanding and peace between the nations of the world.

Mrs. Dyer should have taught us to say:

"¿Es pequeño el mundo? No, señorita, es grande." It's not a small world, it's a large one. But the more we learn to be friends, the smaller it grows.

JULY 11, 1980

A Cat-Astrophic Summer for Liza

This is a terrible summer for Liza, our Show Business Cat.

She's the creature with the beautiful deep gray fur, sea green eyes, and personality you could call outgoing—or ornery and cantankerous, depending on whether or not you like cats.

Liza has been trying to make it in musical theatre since she was a child star. She came into our lives the summer Katie worked in the show at Six Flags. Liza kept hanging around backstage, giving auditions every chance she got.

No one knew where she came from. Maybe her mama brought her. You know how those pushy Stage Mothers are. I have an idea, though, that Liza ran away from home. She obviously had her heart set on the Great White Way.

She's talented, no doubt about it. She sings in a loud clear yowl, Ethel Merman style, that could reach the back row balcony with no problem: "There's neoww business like sheoww business like neoww business I kneoww . . ."

She's a marvelous dancer—tap, soft shoe, even break dancing. Liza was probably the first break dancer in Georgia. We didn't know then what it was. When we dangled a string in front of her, she would moonglide across the room to it, then do spectacular flips, springs and handstands away.

The show at Six Flags didn't need a cat that year, so Katie brought her home and named her Liza Minnelli. She seems fairly content with us, but when that cat food commercial comes on tv ("chow chow chow") she reminds us reproachfully that SHE could have had that part.

We don't dare tell her about the current Broadway show "Cats." She'd head straight for New York.

This summer has been rough on Liza.

We're making her stay outdoors, because last summer she had fleas. That caused our carpets in turn to have fleas, which took three room bombs and two visits from the exterminator to get rid of.

This summer Liza is kept out—and she has never enjoyed camping out. She's a girl who appreciates soft cushions, fine china and the good things of life.

She won't frolic in the grass or chase squirrels or do normal cat things. She just sulks around the house plotting ways to get back in. Our whole life has become a cloak and dagger operation.

Before we take out the garbage or bring in the milk, we crack the door, look to the left and right, and then make a mad dash for our target—just like a James Bond movie.

Usually Liza gets in anyway. She's learned how to flatten herself against the wall. I think she watches James Bond movies, too.

Another problem this summer is that Liza has to share attention with another cat. She likes star billing. We're keeping Patty and David's cat Tisha while they're studying in England this summer.

Tisha (short for an Indian word that means The Hunter Who Stalks By Night) is a lovable calico cat, sweet and gentle . . . except at mealtime. At mealtime Tisha is a tiger.

When we approach with the cat food for both cats, Tisha arches her back, spits, hisses and swipes at Liza. Poor Liza is terrified. She never intended to mess with Tisha's bowl. Now she's afraid to come near her own. I think she's getting an ulcer.

As if that isn't enough, Liza is losing her fur! It's coming out in great tufts and chunks, leaving her beautiful gray coat full of holes. She looks pitiful. Our vet, Thad Riddle, says it's an allergy. It itches and bleeds and she's miserable.

We give her white tablets and pink drops, and rub ointment on her; but Liza is so embarrassed.

When you've been a beautiful show girl, it's sad to lose your looks.

I wonder if perhaps this suffering can deepen her as an actress. Maybe she's ready for tragedy.

Any night now I expect to see her climb up on our garbage can and sing that beautiful number from "Cats"—"Memories, all alone in the moonlight . . ."

It's a tough summer indeed for our Liza.

JULY 26, 1984

The Home of the Braves

Tonight is "Marietta Night" at the Atlanta Braves game.

Mayor Bob Flournoy will throw out the first ball. No doubt, he'll do it with that Flournoy style and panache. And 300 Marietta city employees, dates or spouses will be on hand to cheer the Braves on to—we hope—another victory, leaving the Dodgers further behind in this pennant race.

Ron Ransom, Marietta Director of Parks and Recreation, says that's the extent of our city's part in the program tonight. The Braves office had already lined up someone to sing the "Star-Spangled Banner." I wish Bob and Ron could do it. Both of them are talented crooners. They could even throw in a soft shoe dance and give some great one-liners—we could call it the Skip and Ernie and Bob and Ron Show!

Maybe next year.

Meanwhile, with Braves baseball this summer, who needs anything more?

Aren't they beautiful? Aren't they a team you have to love with all your heart?

This summer has been one of the most wonderful times in our lives, thanks to the razzle-dazzle, give-it-your-all performances they're giving us.

After a long, long, *long* time of supporting a Braves team that never seemed to have it—this summer is too good to be true!

Remember how hard it has been in the past to be a Braves fan?

They were our team so, of course, we hoped they would win. But how could you *like* them, let alone *love* them, when they specialized in leaving men on base, hitting into double plays, making comical errors and dropping an early lead every time?

The men in our family take their baseball seriously: even more than I do. And in the old days, I dreaded every game on the schedule. It meant listening to the ferocious, anguished roars of my husband and sons as they watched the game on tv:

"Take him OUT of there. Good grief, TAKE HIM OUT!"

(They have this delusion that there's a remote control, direct connection straight from our den at home to the Braves dugout and that the Braves managers are anxiously awaiting their advice regarding pitchers.)

It's a good thing our coffee table is sturdy enough to endure the kicks and slams they give it to emphasize their game commentary.

But this season the games are such a pleasure, either watching at home or better yet going to the stadium where not Falcon Fever, but Braves Delirium, reigns supreme.

This season you want to pull for them, win or lose, because they're talented, competitive, star-quality players who win your heart:

Spunky little Hubbard, who doesn't let size mean anything. Chambliss, who works half of the double play magic with Glenn and gets a hit any time we need one. Benedict ("BROOCE"), running right into the opposing team's dugout and falling down the stairs if need be, but what the heck, he keeps his eye on that ball.

Claudell, smashing against the fence to save an out. (Our grandson, Gary, says if the new baby is a brother, he'd like to name him Claudell.) Young Brett Butler, hitting his third homer with such boyish pride you want to pat him on the head.

Raffie of the dark eyes and athletic grace. Chunky, tough Bob Horner slugging the ball—and man, can he slug the ball. Perez, knowing where the stadium is now and how to get there—knowing where home plate is, too.

Niekro with his staying qualities (just wish he'd warm up sooner). Royster and Watson and others, who do so many things well.

And in a class all by himself: Dale Murphy.

The perfect All-American Hero. The sort of guy who makes a miracle play leaping 10 feet into the air for a catch in center field, and tells the interviewer later, "I thought Claudell's catch tonight was better, myself."

What a team! If we don't win the World Series, we'll still never forget them.

We will, though. Our son Stephen, working in Glacier Park this summer, has already written us to be sure to order his tickets. So has my 81-year-old Dad in Orlando (who also thinks he has a direct connection from his living room to the Braves managers when he watches the games).

We'll all be there, to cheer the team America loves (thanks to Ted Turner). But us old Braves fans will cheer hardest of all.

JULY 21, 1983

(Note: Camelot faded again. We traded Niekro, traded Brett—Ted Turner should know that anyone with a name like B-Rhett Butler *has* to play for Atlanta—Horner broke his wrist, Dale hit a slump . . . but wait till next year!)

Cobb Libraries Offer Children the Magic World of Books

Mid-Summer Slump is here.

Dads know summer is half over when the All-Star baseball game rolls around. But Moms know it when their children get over the first thrill of vacation freedom, going barefoot, swimming and goofing off, and start that horrible whine:

"What can I DO? There's NOTHING around here to do."

What you need to do is get them started on a good book. Ruth Inglis from the Cobb Libraries main office called me this week to tell me about the many attractions they're offering children this summer.

Her suggestions will be good news for harassed mothers and whining children.

First, enroll your child—if you haven't already done so—in the Vacation Reading Club. My children always did this and it motivated them to stack their arms high with new reading material every two weeks, and to delve into a book when they were bored. They always wanted to win a certificate and make a good impression on their new teacher in the fall—

but the fringe benefit was that once they started reading, they found out they LIKED it!

The library gives each child who reads 12 books during summer a certificate. If he reads 25 books, he gets a super-duper gold certificate! (That's not bribing—that's "positive reinforcement" and it makes good sense.)

Take advantage, too, of Story Time at the library each week. Every child deserves the privilege of hearing books read to him. Television or records can't match the pleasure of a real, live person reading a real, honest-to-goodness book to a child . . . best when done by a parent or grandparent, of course, while being held in a lap; but a pleasure which is charismatic and enchanting to all children.

You can bring pre-school children to the Main Library for Story Time each Monday morning at 10 or at 11, school-aged children Monday afternoons at 3:30.

Be sure to see the children's room upstairs, where Story Time is held, if you've never been there before. It's such a bright, cheerful place it makes me want to be a child again. The most delightful murals of storybook figures are on the walls. They were painted by sisters Patti Hames and Lucia Hames Phillips (daughters of Judge and Mrs. Luther Hames) and have favorites like Christopher Robin and Big Bird. They march right across the room and straight into your heart!

The libraries also are showing wonderful full-length films every week this summer. Your older children and young teens would enjoy them, too. (They're not allowed to publicize the titles because it would be competing with commercial theatres—but you'd be crazy not to take advantage of this opportunity. Check out the schedule at your library.)

And do you know about the Family Entertainment series on Tuesday evenings? There are programs on every subject you can imagine, with an expert there to discuss them—photography, yoga, gems and minerals, karate, whatever. They are held alternately at the East Marietta and The Main Libraries.

As a confirmed bookworm from the days I used to hide in the old pear tree to cry over Louisa May Alcott, I want to thank Mary Louise Rheay, director of our Cobb Libraries, and her excellent staff for their imaginative methods to open the world of books to children.

Modern communication techniques are great in many ways, but a bad side-effect is that the public reads less. Educators and child psychologists warn that unless a child enjoys books while very young, he probably never will.

It breaks my heart to think of any child growing up without the delights of the *Tales of Uncle Remus*, the naughty escapades of *Peter Rabbit*, the sweet tooth of the *Poky Little Puppy*, the triumph of courageous children over an unfair adult world in *The Secret Garden*, the warm, happy world of Robert Louis Stevenson's *Child's Garden of Verses*, the musical language of *Wind In The Willows*, the British child's world that transcends culture to become *every* child's world in the dear *Christopher Robin* and *Winnie the Pooh*.

Or, for that matter, the Bobbsey Twins and Nancy Drew!

Make sure you open that world to your child and help lead him in.

And thanks to Mary Louise and all the patient, hard-working staff members in each Cobb Library for keeping that special world open for the rest of us. A world where we can find anything we want between the pages . . .

Go, little book
And wish to all
Flowers in the garden,
Meat in the hall,
A living river by the door,
A nightingale in the sycamore.
—R. L. Stevenson

JULY 11, 1978

Mountain Air at Sylva

I hate to tell you where I am right now.

The weatherman just reported 93 degrees in Atlanta today. I'm in the North Carolina mountains and I just closed the windows because the cabin is so chilly.

Charlie and Helen Watson lent me their place this week. It's perched on a mountain on the outskirts of Sylva, North Carolina. You pass through Sylva on your way to Cullowhee. You go to Cullowhee if you're going to Western Carolina University. But you don't really need a reason to go either place—except that they're smack dab in the middle of some of the prettiest country God ever made.

I have the local radio station on (I think it comes from Franklin, about 30 miles away). This morning the announcer said we're supposed to have "far" weather today. At first I didn't know what he meant. Was he telling us the weather was a long distance away? That didn't make sense. Then it dawned on me that he was saying—in perfectly good mountain talk—that it would be "fair" weather today.

Sometimes we flat-landers have trouble understanding the simplest things.

He was wrong about one thing, though. It's not "far"—it's raining. The mountains just across the way from Charlie's mountain, usually a lovely view, have vanished behind a gray curtain.

The white pines near the cabin sparkle with a sheen of misty silver. The hemlocks are a wet glistening green.

I left the door to the sundeck open so I can hear the rain and smell the air. Even though the stated purpose of my trip here is to work on some writing, I haven't touched the typewriter yet. I have another project going just now which is very important: I'm analyzing mountain air.

What is it that smells so good up here? That makes you want to keep breathing in and not ever breathing out—savoring the heady, fresh, wonderful smell? I'm trying to do like those experts do who analyze French perfume or a wine bouquet, trying to figure out the elements that combine for such a delicious aroma.

So far here's my conclusion—what makes fresh mountain air smell so good . . .

1) Basic fragrance: the fresh spicy pungency of evergreens (Charlie has pines, hemlocks, and spruce trees here.)

2) Added sweetness: mixed wildflowers. Any mixture will do. Here at Charlie's I only see a few varieties blooming at the moment—pale yellow and orange day lilies, bright tangerine butterfly weed, dainty Queen Anne's Lace. As far as I know, none of these smell particularly sweet by themselves—but the sweetness floating in this air is light and tantalizing.

3) Mix well in plenty of dark rich wood's dirt. Our dirt at home in Marietta is as hard and unyielding as a tennis court. The dirt here at Charlie's is spongy loam. When you walk outside, you feel you're walking on crepe rubber soles. Mountain dirt has a damp smell that promises shade, birdsong, solitude and peace.

4) Gather altogether and wet them down with cool spray from a mountain stream.

The stream here rushes through the back of Charlie and Helen's cabin and curves around the side—making a merry whooping sound that fills the air with liquid laughter. I'd like to record it on a tape and take it home. It's a drug-free tranquilizer. Lie down at night, listen to that creek, and you're asleep before you can pull up the blankets. By day the droplets glisten in the air like a splintered rainbow over the stream and drift outward spreading free air conditioning far and wide.

There you have it—my scientific analysis of mountain air.

Now, before I start working, there's one more thing I must do: analyze the sounds here in the mountains. The humming insects in the sunshine, the trilling screech owl serenading me last night, that rippling mountain stream . . . with so many things to be done here, how can I possibly do any writing?

JULY 19, 1984

Neonatology Is a Beautiful New Word

Do you know what "neonatology" is?

Two weeks ago I didn't either.

It took a phone call from Texas and a baby from Savannah to teach me. And it took my own four-year-old niece, little Joelle Ryle in Pensacola, Florida, for me to know how truly beautiful it is.

"Neo" means new, of course. "Natal" means related to birth. "Ology" is a science or branch of knowledge. Put them together and you have the science of caring for newborn babies.

Most babies don't need special care. It's all natural. They bounce into the world, get spanked by their doctors and fed by their mothers, and proceed to kick, cry, wet, sleep, live and grow in the natural, marvelous development of human life.

Some little ones, though, aren't so lucky. They can't make it on their own. They're born too soon, before their lungs are fully developed, before their brains can "tell" lungs to breathe and hearts to keep beating in the cold outside world.

Others may be full-term babies who become critically ill or have serious congenital problems.

Treating these special babies is a new medical specialty. Med students now can specialize in neonatal pediatrics; nurses get special neonatal nursing training.

We have a Neonatal Intensive Care Unit (NICU) now at Kennestone

Hospital, presided over by Dr. Brenda Marino and her team of nurses and workers. The center opened last August and has treated about 250 babies in its first year of operation.

The phone call that put me in touch with NICU here was from our son, Buddy. He was calling from Austin, distressed over news from his girl friend, Peggy's, brother and wife in Savannah. Their first baby had been born prematurely, at six months, and weighed less than two pounds. Doctors gave little hope the baby would survive.

"Mother, the Savannah hospital was too crowded and they sent the baby in a helicopter to Kennestone Hospital! They have something called a 'Neonatal Nursery' there. Would you please go check on the baby? They're all so worried—it's their little 'Gary,' you know."

I knew. Gary was the first grandchild in our family—this was the first in Peggy's.

And that was my introduction to the NICU at Kennestone.

This week I talked with Dr. Marino and learned more. The dark-haired, dark-eyed young woman (New York native, Georgia Medical College grad, directed the NICU at Memorial Medical Center in Savannah for six years before coming here; husband Bob Fuller teaches math at Marietta High, three children, "and we all love Marietta") sparkles when she talks about her work.

"These babies do so much better than you think they could!" The survival rate is 85% and of those babies, 80 to 85% will be normal children. No wonder Dr. Marino fights so hard for each tiny patient.

"They accuse me of being willing to resuscitate a doorknob," she laughs.

The hardest problem is the proper balance of oxygen. "Oxygen is a poison—too much will damage the eyes, but too little will damage the brain." In the tertiary care unit, where there are four beds or isolettes, the babies are on life support systems (respiratory and intravenous feeding) and monitoring equipment. Each little patient has a full-time nurse.

Kennestone is the closest hospital to Tennessee which has tertiary care for newborns. Babies are flown here, too, from Florida and south Georgia. They come in helicopters which have the necessary equipment. An entire helicopter is needed for each baby—twins came to Kennestone, each in his own vehicle!

In the eight-bed intermediate unit, the life support is removed but full-time monitoring continues, with one nurse for four patients.

They let me put on a white smock and tiptoe into this section to see the babies. Lying under their clear coverings, they look exactly like Tiny Tears dolls in plastic boxes—so small and precious.

All I could think of was our darling niece, Joelle, who was also a "miracle baby." She and her twin sister were born to Dallas's younger brother, Sam, and his wife, Patricia, almost three months prematurely. Unlike the baby of our Savannah friends, and unlike her own twin sister, Joelle won the fight for life. Today she's a bright, perky little girl whose only physical problem is needing glasses.

The price tag for all that early care was out of sight, but Joelle is beyond price. Today, because of their gratitude, Sam and Patricia both serve as volunteers in a parent support group at the hospital in Pensacola, and Sam serves on the hospital board of directors.

I didn't know three years ago, when Joelle was born, what "neonatology" was, but it's a beautiful word. If you can't say it, you can just say miracle care. It's about the same thing.

JULY 28, 1983

Joy Is Having Your First Grandchild

A new baby. Close encounters of the very first kind.

If you're bored with cliché grandparents who whisk out pictures, turn the page fast. You're getting ready to read a whole column about my new little grandson.

Name: Gary Ryle Minor. Born August 16, 1978, at Kennestone Hospital. Weight: 9 pounds 6 ounces. Length: 22½ inches. Hair: reddish gold. Eyes: blue.

A "Minor" baby, a major event!

Certainly I could write about nothing else just now. Gary has been the only thing in our lives since he entered our world last week. On Monday he went home and I went out to help Dixie and Ken take care of him.

A new baby is like the other milestones in life. It all happens too fast, the feelings go too deep. Events, impressions, thoughts tumble together and you feel it's a movie shown at the wrong speed. You want to slow it down, sort it out, enjoy it slowly—but there's no way.

It happens in a glad rush, and you have your own private rerun later, with your snapshots and souvenirs and memories.

Here are my first impressions of close encounters with our Gary.

First, the ordeal of waiting. Time telescopes, and the last nine months seem much shorter than this last day. Grandparents can stay in the fathers' waiting room—so now I know how it feels on the other side of that delivery room door.

My compassion for new fathers is boundless. Each young man knows the one he loves is suffering, and so he suffers too. Whether he sits with her in the labor room as Ken did—having learned all about having babies in Lamaze classes—or paces the waiting room in the traditional way, red-eyed, smoking nervous cigarettes. (To their disappointment Ken had to join us finally in the waiting room, as Dixie delivered Gary by Caesarian—since Gary was determined to come into the world feet first rather than head first, by golly.)

What a relief and joy to hear the announcement: "Mr. Minor, would you like to see your new son?"

Our mad scramble, all four grandparents close at Ken's heels, to peek at little Gary in his incubator before they wheel him off to the nursery to be cleaned, weighed and measured.

The indescribable, jolting impact of seeing your grandchild for the first time—wise, puckered little face; calm eyes; the utmost dignity; not bothered one bit by all these flurried, hysterical grownups around him; an adorable, perfect miracle.

The comfort of good doctors—and an extra bonus because Dixie's obstetrician and pediatrician had been my doctors, too. The excellent care at Kennestone—including special, personal instruction each day for mothers who want to breastfeed their babies. A festive dinner on their last night, when Dixie and Ken joined other new parents for a candle-lit dinner at the hospital, with steaks and sparkling grape juice! (There were 37 babies born at Kennestone last weekend . . . and there was a full moon!)

Now I'm learning new ways to care for babies: no baby powder, a better way to burp (rubbing, not patting), wrapping him tightly so he feels secure. I'm still clumsy with safety pins, and fearful of handling this tiny person—until forgotten skills return and I get the hang of it again.

The marvel and wonder of such a perfect little mouth, hands, and feet. A body barely the size of two hand spans, yet solid and heavy and strong enough to push out of your arms if you're not careful. Dr. Spock—still the hope and mainstay for new parents. The bursting pride of his other grandparents, Jim and Jerry, Dallas and me, not to mention his five young aunts and uncles.

We could spoil Gary in a hurry. Luckily he has parents who won't let us.

We've been singing the old lullabies that we used to sing to his mother.

"Toora Loora" and "Mighty Lak A Rose." But I like a new one my daughters have taught me—it's by Carly Simon . . ."Julie, through the glass, smiling up at me, you've just got to be the sweetest thing I've ever seen."

Gary through the glass, Gary at midnight alone with me on the sofa, Gary snuggled warm and small on my shoulder, Gary anywhere and anytime at all, I love you.

AUGUST 25, 1978

My Husband, the Pot-hunter

My husband is a pot-hunter.

He doesn't go around looking for marijuana. He's not a narcotics agent for the Feds. What he is is an amateur archaeologist.

Professional archaeologists, who worry (often with reason) that amateurs will disturb or destroy valuable evidence of the past, give it the slightly derogatory term "pot-hunting."

It's a hobby Dallas finds fascinating. As often as he gets out his golf clubs or rod and reel, My Husband, The Pot-Hunter, dons baggy old overalls and muddy boots, grabs his maps, and heads for the countryside.

The objects of his searches are Indian artifacts, and our Georgia clay is rich with such relics for those with the skill and patience to find them.

Dallas began this hobby only three years ago but his collection already numbers several hundred pieces. Besides arrowheads and spear points, it includes tools such as knives, drills, scrapers and hafters (used to notch arrow shafts), pottery fragments, ornamental discs, throwing stick weights, and—probably his favorite—a large, well-used old stone hoe.

Some were made by the Cherokees—but many are much older. They cover periods from Archaic to Modern Indian.

The first time Dallas told me that one of the points he had found was probably 6,000 years old I gave him a hard time. That sounded incredible to me. (I'm a doubting Thomas anyhow—I wasn't sure much of his stuff was anything but plain old rocks, 'til he showed me enough pictures in his reference books to convince me!)

Then I saw the display last year at the Joanne Stratton Library, which had identical pieces to his, and I was a believer. They were indeed very, very old.

Now that he's taught me more history of our continent, it's not so surprising: North America has been inhabited by man for 10,000 to 30,000 years, depending on which theory you accept. With early Indians roaming America 25 times longer than Western man has lived here, no wonder so many traces of their culture remain.

Many friends wonder at such a strange and weird hobby! Why would anyone want to walk miles and miles in the boondocks, scratched by brambles and slogging through mud? (Dallas once found himself shoulder high in wet sand, a frightening predicament it took 30 minutes to free himself from.)

What could be the fun of picking up and discarding hundreds of dirty little rocks before seeing two or three worth keeping?

There are several enticing reasons for pot-hunting:

First is the thrill of discovering the handiwork of early man. There's something intensely moving about holding in your hand a knife shaped by a long-ago hunter, or a piece of a cooking vessel used by his wife.

You learn that, though his lifestyle was rough and primitive, he cared about beauty. He pressed fabric into clay or scribed with a stick and made a pottery design. You respect his cleverness in shaping arrowheads (broad base, indented base, beveled, many other varieties of this small tool).

He existed because he adapted to the world around him—and you wonder if you could have done half as well if you had "walked in his moccasins."

There's also the fun of the search itself. When My Husband, The Pot-Hunter, spreads out his topographical maps and notes, and begins poring over them to plot his next expedition, it reminds me of a little boy playing at treasure maps and buried gold. What could be more fun?

He has learned where to look and how to go about it. Indians encamped near water, yet high enough to be above the flood plain. Therefore, *voilà*! A high, level bank along converging streams, or the confluence of a stream and a lake, makes an ideal spot to search.

He tries to avoid digging—anybody who gardens in the rock-hard Georgia clay can understand why! He explores areas where the earth has already been turned up, such as a ploughed river bottom, a lake shore in winter (when the water level is low), or a newly excavated building site.

It takes practice to know which stone chips or mud chunks are actually Indian tools or pottery. But then it takes practice to be a par golfer or champion tennis player, too. And just think—no court reservations, no greens fees. It's all there, free for the taking.

Pot-hunters need to know that antiquities law strictly prohibits digging on government property. Also, if you ever luck up on an important Indian site—such as a mound or lithic station—leave it alone! Call your nearest chapter of the American Archaeological Society.

Disturbing such a site would be like tearing out the pages of a rare old book, destroying forever the truth it could teach us.

With that stipulation—anyone for pot-hunting?

JULY, 1977

The Art of Cooking

If you can't stand the heat, don't get out of the kitchen. Stay in there and whip up something good for supper!

You're going to be hot anyhow. Why not make it count? Summer eating is the best kind of all. Now's the time to glory in the good things at the farmer's market or growing in the garden. Crisp fried okra, fresh butterbeans and crowder peas, tangy home-grown tomatoes, sweet thick slices of Vidalia onions (Georgia's gift to the world), corn either on the cob or better yet, cut and cooked in the skillet . . . umm! Summer is no time to count calories.

My husband undergoes a personality change in the summer. In fall, winter and spring, he's a liberated husband. He never complains when I set an uninspired meal before him—he'll even whip up an omelet himself.

But in the summer, he gauges the success of the season by how many times we have homemade ice cream, butterbeans, and crowder peas.

In fact, he counts. He'll say about the last of July, "Did you know we've only had fresh crowder peas three times this whole summer?"

Fortunately, it's not a problem in our marriage because I truly love to cook. In other domestic skills, I'm not so great. I never learned to sew more than Jiffy patterns (those that come in three pieces.) And I don't clean house 'til we can't find anything any more. But cooking to me is satisfying and creative. Some of my happiest times are when I can spend time in the kitchen without interruptions measuring and stirring while the radio plays some easy listening tunes. It's as much fun to me as writing a column that goes well or working out a Bach passage smoothly on the piano.

Like any art form, cooking varies with the artist. Most men who like to cook seem to have a cavalier attitude about ingredients and measurements—have you noticed? They'll dump in whatever they have at hand, try an herb or spice they hadn't thought of before, or tackle the most intricate, complicated recipes without blinking an eye.

Two of the best cooks I've ever known are my mother and my husband's mother. Each has her own style and flair—complete opposites from each other.

My mother cooks easily and quickly, doing proportions by instinct, trying incredible new recipes (she has a marvelous collection of cookbooks) and improvising her own. She makes her own chutney for curried chicken, just thinking up what ought to go in it. I wouldn't know where to *start* with chutney. She entertains beautifully, often spontaneously, and one of her greatest gifts as a preacher's wife is the gift of hospitality. From quail dinners for the elders and deacons, to Sunday night sings for the young people, to lunch and supper invitations to singles, widows, whoever needs "tender loving care"—cooking for them is her pleasure.

My husband's mother works as slowly, carefully, and thoroughly as a scientist in the kitchen. She uses measurements so exact that one of her recipes (for "hermit cookies") calls for $3/16$ teaspoons of each spice. She has also measured what a "heaping teaspoon" is, and notes it's actually one level teaspoon plus $3/4$.

She's an artist with her cooking, too. She spends almost an hour beating her pound cake ingredients . . . and the result is buttery perfection. No matter how I try, I will *never* be able to make a pound cake like Mother Ryle's.

She enjoys having company, too, but plans far ahead for every detail. She laughs that she can't do anything in a hurry—but she's a true artist in the kitchen.

No matter what your style is, if you like to cook, you do need to do it without interruptions. It's frustrating to wedge it in between car pools, or after a long day at the office. And you need to try new recipes now and then or it gets so boring you lose interest.

I hope your summer vacation offers enough leisure time to indulge in the art of cooking, if you enjoy it. Here are a couple of my favorite recipes that may interest you . . . I'd love to get one of yours.

Mother Ryle's Deep Pan Apple Pie

(This makes enough to satisfy our family of 8, with a little left-over. You may want to half it.)

10 c. tart cooking apples, peeled and sliced thin
  (slices should be the same thickness if possible)
2 and ¾ to 3 c sugar
¾ tsp. spices: ⅜ t. nutmeg
  ⅛ t. mace
  ⅛ t. cinnamon
  ⅛ t. cloves
Mix spices with sugar
Juice of 1 lemon
⅛ lb. margarine or butter, cut in thin slices.
Pastry (I cheat and use pastry mix for this!)

Put pastry around sides of deep pan and on top of pie (not on bottom). Make two layers of apples. Use half of all ingredients on top of each layer. Bake medium oven about 45 min. 'til apples are tender.

(Some of you may remember the apple pie at the old Mammy's Shanty Restaurant in Atlanta . . . this is even better!)

I chose one of my mother's bread recipes to share. She keeps her freezer full of homemade rolls, muffins, coffee cake, breads of all kinds, and they add so much to any meal. This is a traditional Southern favorite, Sally Lunn. It's slightly sweet, so it's good not only as an accompaniment with meals but as a dessert or coffee break sweet. I learned recently the name derives from the French "Sol Et Lune," meaning "sun and moon." (Maybe because it's equally good at breakfast, lunch, or dinner!)

Mother's Sally Lunn

1 pkg. yeast
2 tablespoons sugar
1 cup milk, scalded and cooled
¼ cup Crisco or cooking oil
2 eggs
½ tsp. salt
3 cups flour

Soften yeast with sugar in the lukewarm milk. Add shortening, well beaten eggs, then salt and flour. Beat thoroughly until smooth. Pour into a well-greased tube pan and let rise 'til doubled in bulk. Bake 350° 25–30 min. You can sprinkle sugar over it, but not if using for dinner.

Serve warm, with plenty of butter!

AUGUST 4, 1978

Georgia Governor's Honors

What in the world was I doing, I kept asking myself, driving alone down I-75 to south Georgia to spend two of the hottest days in the summer in Valdosta?

My husband couldn't get away to go with me. I'd never been anywhere overnight alone in a motel. And if I were picking places to go this time of year, the last place would be Valdosta!

Even my advance reservation was a mistake. The motel I'd chosen was two exits away from where I thought it was. I changed to the King Of The Road Motel, because I thought they advertised a Davis Cafeteria. Wrong again. It was the Jolly Inn across the way that had the Davis Cafeteria.

Anyway, I signed in, pretending I was a career woman who traveled. And once I lugged my suitcase to my room and followed the desk clerk's directions to Valdosta State College, things looked up.

The next two days were filled with exciting, happy experiences.

I wish everyone in Georgia could see for themselves the six weeks honors program for high school students called The Governor's Honors Program in operation. We may not do everything right in Georgia—but this program is one we've got right. It should make us very proud.

Our Stephen was fortunate enough to be there this summer. We'd always hoped one Ryle kid would make it. Dixie almost got there. She was a runnerup ("alternate") in music. She said she blew it when they asked her who was her favorite composer and why, and she answered Bach because he was so melodic. (Bach is a lot of things, but melodic he's not. You don't walk around the house whistling a Bach tune.)

So here I was, seeing for myself what went on at G.H.P. and why every young person or staff member who goes thinks it's so special. Over and over we've heard them say it's one of the greatest experiences of their lives. Now I would find out what it was like.

It's hard to put G.H.P. into words—but even on a brief visit you feel the impact of incredible energy and emotion. Boys and girls intensely concentrate on special projects, free to stretch as far as they can stretch, take on goals that sound impossible—and carry them out. Most of what I saw certainly was college level stuff. And they were loving it.

You also sense tremendous caring on the part of everyone—faculty, counselors, and students. I wasn't expecting that. Teenagers are fairly reserved—not into making instant friends as a rule. G.H.P. is different. On the last day at Valdosta I never saw such an outpouring of love, hugs, and tears. Dr. Jean Fant, the state director of the program, says, "I've learned to take a box of Kleenex around with me the last day."

One student wrote in the G.H.P. weekly newspaper this summer:

"Here no one is out to prove their superiority or point out someone else's inferiority. People share and give freely of themselves, are open and loving. I have changed. I've learned about myself and I've learned how to understand other people, grow with them and learn from them. All mean more than I can describe."

Most of the counselors are "alumni" of the program. Marietta's Lonnie Love, on the state's administrative staff for G.H.P., who hires them, says, "They know it's one of the most special situations they ever experience."

What goes on, exactly?

These 400 students at Valdosta (and another 200 in the G.H.P. program at North Georgia College, Dahlonega) have intensive study each morning in their major subject, one of the following: language arts, foreign languages, science, math, social studies, vocational management, or one of the arts—art, dance, drama, vocal or instrumental music.

In the afternoons they spend several hours in an interest area.

One teacher told me, "It's the ideal teaching situation: teaching students who want to learn as much as you can give them."

Dr. Fant says the program is designed "to provide gifted 10th and 11th grade students challenging, enriching education not usually available during the school year, and to assist them in recognizing their potential."

It's a heady, exhilarating experience for these kids.

Their nights are filled with concerts and plays (by themselves and by guest artists and groups), and plenty of fun, games, and parties.

How do they feel when it's over?

One of their speakers said in the closing ceremony: "Reaching deep inside to draw out our best has been an everyday activity for us. We've learned not only new strengths and talents in ourselves, but most beautiful of all, we've learned about others . . . that each person is unique and special. *Never anywhere else will we know so many special people.*"

They probably never will.

Stephen had been hesitant about going to G.H.P. this summer. Giving up a whole summer vacation—going to school—in *Valdosta*? (By the way, it's a beautiful town, and the campus is lovely.)

On the last day he hated to leave.

If you're a parent and your child has the choice, encourage him or her. It's a rare opportunity and should not be missed!

I'm grateful our child had the chance. And as a Georgia taxpayer, I'm glad this is one state program we really do right. Enabling these kids to reach their potential should help the future world for us all . . . which is sooner than we think.

AUGUST 8, 1980

The Girls Club: Bubbly, Black, White, Short and Tall

Question: "What bubbles over, yet constantly grows? Is black and white and short and tall? Has 650 legs, a heart as big as all out-doors—and sparkles?"

Answer: The Cobb-Marietta Girls Club.

Joyce Parker gave that captivating description in her message as outgoing president of the board of directors last year. When I peeked into their club building on Manget Street the other day, I found it an apt description.

There weren't 650 legs there at one time, of course, but it was raining so the place was jam-packed. (Drive down that muddy hill and you know why a paved driveway and parking lot are high on their "wish list.")

And yes, despite the dark day, there was a sparkle and a brightness. It's a happy place. You see it in the girls' faces, sense it in the friendliness of the counselors, hear it in the laughter and squabbles (most of the fusses—did you ever know two children to play without having one?—seem to be settled by the girls themselves).

Little girls were playing fierce games of ping-pong and table hockey and bumper pool. One girl has her arms around her little sister, pretending to let her use the cue stick. Older girls listened to records or gave each other new hair-dos. Tiny girls wandered around big-eyed, thumb-in-mouth, but contented.

In the art room small girls were winding colored yarn around glass bottles—the special project that week for 6- and 7-year-olds.

While they worked, one of the counselors, a teenaged boy, came to stoop down beside one and talk confidentially to her. "I've been talking to your mama. She said you told her you had to stand in the corner yesterday." A nod of five pigtails, fastened with bright blue bubble hair clasps.

"She wanted to know why you had to stand in the corner. I told her." Another nod of pigtails. It was o.k.

Janet Millard, executive director, a small young woman with long straight hair who looks like one of the girls herself, is quick to praise her assistants. This summer 10 CETA employees are serving as counselors, along with her regular coordinator Jo Ann Harris. The board of directors is headed by Dr. Jim Cole.

Janet began working with the club a few months after it opened in 1976. "I love it; when I'm 55, I'll probably still be directing the Cobb-Marietta Girls Club."

Tragedy revealed the urgent need for such a facility in our community. A little girl was kidnapped, raped and murdered—she had been abducted from the laundromat at Marietta Place, the only "hang-out" then for girls in that neighborhood.

Joyce (Mrs. Sidney) Parker and Irma (Mrs. John) Glover showed insight and leadership in establishing the Girls Club. The Cobb Chamber of Commerce recognized them with Public Service Awards this year.

A look at the club scrapbook shows many others, also, who have been involved. It's a wonderful example of what can happen when city and county officials, civic clubs and individuals work cooperatively to make a dream come true.

Now, after only two years of operation, the building is going to be doubled in size thanks to a Community Development federal grant—giving more space for activities, office, and kitchen.

Janet has vivid memories of working in that tiny kitchen last Christmas! She cooked a dinner for 80 kids—macaroni and cheese, potatoes, a 23-pound turkey and all the trimmings.

The club is now a United Way agency with a full program every weekday in summer; after school and weekends during the school year.

The uppermost goal is to provide a safe and happy place for girls to gather and to offer them a program which helps them realize what "better" is and how to achieve it.

The first "alumna" of the club is Stephanie Grogan. She was an aide from the beginning, coached the basketball team (they lost every single game their first year but last year walked off with the city championship), and has been involved in all the club activities. Now Stephanie plans to attend Truett-McConnell College and wants to study physical education and religion "so I can help girls in a lot of ways."

The girls and their counselors held a special election this summer and awarded beautiful trophies in a program last Friday to the winners:

Most popular, Maureen Gober; 2nd place, St. Mary Grogan; Nicest,

St. Mary Grogan; 2nd place, Sheilah Norah; Friendliest, Zabrina Jones; Most Helpful, Kim Glaze; Best Athlete, Kelly Wright; Best Artist, Terri Harris; Best All Around, Sheilah Norah; Best Volunteer, Marie Young; and Best Staff Aide, Stephanie Grogan.

AUGUST 11, 1978

Family Reunion

The letter was carefully printed in pencil on lined stationery. The stationery was decorated at the top of the page with a little bluebird and at the bottom with a brown puppy.

In between the bird and the puppy, in an 8-year-old's own spelling, it said:

Dear Aunt Nancy,

How are you? I am fine.

Thank you for my teddy bear neckles for my birthday. I love it.

The picture is my recital. For my recital I played "Blue Windmill" and "First Corsage." I will play those for you in the summer and more. I like the piano.

I'm glad when it will be summer when I can see all my relatives. I love you a lot.

Mary Jo

P.S. I'm glad when I can see Gary.

Enclosed was a photograph of a little girl with short brown curls, wearing a long party dress and a corsage (was it her "first"?). There was another picture, too, of her big brother at his junior-senior prom. It's hard to reconcilc these with the five-year-old tot and the thirteen-year-old boy we last saw three years ago.

I wish I could have heard Mary Jo's piano recital and seen David and his date all dressed up for their big night at the prom.

But California is far away, and my only niece and nephew are growing up hardly knowing us at all. We talk on the phone some. We write—but I'm an unreliable letter writer, always meaning to write and almost never doing it.

Mary Jo wasn't the only one that would be "glad when it was summer and she could see all her relatives." Me, too, Mary Jo, me, too.

Last Thursday was the big day!

They rolled down our drive that afternoon: Mary Jo, David, their mom Judy, and their dad Marshall. (I call him "Bubba". So what if he's bearded, dignified, pipe-smoking and paunchy? He's still my little brother whom I fought and fussed with and love dearly, and, because we're seldom together, he tolerates the nickname.)

They also brought Muffin along, a tiny bit of canine fluff they couldn't bear to leave at a vet's so long.

We were still trying to keep our cat, Wendy, from destroying Muffin, and explaining to our dog, Ginger, that just because Muffin was allowed inside the house didn't mean Ginger was—when the Florida grandparents arrived. They came loaded down, as always, with "just a few things to help out" . . . a ham, a turkey, Mother's watermelon rind pickles and her pear preserves, and from their freezer a sentimental souvenir of the last reunion we all had together: the top layer of their Golden Wedding Anniversary cake.

And so it began. Four exhausting, confused, glorious days and nights of togetherness.

Except at bedtime, when the visiting adults escaped to a motel, we had more action going on here than Wall Street at closing time.

Our baby grandson Gary crawled under everyone's feet, showed off his pat-a-cake trick, and gleefully chased Ginger.

Ginger chased Muffin.

Muffin, trapped between the two, leaped to a safe sanctuary . . . right into the lap of a very surprised Granddaddy Dendy.

Mary Jo, serenely isolated from it all in her dream world at the piano, played "Blue Windmill—and many more" for us as she had promised. She's good, too. She can negotiate the rolled chords and the crossed-over hands of "The Faerie Harp" in the red John Williams book, which is no small feat, let me tell you.

David and Stephen, only one week apart in age, have always been unusually close and compatible. They had fierce games of basketball in the driveway, joined by Ken and Buddy after work, coming sweat-soaked to meals and eating, by mutual agreement, at a separate table.

Ken baby-sat with Gary so that Dixie and Patty could take the younger cousins to play putt-putt. Uncle Bubba showed my children, one more time, the scar on his arm which he claims I made once with a particularly nasty pinch. They love it.

Mother, Judy and I moved in continuous circles like figures on a Swiss clock, from stove to table to sink, serving endless paper plate meals on the back porch. (I can remember formal meals in the dining room at my grandmother's house . . . thank goodness casualness is the keynote today.)

Now they're all gone. The once bulging refrigerator is empty. Wisps of Muffin's hair lie on the carpet. Mary Jo's picture of a rose, which she colored while she and Nana and Dendy listened to "Moonlight And Roses" on the Lawrence Welk show, has gone up on the kitchen bulletin board in place of the letter with the bluebird and the puppy.

Will she remember how she and I slipped up to the girls' room at bedtime, and read "Christopher Robin" and "How Do You Like To Go Up In A Swing" together?

Will David remember how he put his arms around me and told me I made really great iced tea?

Will the cousins keep up with one another through the years, so far apart?

California is entirely too far away.

JULY 20, 1979

Callaway Gardens: Georgia's Beautiful Get-away Place

Last week we managed a short vacation trip with some of our grown children down to Callaway Gardens near Pine Mountain.

Callaway Gardens.

What happy memories—though not necessarily peaceful or idyllic ones—that name conjures, of other times there when our children were small.

I'm sure the lake was just as sparkling and clear then, the sand as pretty and white. But I never saw them at all. I spent all my time sitting on the beach, doing that swivel-headed, rolling-eyes act that mothers of young children do on beaches. Trying to look in three directions at once, from the baby under the umbrella to the tot at the water's edge to the three other kids further out.

"Yes, I see you swimming. Yes, you can kick really well. Could you kick a little easier so you won't splash that nice lady?"

"No, you don't need drinks yet. You just think you do."

"Stop throwing sand this minute. *Do you hear me?*"

"No, you don't have to go to the bathroom yet. You just think you do."

"Yes, we'll go out in a paddle boat when Daddy finishes his golf."

A paddle boat . . . famous last words.

My son, Buddy, and I got off to a terrific start, as I remember. We were zooming merrily out in the middle of the lake when my brain slowly clicked and I realized our folly: we had used up all our energy getting *out* there. How would we ever pedal *back*?

I remember trying to pump my legs weakly in circular motions, the beach seeming further away the harder we pedaled. I remember my panicky thoughts . . . did they send a rescue crew for mothers too pooped to pedal? Would they miss us when the sun went down? How did you signal "help" in semaphore? (I wished I'd been a better Girl Scout.)

It was my first and last paddle boat ride.

We stayed in the motel inside the gardens a couple of times when the children were young. Once we shared an A-frame cabin with our friends Mary and Bill Lee from Macon and their two boys. That was the year little Billy Lee walked through the sliding glass door of the cabin and had to have 12 stitches in his head.

Last week we made a mind-boggling discovery. We found there's a whole world at Callaway Gardens we never encountered before. They still have the children's world—beach, FSU circus, ski shows—but they also offer a world of peace, natural beauty and elegant style for a perfect adult get-away spot.

The Callaway Inn prices are higher than the average motel—but it's well-staffed to give excellent service and serve sumptuous food, and as a guest, you have access to the many attractions of the Gardens.

Callaway Gardens itself is a non-profit organization, financed by a foundation established by the Callaway family. The purpose is "to create and maintain a place where all may find beauty, peace, inspiration, knowledge, and wholesome recreation." And we found them all.

We just wished we had longer—three days is not enough.

We drove the scenic five-mile drive through lovely woods (the children did it on tandem bikes), saw azaleas incredibly blooming at the end of August, deer so friendly they almost waved to us.

We visited the new John Sibley Horticultural Center—a new concept in greenhouses designed especially for the South. Solar radiation, natural cooling (a 22-foot waterfall inside, surrounded by a charming rock garden the size of a small mountain), sliding walls, removable roofs. As we strolled among the lush greenery and delicate blossoms, I understood why

Marvina Northcutt, president of the Georgia Garden Clubs, is so enthusiastic about this new center.

We found the small chapel tucked in the woods at one end of the lake, in an area set aside for a meditation retreat. Its glowing red, blue, and green windows are etched with leaf and flower designs, and the interior combines contemporary and traditional elements, achieving a lovely, worshipful atmosphere. Part country chapel, part miniature cathedral—a perfect place for prayer.

Katie and I loved the little rustic cabin in the Gardens. It was built in 1799 in Troup County of hand-hewn pine and is furnished authentically—a hanging "Betty" lamp, charming tattered quilts, old petticoats trimmed with tatting hanging on the hooks, ready for a pioneer woman to step into and start her day.

Of course, there's golf—four courses—tennis, fishing, sailing, a fitness center and miles of beautiful walking trails.

One highlight for us was the nightly entertainment by the Musicana Singers, talented young people who captivated us in a two-hour show with songs from Gershwin and Sondheim. There are two Musicana Productions at the Gardens: one in the Vineyard Lounge at the inn, another in the Garden Restaurant.

The only disturbance of the place was . . . us! We took our Trivial Pursuit game. Naturally we got a little rowdy. A darling honeymooning couple from Marietta, Mike and Laura Gross, joined us for our cut-throat competitions.

Cason Callaway, Sr., and Virginia Hand Callaway established a world-class facility, comparable to the Bok Singing Tower in Florida, the Kew Gardens in England, when they established their lovely gardens. We are fortunate to have them here in Georgia. The more urban our lifestyles become, the more valued it will be.

SEPTEMBER 6, 1984

A Message to the Ku Klux Klan

Marietta has been my home for half my life. I love it and I'm proud of our city. But I've never been prouder than I was last week when our city council adopted their "Resolution of Non-Hospitality" to the Ku Klux Klan.

Their statement shines with truth and integrity, underscored with just enough irony to give it clout. To John Hammond, the author, and every member of the Marietta City Council, who voted for it unanimously, thanks! You did us proud.

As far as I know, there was only one news account of their action. (Good news doesn't go far. Bad news does. You'd better believe if the Klan holds its planned march on the Marietta Square Labor Day weekend, every news medium in the state will pick up the story.)

I'll tell you about the resolution in a minute, in case you missed it.

First I want to say something to the Klan.

I don't know any of you personally, but some of you do live in Cobb County. If you're a Klan member now or know one, please read this and pass it on.

First off, you need to know that I'm a Southerner too, through and through. As Southern as grits, fried chicken and Scarlett O'Hara.

My roots go deep in South Carolina, where I was born. My ancestors fought in the gray uniforms. My cedar chest has old Confederate money and old letters from the soldiers fighting in the Lost Cause. In our front yard is a black washpot with red geraniums in it. My husband's great-grandfather "borrowed" it up in Virginia after the war, to cook for his fellow soldiers on the train coming home.

I know all the words to "The Bonnie Blue Flag" (that's the great background music in "Gone With The Wind") . . . "Hurrah, hurrah, for the

Southern states, hurrah! Hurrah for the Bonnie Blue Flag that bears a single star!" My favorite books as a child were "The Little Colonel" books. I still have the whole set. Heck, we even named our first child an old family name we liked a lot—Dixie.

My blue cameo brooch belonged to my great-grandmother, Nancy Casey, who nursed her two brothers when they came home from the war with tuberculosis. After they died and her parents, who caught the disease, died, Nancy lived alone in their farmhouse for a year, with only one servant, so she could be sure she was free from tuberculosis herself and could marry my great-grandfather.

It's a romantic story. So were "The Little Colonel" books. But I heard other stories, too. The terrible, tragic, not-so-pretty stories of the war and the time afterward. South Carolina, as the first state to secede, was the last state to be pardoned. The "peace" terms inflicted on the South were the harshest the U.S. ever gave a defeated enemy. For 10 long years until 1875, South Carolina whites were not allowed to vote or hold office and were devastated by poverty, without any relief.

I understand the bitter Reconstruction background that spawned the Ku Klux Klan.

But I know in my heart the Klan was wrong as slavery was wrong. The principles of the Klan offend anyone who believes in our American Constitution and certainly anyone who is a Christian—as now and then a Klansman claims to be.

Get straight in your minds right now, Klan members, that the Bible states no person should ever be judged by race, sex, age, or any physical criteria. It's right there in Galatians 3:28. When you hate instead of love, you hurt yourself most of all. Why not disband and join the 20th century—before it's too late?

To use a cross as your symbol is the ultimate obscenity. The cross is a symbol of love. The one who died on the cross gave love as the great commandment.

The Marietta City Council speaks for ALL of us when they declare "deep displeasure in your message of destruction, divisiveness and hate" and call the Klan "that neanderthal of twisted, warped and cancerous element, a minuscule band of social deviants" and "a threat to the fundamental principles we in this city hold dear.

"We don't want you, we certainly don't need you, and you are most vehemently unwelcome in our community, but we do wish you a speedy departure."

AUGUST 18, 1983

(Note: When the KKK claimed their constitutional "right to assemble" to parade around our town square, our city council planned an alternate event: an interfaith, interracial service led by Jewish, Catholic and Protestant ministers and civic leaders. It drew an overflow crowd of over 1000; the Klan march, about 60 spectators.)

Hate Loses, Good Will Wins

If you ever had doubts Cobb County is a good place to live, last Saturday should have cleared them up for you.

It was a long holiday weekend. The Labor Day break was a good chance for a last trip before settling in to school-and-work routine. Dove season opened. And that lovely, wonderful rain after two months of drought softened our Georgia clay and made it a fine time to work in the yard.

But 1200 Cobb Countians let other plans take second place—to demonstrate their belief in "Faith, Brotherhood, and Mutual Respect," the focus of the interfaith, interracial prayer vigil in downtown Marietta as an alternative to the march of the Ku Klux Klan.

It was an amazing turn-out.

By necessity, it was a last-minute plan. There was little time to notify the churches of Cobb, and no official organization sponsored the prayer vigil. It just happened . . . because a few pastors responded to Mayor Bob Flournoy and the Marietta City Council's request to help plan something to counteract the KKK event.

The tremendous community answer was loud and clear: we believe in peace and brotherhood!

It resounded through the talks at the prayer meeting, representing many denominations and creeds. It rang out in the music—from Beethoven's "Hymn To Joy" (*Teach us how to love each other . . . All who live in love are thine*) to the moving spiritual sung by Zion Baptist Choir, "I been 'buked and I been scorned."

It echoed in Old Testament words—*And what does the Lord require of thee, Oh man, but to do justice and to love mercy, and to walk humbly with thy God*?—words of faith to Protestants, Catholics, and Jews.

And it showed most of all in the response of the people. They applauded louder and longer at each part of the program and at the end were holding hands 1200 strong.

The best way to describe it is to say it was the "Christmas Spirit" of good will, come to Cobb County on Labor Day weekend.

John Hammond, Marietta city councilman who helped to plan this event, said, "I'll admit it brought tears to my eyes. Then I looked at the mayor when he got up to speak and saw tears in his eyes, too."

The Rev. Cecil Fike, chaplain of Kennestone Hospital, said, "I was really impressed by the turnout, by the cross-section of people there and the spirit of togetherness."

The Rev. David Wayland, rector of St. Catherine's Episcopal Church and past president of the Cobb Ministerial Association, said, "Many people have said we should do this more often. We might plan something like this once a year."

My own pastor, Charles Lloyd, who offered our church, First Baptist, to host the event (and of whom I am very proud!) said "We wanted simply to underscore what every American stands for—that we respect one another despite our differences." And Barbara Owens, whose husband Phil is another Kennestone Hospital chaplain, said "The meeting was so wonderful, I didn't want to leave when it was over!"

Dr. Harris Travis, vice-president of Southern Tech and respected black leader, said, "We stand together in mutual love and there is no place for intolerance and hate in our city. I say to the Ku Klux Klan today, 'Come out of the darkness and come into the light.'"

Bob Flournoy deserves special thanks ("Cobb Kudos") for the idea of this vigil, and for writing the *Declaration of County Conscience* which citizens could tear out of our *Marietta Daily Journal* and *Neighbor Newspapers* and mail to city hall.

I checked on Tuesday with Barbara Goscha, city clerk, to see how those petitions were coming in.

"So far we have 1700 names," said Barbara. "But we haven't gotten today's mail—meaning the holiday weekend mail—yet."

Bob tells me most of the response has been from families, with children printing their names in big letters. Many, he says, have added a message on their petition "This is beautiful," or—"We can't be at the vigil but our prayers are with you."

They have come from all over our county—Powder Springs, Mableton, Smyrna, Austell.

"And remember," says Bob, "this has not been an organized effort. There was no way I could run around the county getting signatures."

Hate lost last Saturday. Good will won. Blessed are the peacemakers. And hurrah for Cobb County.

SEPTEMBER 11, 1983

Mr. Ruddell—
Sunny Side Up

On Tuesday, supper at our house is usually scrambled eggs and grits or maybe a ham omelette. This is for two reasons. First, by then Sunday's roast beef is all gone. Second, Tuesday is the day "The Egg Man" comes.

"The Egg Man" is Mr. J. S. Ruddell, who for almost 20 years has been delivering to our front door the biggest, freshest eggs you ever saw once a week.

You may have seen him climb out of his red pick-up truck with a big basket of eggs or, in summer, some of his vegetables. What you probably didn't see was that his basket was swung over a hook in place of his lower left arm, for Mr. Ruddell handles his handicap as he does all of life: jauntily and happily.

That hook on his left arm is what got him into the egg business.

For most of his life he had been a railroader. He grew up in Calhoun, Ga., married in 1918, and in the same year at age 21 went to work for the Nashville, Chattanooga, and St. Louis Railroad Company.

Those were the boom days of railroading. The NC&StL had seven passenger trains a day coming through Marietta, not to mention the numerous freights. Mr. Ruddell and Mama, as he calls his wife, and their three children lived in Calhoun in the section houses provided by the company. His work took him from rail repair to being on the "extra gang" working various locations including the Union Terminal area in Atlanta, to finally becoming a section foreman.

With only a grade school education, he became a respected foreman until the train accident that injured his arm and forced early retirement, after 38 years with the railroad.

By then the company had transferred him to the Marietta area. He and his family lived with other railroaders in section houses, now vanished, near the trestle bridge on old Highway 41, just north of Kennesaw Battlefield Park Museum.

Mr. Ruddell had worked since he was 12 years old, when he plowed fields for 50¢ a day. He says, "I wasn't about to sit on a stool and do nothing." The idea came to him of having chickens and selling eggs.

He and Mama moved to a big, comfortable home on Burnt Hickory Road, built their chicken houses, invested in white Leghorns (eventually 3,000 of them), and were in business.

Always it was hard work. Eggs had to be gathered at noon and again in the evening. Then far into the night working in their basement, the Ruddells would sort the eggs and "candle" them to detect cracked or blemished eggs.

After Mama died and help became harder to hire, Mr. Ruddell phased out having his own chickens, but continued to distribute to his same customers from a supplier who, he feels, maintains his high standard of quality.

He makes 200 deliveries each week, and many others come to his home for their eggs.

Often one of his eight grandchildren helps with his route work. The current helper is Lisa, a recent graduate of North Cobb High School. Now at 78, he's going strong as ever.

He did have to take a few weeks off last year to have major surgery. He talks with pleased astonishment of the big box of get-well cards from his customers and laughs about what happened while he was in the operating room waiting for his surgery. Dr. Bob Sessions dashed in, calling out, "Do you have my egg man in here?" It seems the Sessions had missed him and wanted to deliver a late Christmas present.

Mr. Ruddell now lives a little way down the road from his earlier home, in a small, neat white house with his unmarried son, Eugene, next door to his daughter and her family. Although Mama's flower beds are mostly gone, he still has a nice vegetable garden and goes fishing often. "That's my real weakness!"

He seems a good walking advertisement for his own eggs: cheery, fresh and sunny side up.

SEPTEMBER 20, 1976

Please Remove Label

It's my husband's birthday. The family at dinner watches him open his gift. The one from my daughter and her husband is in a long slim box, obviously a tie. He doesn't usually like gift ties—I hope he can fake it when he thanks them.

But he doesn't have to fake it. He loves this tie. Who wouldn't? It's beautiful—a soft, silk fabric of the finest quality, in a lovely shade of burgundy with white dots; a very classy tie.

But centered near the bottom is a tiny monogram, and it's not his. Not DMR. These initials are YSL. Oh—Yves St. Laurent, the designer. Wow.

This tie states a subtle message: "Look folks, this is not your basic, ordinary polka dot tie. This tie is special. See the label?"

We're living in an age of labels—turtles, alligators, designer names splashed over scarves, tiny tags on jeans pockets. And these labels stand for quality.

But sometimes, a label doesn't really matter. Sometimes a label needs to come off.

One night recently I had a terrible time going to sleep. As I flopped and thrashed around, I gradually became aware of something strange—each time I turned my head on the pillow, I heard a rustling, crackling noise, right in my ear. It seemed to be coming from my new pillow. What on earth?

Yanking off the pillowcase, I discovered the problem: it was a stiff label, sewn in the edge of the pillow. You know those labels—they identify the contents of the pillow, and then warn you in big capital letters, "Do Not Remove Label Under Penalty of Law."

Now, I knew that such a label only applies in the store before the merchandise is bought as protection to the consumer, but I somehow felt reluctant to snip off the warning tag.

Suddenly I could envision a big, burly policeman popping out from under my bed and pointing his finger at me: "Aha—gotcha! You were removing the label from this pillow. You are now under arrest."

Ridiculous.

But no more ridiculous than some other labels I keep in my life. Labels that I unconsciously apply to others, placing people in categories so that a rustling, irritating tag keeps us from relating closely as one human being to another. Can I work on them, too?

Former Gov. Leroy Collins of Florida tells in his autobiography of walking on the beach with his little granddaughter, looking for shells. She chose a shell which had a hole in the center. The governor tried to discourage her—"Why do you want to keep this one? Look at the hole."

But the little girl just held it tighter, showing her granddaddy the pretty color and the shape. She didn't mind the hole.

Collins recalled this experience when he talked with a physically handicapped citizen and asked the man what his greatest problem in life was. The man answered, "Trying to get people to think of me, not as a handicapped person, but as a person who happens to have a handicap."

So many labels. Can I take them off? A person, who just happens to be black. A person, who just happens to be older or younger than I. Labor and management, Protestant, Catholic, Jew. People first, labels second—or not at all.

Herb Barks, in *Prime Time,* writes, "The stuff of the Christian faith is found in the matter of if and how I relate to people. Unless I am in deep relationships with others, unless I walk and talk and come to know others, I am never going to be satisfied."

"Please Remove Label"—under penalty of divine law. Even when it's hard.

SEPTEMBER 26, 1980

FALL

September Goodbyes

September is a time of good-byes.

Last Tuesday was the first day of school. I planned to phone my daughter early that morning, but she beat me to it. Her voice was quavery.

"Well, I took him . . . it was so sad!"

"How did he do?"

"Oh, *he* did just great. No problem. The only problem was *me*. He had on his new little Jedi backpack and he was so excited! His teacher was waiting in front of the school for all the kindergarten children. They sat together on a stone wall until everyone got there."

Her voice breaks, "He looked so little."

I feel teary myself. He *is* little. He just had his fifth birthday. I remember his sparkling blue eyes, his proud, self-conscious smile as his friends sang "Happy Birthday, Dear Gary." (At least the little girls sang—the little boys were busy wrestling.)

But nowadays five-year-olds go to public kindergarten. Gary rides on a real school bus. He goes inside a real school building. His life is already regulated by school bells and rules and a teacher to whom he's only one unknown little boy out of 25 boys and girls in her room.

She doesn't know he's a very special little boy with shiny red-gold hair and a bright happy disposition who can name the batting order of the Braves but still needs his cuddle bear and rabbit to sleep with at night. A little boy who has no reason, so far, not to believe this world is a wonderful place.

Now Gary's young aunt gets on the extension telephone, "What time does he get out?"

"Ten o'clock," his mother answers, and all three of us burst out laughing. We're mourning and keening for a little boy who gets back home again in two hours.

It's the symbol that hurts, of course—the first rite of passage.

Welcome to motherhood, I silently toast my daughter. *Being a mother is learning how to say goodbye*. The Lamaze classes, the birthing, the colicky sleepless nights, the toddler years of non-stop business and responsibility—that was just an introduction. Welcome to the real thing.

Nurturing your child so that he can make it on his own is what parenting is all about.

My mind races back to *her* first day of school. We hesitantly entered Allgood School holding hands tightly. She slipped into a big desk. I squeezed into another, filled out the forms (date of polio shots, smallpox vaccination—who remembers?), took one last look at her earnest little face, and fled to a friend's house. Ella Jo had just put her little girl in the first grade, too.

We laughed and cried and drank coffee all morning, trying to ease the lump in our throats.

I think of the day we took this same daughter to college. We kept all our children home from school that day (the excuse was a "family emergency," loaded up the station wagon until it sagged and children hung from every window, and headed for Furman University). Heavens, what a spectacle we must have made—her dad and mom and four little brothers and sisters, crying goodbye in front of her dorm!

When we got back home I kept forgetting and setting an extra place at the table. The lump in my throat took weeks to dissolve that time.

Each goodbye for every child has its own pain. A time for self-examination and regrets. "Did I do o.k.? Did I give him/her enough? I wish I had handled it better."

The best book I know about loving and living—parenting, marriage, friendship—is *The Road Less Traveled* by M. Scott Peck, M.D. (Simon and Schuster). Peck writes, "Love is being willing to extend oneself for the spiritual growth of another." (He defines "spiritual" as meaning the mind, emotions, everything that makes up the inner person.) Anything less is not real love.

"Dependency may appear to be love, because it is a force that causes people to fiercely attach themselves to another. But it is not love; it is a form of anti-love. It works to trap and constrict rather than to liberate. It destroys rather than builds up people."

So it is that mothers and fathers say goodbye a lot. And September is a hazy month.

Partly because of the weather and that misty, golden atmosphere we call Indian Summer.

But partly because of the tears in our eyes.

SEPTEMBER 1, 1983

Off-to-College Advice from a Great-Great-Grandmother

Anyone who has ever sent a daughter off to college will appreciate a wonderful letter shared with me by my friend Sarah Fortson.

Sarah's daughter Becky a student at McGill University in Montreal, recently did a research paper on the life of women in the southern United States at the turn of the century.

Among some old family papers and pictures, Becky discovered this jewel. It was written by her great-great-grandmother to her oldest child, a daughter who had just left home to enter Coxe Female Institution in LaGrange, Georgia.

It shows that what mothers worry about hasn't changed much in 100 years: the practical worries; the love and the missing, which makes a goose-sized lump in the throat; the dreams and hopes for her daughter's future.

It also reveals an extraordinary lady, whose advice from beauty hints to thoughts on being a woman, would be just as appropriate in *Seventeen* magazine today!

Headed November 17, 1878, Edgefield, South Carolina, and addressed to "Darling child," here are some excerpts.

"I can think of no pleasanter way to spend this Sabbath afternoon than writing to my absent one . . . brought your letter, which met with a warm reception, for we were getting very anxious to hear if you had received your box. We were glad you were pleased with your things. Accept the kisses, wish we had them fresh from your sweet lips.

"I think you have enough winter clothes now. Thought you would like your waterproof. I did not admire the make of your dresses much myself, but they are only calico and if they fit your figure nicely they will do . . .

"Be careful my child and mind how you ride on your F.Q." (Sarah and I wonder if this means a four-quartered horse—but we're not "horsey" and we don't know.) "Remember your back is not very strong anyway and a fall might make you a cripple for life. When in those rough, boisterous plays wear your wrapper, never be ashamed to take care of your clothes . . . Please keep your clothes in order, never wear a garment with a rent.

"And your trunk—have a place for everything in there, and keep everything in its place so when you want any article you can get it without tumbling your entire trunk. About washing, remember if the skin is cleared from every impurity before retiring, it causes it to look clear, bright and pretty.

"The independent, highminded, Christian woman has to be careful of personal appearance, or should wield no influence for good. Walk erect, carry yourself as if you were proud of the stature God has given you, and do not try to stoop your shoulders, stand 'hip shot,' etc. to make yourself appear not so tall. I would not if I could take an inch from your height, or have you one bit different.

"You can make of yourself just what you will, by cultivating taste in your dress and arranging your hair becomingly, always wearing a sweet smile, having a kind word for and about everyone, and lastly a mind well stored with useful knowledge, and you would be far more admired by persons of worth than a dwarfed, wax doll, expressionless, silly beauty. It is an old and true adage 'Pretty is as pretty does.'

"Don't think, my darling, 'Mama' has nothing to do this even, and is merely writing to pass off time. Far from it, every word comes from my heart.

"Papa is slow about writing his 'yellow pink' but still he loves you and is always when about the house talking and wishing to see you.

"Oh, my dear child! Mama is so anxious for you. It is my wish, my prayer, that you may now lay the foundation for a true, noble woman that can yield an influence for good to the age in which she lives."

And also to the ages still to come . . . as this ancestor of Becky's, who crosses a century from her generation to ours.

OCTOBER 21, 1977

Back to School at Candler Street . . . Remember?

These hot, dry Dog Days are beginning to have a wonderful autumn nip to early morning, and somehow it brings a rush of back-to-school memories of long ago.

For me it was Candler Street School in Gainesville, Georgia, in the 1930s. (So far in the past my children say my scrapbook pictures look like "The Waltons.")

My first grade teacher was sweet, gentle Miss Leland Gilbert. She taught generations of Gainesville children not only to read and write but to learn that school isn't so scary after all.

I remember how embarrassed I was to tell her my name because I had just lost two front teeth and no matter how hard I tried it came out "Nanthy."

Way back in the summer we had gone to Estes Store on the square to select material for my new school dresses. Plaid ginghams—brown and yellow, blue and red. I remember how cool and smooth the cloth felt, how excitingly new it smelled. My Grandmother Copeland, who lived with us, made them on her treadle Singer machine and Mother added the special trimmings: rickrack or homemade tatting around the collar, maybe an applique design somewhere, or a smocked yoke. Every dress had a big sash that tied in the back.

I hated to try them on. No matter how careful we were, a pin stuck me. But Grandmother would jokingly admonish me, through a mouth full of pins, to "stand still or I'll hop you."

She always made a matching pair of underpants to go with each dress. They were short, bloomer–like affairs. I don't know if other little girls had those homemade pants or if Grandmother dreamed up the idea by herself. At any rate they came in handy when I skinned the cat on the monkey bars at recess.

For my school shoes we went all the way to Atlanta. They were the identical shoes year after year—sturdy, brown, tie-up oxfords. They had to be sturdy. We walked a lot. No school buses or car pools for us! We not only walked to school—down Brenau Avenue, turn the corner on Boulevard, down to the end of Boulevard to Candler Street—but we walked home at noon for lunch. Not lunch, dinner. Vegetables and cornbread.

To complete my fashionable school ensemble, my short, straight hair was always garnished with a huge taffeta bow pinned on top, dead center. How I loved choosing new hair ribbons from the rolls of rainbow colors at Rose's 10 cent store! Sometimes Mother rolled my hair on the curling iron for corkscrew Shirley Temple curls (our idol). Unfortunately they would start slowly unwinding to their natural state of straightness almost immediately.

My new school supplies were carefully chosen at Roberts Book Store: a new pencil box (how I loved my pencil box), which had colored pencils and a pencil sharpener shaped like a tiny world globe, a 25 cent notebook, Blue Horse paper, and a new book satchel. Mother disapproved strongly of book satchels which strapped to your back, convinced they could cause

poor posture and a bent-over back. I always had a book satchel to carry in one hand by a handle—probably causing poor one-sided posture instead.

We had no band instruments to worry about. Our school band was a rhythm band—triangles, bells, and rhythm sticks. We also had singing sometimes. We would all clatter up the wooden stairs of Candler to the upstairs hall where there was a piano. While Miss Linda, our principal, played for us, we lustily raised our voices in song. We may not have been the Vienna Boys Choir but I still remember all the words to Santa Lucia and Juanita (Nee-ta, Wah-ah-ah-nee-ta!)

When I was in the third grade, my little brother began school and walked with me—wearing corduroy knickers that whistled at every step. We met Joanne Cheves and her brother Charles on the next corner on Brenau Avenue.

Joanne was one of my "best friends." We had a special bond—her father was the school superintendent, mine the preacher. This was a terrible social stigma among our peers that we had to overcome!

The teachers at Candler Street were always the same: Miss Gilbert, followed in order by Miss Bessie Bickers, Mrs. Dent, Miss Lay, Mrs. Castleberry, Miss Linda and Miss Self. We called them "Miz"—long before this Ms. got started.

A teacher reigned supreme. The only time I doubted she was an oracle of divine wisdom was one year (I forget which) when the teacher asked us what season of the year we thought was most beautiful. The whole class voted for spring—except for Heyward Hosch and me. We voted for fall. Our teacher told us we were wrong, wrong; *spring* was the most beautiful.

What close friendships we made in that school, playing together at recess, going home with one another after school, spending the night in a friend's home. I moved away in the 6th grade but the bonding was firm, and every year or two we arrange a luncheon meeting in Atlanta or somewhere: Felicia Jackson, Beverly Burns, Harriett Woodcock, Nancy Curtis, Elizabeth Pendergrass, Joanne. Mildred Wright died of cancer several years ago and left a special place no one can fill.

Candler Street School . . . a secure childhood, a good education with no frills but teachers who gave all they could to their children, lasting friendships.

It's nice to remember how it was in Gainesville so long ago.

September 12, 1976

(Note: Joanne Cheves, my childhood "best friend," and her husband, Bob Davis, as one of life's happy surprises, now live in our Marietta neighborhood. Her dear father, Mr. C. J. Cheves, was honored in Gainesville in

1983 when the new Gainesville High School Media Center was named for him. The old Candler Street School, now a commercial office building, is listed on the National Register of Historic Places.)

Hemlock Inn

We shouldn't have been surprised when Ella Jo and John broke their news to us—but we were.

They phoned one day, a few years ago, and asked Dallas and me to come to their house that night for dessert and coffee. They had some special news they wanted to tell us.

Sarah and Ralph Farrar were invited, too.

The three couples, plus another couple now living in California, had been unusually close friends through the years and had enjoyed a special vacation trip together each year. Our children were friends. We had season tickets at the Marietta High football games together, belonged to the same supper club, shared problems and hopes and dreams as only good friends can do.

Now John (we usually called him "Buddy") and Ella Jo had some astounding news for us. They were going to move away from Marietta.

They had been able to buy the Hemlock Inn, up in Bryson City, North Carolina, and would move there and operate the hotel.

Of course it was a fantastic opportunity for them—and we all knew they would be perfect for the job.

Now everyone else knows, too.

We miss them in Marietta (both were active leaders in the community), but they've given us all an ideal vacation spot to visit!

Their inn is a charming country inn (it's included every year in the well-known guide, *Country Inns and Back Roads*, edited by Norman Simpson, published by Berkshire Traveller Press.). Its location is one of the prettiest in the Smokies—high on the crest of one range overlooking another, outside Bryson City (the closest city to the Cherokee Indian Reservation).

The guest rooms are in a comfortable lodge, but guests gather most of the time to a row of rocking chairs on the front porch outside the dining room.

Those chairs get a lot of action. Guests rock there before meals, smelling the good smells floating out from the kitchen and waiting for John to ring the dinner bell. They return there to rock after meals, trying to recover from overindulgence. You might call it a "rock festival," with all the rocking on the front porch of Hemlock Inn!

Ella Jo sets a fine table: country ham, fried chicken, fresh vegetables and casseroles—but best of all are the biscuits—incredibly light, easy to lose count of how many you eat—especially with country butter and homemade pumpkin chips or apple chips—the Hemlock Inn specialty.

You leave Hemlock Inn lighter in spirits—but heavier everyplace else!

This Labor Day weekend Dallas and I went there for another relaxing, delightful time. The Farrars joined us. We found John just the same—genial, laid back, and as friendly as a puppy. He and Ella Jo are born innkeepers, hospitable and friendly because they can't help it. Everyone is not just a paying guest but a personal friend.

John points out that you won't find a tennis court, swimming pool, or even a television set on the place. And the "rowdy" activities, as he calls them, are on the back patio—shuffleboard and horseshoes.

We took part in the "rock festival," gazing out at the mountains seen from the front porch of that little inn—range after range, rolling away into a sky so blue I'd forgotten it could be that blue.

The only action we had was the duel between Dallas and Ralph to see who could turn the Lazy Susan tabletop the fastest.

SEPTEMBER 9, 1977

Clyde—Our Children's Friend

I wish every youngster could have someone like Clyde in his life.

Clyde Kirk is an adult whom my children consider their special friend. Though he's a neighbor, I hardly know him—which makes it all the better as far as the children are concerned. He's not someone from their parents' world. He belongs to them.

They "discovered" Clyde for themselves, finding his house while exploring the woods back of our new home several years ago. Since then, he has become very important to them. One by one, each of our sons and daughters has gone often to visit Clyde.

Sometimes months go by without seeing him, but he's always the same, his door ajar (he never closes it when he's at home), ready with a welcome.

They listen to his stories and later re-tell them to us. They watch him puttering around his place—making muscadine jelly, working in his garden, cutting up apples from his trees to spread them out to dry in the September sun.

Often he joins them for a ramble on Kennesaw Mountain, pointing out a chestnut tree he knows of that hasn't yet been hit by the blight, or where moonshiners once had their still, or the old rock quarry.

Clyde calls himself, "just a run-down old man living in a run-down old house," but of course the children and I know better.

His house is a rarity in Cobb County now—a symbol of another age and filled with memories. And Clyde himself is a rare individual, an adult who sincerely likes young people and who inspires their confidence as their true friend.

He has a unique rapport with teenagers that many a guidance counselor, teacher and parent could envy.

He's Huck Finn and a favorite grandfather rolled into one, and he fills a special place in our children's lives that neither peers nor parents can fill.

We didn't know for a long time what Clyde's last name was—all the children cared about was that he was just Clyde. It's Kirk—and he's a member of one of Cobb County's oldest and most distinguished families. Clyde himself had seven brothers. We know many of the Kirk clan and count them friends (Dempsey, Jr., Cleve, George, Adrian, Mary Kirk Underwood. . . .the list goes on).

Clyde lives on a little dirt road off Kennesaw Avenue, just as close to Kennesaw Mountain as you can get without trespassing in the national park. Actually he was born on what is now park property. The old home place has been torn down but it was only a stone's throw from Clyde's present home.

His parents, the George Washington Lee Kirks, sold 40 acres of land to the park service in the early 1930s, when Kennesaw Mountain National Battlefield Park was begun. The house Clyde lives in now (which they moved into then) was built in 1900.

Clyde was the first local employee at the park, riding his horse, Old One-Eyed Dan, up the mountain (no trails then) to the lookout tower to watch out for fires.

He's tried his hand at other jobs, too, through the years, working in Detroit and in Miami and serving in the U.S. Army. Now he seems thoroughly content in the old home place, living his bachelor life surrounded by cheerful clutter of by-gone years.

There's the old treadle sewing machine and flatiron that were his mother's; the hewing ax his father used to build a log cabin; the wardrobe that belonged to his grandmother (but Stephen thinks it's neat that Clyde hangs his clothes on a nail); the old smoke house out back; a little half-pint glass milk bottle, used back when Clyde and Dempsey delivered milk in their fine red one-horse wagon, and later in a 1925 Model–T pick-up truck.

Clyde spins his yarns from the past and the children feel history come alive.

He shows them where the Indians passed through our woods between Big and Little Kennesaw Mountains. He tells them about the old C.C.C. camp in the park, and about Kennesaw Avenue and Church Street becoming the first paved roads here.

He tells them about the quail, foxes, rabbits and raccoons around him—deer too, every now and then. They don't stay long—but they come from Paulding County during hunting season.

And just as important, Clyde knows how to listen. The children share their news and their feelings with him. He never seems to forget. Sometimes years later he'll ask them about one of their friends by name, or inquire about an interest they told him about.

The sign on the little dirt road leading to Clyde's place says "PRIV DR." I suppose that means "Private Drive;" but to me it has another meaning—Privileged Drive. It leads to my children's special friend—a privilege every child should have.

The world could use a few more Clydes.

September 16, 1977

Autumn and Miss Annie

It's a golden morning in late September.

Later today it will be hot but right now the air is cool and fresh. Tell-tale color accents the green leaves—here a brown oak leaf, there a rose or yellow dogwood leaf.

In our arbor the scuppernongs are getting ripe, burnished green-gold balls hanging from heart-shaped leaves. The squirrels were merciful and left them alone after mutilating our peaches and apples.

The biggest change of the season, however, has already occurred—our household is quiet and deserted.

Buddy has gone back to Athens, wagging his U-Haul behind him. Patty moved from home to a place of her own in Atlanta—a real working girl. Katie and Stephen are back in school.

This morning it's so quiet after the noise and nitty-gritty group living of summer that I can't handle so much silence at once. I've turned on the radio to keep me company.

I've been thinking this morning about "Miss Annie" and her apron.

"Miss Annie" is what everyone but the family called my husband's darling grandmother, Mrs. Annie Watson (we called her "Mama"). She lived in Marietta most of her life and many here still remember her.

Recently, Judge Luther Hames told me a wonderful story about Miss Annie which has special meaning for me this fall morning.

Before I tell it to you, I need to tell you about Miss Annie.

I first met her when Dallas and I had been dating a while in college and I went home to meet his folks down in Perry. He'd already told me much about his grandmother. I knew that Mama was a remarkable lady whom he adored.

She grew up in the Lost Mountain community of west Cobb and married her childhood sweetheart, Sam Watson (also from Lost Mountain). Sam went to work for the newly formed Life of Georgia company. We have a charming group picture of five or six men, the first agents of the company and their president, dressed in the style of the day (high collars, severely parted hair), seated in an ornately furnished Victorian room.

The young couple lived in Atlanta and had one child—my husband's mother. Sam developed tuberculosis and they moved to Texas for his health. He died there when he was only 29. (He was Mama's true love, and she never considered marrying again though several men wanted to marry her.)

Young Annie brought her child back home to Georgia and managed to raise her alone and send her through college, and also to make a home for her mother and invalid brother.

The courageous and resourceful young woman first opened a private school in her home (East Dixie Avenue in Marietta). To show how good a teacher she was—when Mother Ryle entered Marietta High School for her last year, after Mama's schooling, she graduated class salutatorian.

Then Annie went to work for the U.S. Postal Service at the Marietta Post Office. She handled the money order window. During World War I when there was a manpower shortage, she carried a route for a short time on her slim shoulders—down Lawrence and Washington Streets.

She always made time for her church, Crestview Baptist (then called Second Baptist Church), where she taught a class of girls and led the youth in B.Y.P.U.

When she retired from the post office in the 1940's, she sold her house and moved to Perry to live with her daughter.

I knew her as a frail little lady, bent with arthritis, walking slowly and carefully with a cane, but with a lively mind, sharp wit, and merry disposition.

Everything she did was done slowly, methodically, and perfectly. If Mama strung the green beans, you didn't find a string. If Mama wrapped a package, the corners were neat and tight (not bunched together like mine.) She wasn't able to go to church but she was the treasurer each year for the W.M.U. because they knew how efficient she was—and so beloved that one of their circles is the Annie Watson Circle.

Our children loved her just as their daddy did. They spent long hours in Mama Watson's room listening to her wonderful yarns of long ago. (Their favorite was about a buggy race between Sam and another suitor).

I always felt a little uncomfortable, though, around Miss Annie. In those days I was caring for five little children. I was always rushing in three directions at once. I felt harum-scarum and scatter-brained. I wished I could slow down and do things perfectly like Miss Annie. I wondered if she was dismayed by my way of doing things, if she thought Dallas could have done better!

Not that she was judgmental, ever—quite the opposite. She was a dear, loving lady.

Now . . . about Miss Annie and her apron.

Not long ago Judge Hames said, "Nancy, I'll never forget about Miss Annie and her apron!"

What? I didn't know the story.

"Well, you know she was the leader for our young people on Sunday nights at Crestview. And—as you know—she was always on the run, in a hurry."

Now my astonishment showed. *Miss Annie—always in a hurry?*

"One night she came in late to B.Y.P.U., hurrying across the street from her house. She stood up to announce the first hymn—and we all started laughing. We snickered and giggled and couldn't even sing."

"Miss Annie didn't know what was wrong. Finally she looked down and saw—she still had on her apron! She'd been in such a hurry she forgot to take it off."

What a revelation!

And yet I should have known. How else could this amazing woman have supported a large household and done all she'd done without being pushed for time, without hurrying?

I had known her only as a patient little lady accepting her last years with calm dignity and grace.

A woman for all seasons. . . .forgetting to take off her apron, or rocking in her rocking chair.

Will I cope with my life seasons as well? At least now I know, if I goof up sometimes when I hurry, so did Miss Annie long, long ago.

Car Pool Mania

Our Marietta City Council members and mayor will soon be ending their terms of office. Regardless of who's up for reelection, I have a special message for our outgoing city fathers: thank you, from the bottom of my heart, for installing city school bus service!

Free at last, free at last!

After all these years of car pools, I hardly know what to do with myself. I have the heady exhilaration of a Liberated Woman. I didn't have to wave signs, burn my bra, or march on city hall. You took care of my liberation when you voted to install the school buses in our town.

My sudden emancipation has caused an identity crisis: if I'm not the Family Chauffeur, who am I? That's all I know how to do.

It took a little while for me to flex and unflex my fingers on the steering wheel, lift my foot from its rigor mortis position on the gas pedal, find my way into the house from the driveway (the closest I usually got), and hang up my car keys.

Wow!

Before you made your Great Bus Decision, I had been driving my children to school in Marietta for 16 consecutive years. By then two had graduated but three were still matriculating.

Think about it—16 years! Twice a day. Five days a week. Four weeks a month. Do some multiplication and that's 5,760 round trips to school!

And that leaves out some of them . . .

For one thing, the kids weren't ever in the same school at the same time. One horrible year I had them in four—count 'em, four—schools at once: kindergarten, elementary, junior high, and high school.

The only way I survived those years was by car-pooling with Joanne Walker, my next-door neighbor. As a mother of four boys, she had the same horrendous situation. Each day we took turns piling the five Ryles and four Walkers into our station wagons and circling Marietta, ejecting the proper children at the proper locations.

(Last summer I thought it was perfect that when our daughter, Dixie, got married, it was Rob Walker who drove the bride and groom in the get-away car for their honeymoon. After all, Dixie and Rob had *always* car pooled together!)

That basic school car pool, however, was just the beginning. Mothers drive as many car pools as their children have activities. Before-school car pools for Safety Patrol. After-school car pools for band practice. The car is our home away from home. . . .or is it the other way around?

Each car pool has its own modus operandi, requiring us to keep meticulous notes so we won't goof up . . . "Drive ballet car pool on 2nd and 4th Mondays, unless the month has five Mondays" . . . "Soccer car pool goes alphabetically, but Tommy's mother switched with Bruce's so M comes before G."

These intricate arrangements rival the French Connection, and the logistics needed to drive *one* car pool while helping siblings make contact with *other* car pools would drive a seasoned traffic controller bonkers. One choked intersection, one poorly timed traffic light, can throw the entire day out of kilter.

I'm not sure that men could handle it. The only fathers I know who have ever volunteered for car pool duty were Rupert Raines, of the Marietta City Police, and Glenn Gray, test pilot for Lockheed. Think about it.

Of course, the new city school buses won't solve all these problems, but they're definitely a help. It's lovely to sit at the kitchen table and enjoy a second cup of coffee while that beautiful yellow bus goes roaring by.

I no longer think of myself as a sphinx-like creature—woman from the waist up, four wheels and a chassis from the waist down.

The City Council said they hoped the buses would help solve the energy crisis. I can tell them, personally, that I have the most energy I've had in a long time.

OCTOBER 7, 1977

How to Read in Bed

People fall into two basic categories: those who like to read in bed and those who don't.

For some reason, people of one type seem to marry people of the other.

My husband does not read in bed. He loves to read but not in a prone position.

His favorite place is on the screened porch. He likes to rock in the glider, smoke his pipe, listen to the tree frogs at night and enjoy the fresh air. If it's too cold, he reads in the den.

He says he can't get comfortable propped up in bed. He doesn't even like breakfast in bed. For years we brought him a tray every birthday and Father's Day. Finally he told us he hated it. He didn't like cutting up his egg on a plate that bounced up and down, or having to lie real still so he wouldn't slosh his coffee.

On the other hand, breakfast in bed is my idea of utter, supreme luxury. And I see no earthly reason to read at night while sitting up in a chair, if you can do it lying down instead.

Having been a bedtime reader since I hid my Little Colonel and Gene Stratton Porter books under the cover and used a flashlight, I've developed certain skills. In fact, I have the art of reading in bed down pat. Reading in bed is probably the only thing in life that I do really well.

If you like to do it, too, here are my special "How To Read In Bed" tips, culled from careful research, that I'll pass along:

First: *How to prepare.*

Get completely ready for bed first. Your goal is to read yourself into oblivion without having to get up again. Brush your teeth, put out the cat, turn off the overhead light. And make sure everything you need is placed on the bedside table: book, bookmark, reading glasses, snack.

Second: *How to be comfortable.*

Two pillows behind your back do fine, but a bedrest is wonderful—

one of those padded, contoured things that looks like a broken armchair. Keep your pillow nearby, though. As you get sleepier and slide down lower in the bed, at the very last minute you can grab your pillow, place it under your head and put your bedrest on the floor. (Be sure you remember it's there if you get up during the night. Padded bedrests in the dark can be dangerous.)

Third: *How to hold your book.*

Prop it up on something. Holding a book in your hands is hard work, especially if it's not a paperback. You can put it on a small cushion in your lap, but I've made another great discovery: those beanbag lap desks. They're perfect. One of those can hold a book and a snack at once—a marvelous convenience.

Fourth: *What to read.*

This is your most crucial decision. You need a book exciting enough to block out worries of the day. On the other hand, if it's too exciting, you'll still be reading at 3 a.m.

For me these are best: poetry (amazing how much fun it can be sometimes), travel books, historical novels (Eugenia Price can't be beat), essays—especially about living in the country (Gladys Taber, Celestine Sibley are my favorites) and English novels. Here's my special English novel list, culled by long, careful examination: any books by Barbara Pym, Jane Austen, Elizabeth Goudge, Angela Thirkell, Miss Read, Margaret Drabble, Elizabeth Taylor, or Rumer Godden.

But the quintessential bedtime reading is—beyond a doubt—a mystery or spy novel: one with good clean murders (not gory ones that cause nightmares) where the detective or the chief inspector gets his man. If it has a floor plan of an English great house in the front, you *know* it's good.

Some of my favorites here include (omitting the obvious, like Christie, Rex Stout, Dorothy Sayers, all of whom can be read over and over): Ed McBain (New York precinct cops), Dick Francis (English horse racing world), Emma Lathen (Wall Street), P.D. James, Ngaio Marsh (behind the scenes theatre world), Georges Simenon (Inspector Maigret just sits quietly, smokes his pipe, and wins the killer's confidence), Lucille Kallen (her C. B. Greenfield and Maggie make a fine New England pair), and someone I've just discovered (who works in wonderful recipes!), Virginia Rich.

Finally—here are some tips for that special problem many of us face:

How to read in bed when your roommate doesn't:

Never—repeat, never—read a newspaper. The rustling noise is grounds for divorce.

Never read Lewis Grizzard, Harold Martin, or Erma Bombeck. You'll laugh out loud in spite of yourself.

Choose quiet snacks. Apples are out. Peanut butter is in. Keep cracker crumbs on your side of the bed. And don't munch your ice.

Pull the lamp as close as possible. A crookneck lamp is best. Bedtime reading is often spoiled by a mate who mutters, "When are you going to turn off that light?"

Night night, happy reading. And send me your tips, please. I'm about to run out of mysteries and English novels. It's enough to give me insomnia, just thinking about it. All propped up and nothing to read? Horrors.

October 25, 1984

Memories of the Frances Virginia Tea Room

Do you remember the Frances Virginia Tea Room?

You probably do if you grew up in Georgia when I did. Going to the Frances Virginia was one of those special things you did when you went on a shopping trip to Atlanta. It didn't happen often. It was a rare treat, like visiting the Cyclorama or going to the Fox and looking at the stars on the ceiling.

The very name, "Frances Virginia," conjures up childhood memories for me . . . of coming to Atlanta once a year to buy my new school shoes at Thompson-Boland-Lee . . . going to see the *real* Santa Claus at Rich's (all the others were helpers, he was the real Santa and toyland at Rich's was like fairyland, magnificent and dazzling) . . . the crowds on the sidewalks of Peachtree (we usually walked from Davison's to Rich's but sometimes we splurged and rode on the "Shoppers Special") . . . the clang of the streetcars . . . the awesome vastness of the stores, making you feel very small, so you clung to your mama's coat down the long aisles of elegant gloves and hats and perfume . . . riding the elevators, listening to the operator call out the merchandise on each floor, feeling your stomach lurch at every stop (those new-fangled escalators came much later).

If my father and little brother went to Atlanta with us, we'd probably eat at the S&W. I liked it. It smelled like vegetable soup inside and had a big goldfish pond inside with *real* water and *real* fish, an amazing wonder that boggled my mind.

But if it were just all "girls"—my mother, my grandmother, my Aunt Marion, and I—we'd go to the Frances Virginia. It was close to Davison-Paxon's, and after a busy morning shopping, we could shove our bags under the table and rest our feet while waiting for the waitress to bring delicious things we never ate at home.

Now that I think about it, the Frances Virginia must have been the first restaurant I ever went to. I certainly don't remember ever eating in a restaurant in Gainesville, where we lived then. The Dixie Hunt Hotel did have a fancy dining room, and sometimes when my friends and I went to a movie, we would sneak inside the hotel when we passed it walking home. We thought the dining room was so fancy and beautiful. No one we knew ever ate there—just mysterious, obviously wealthy strangers from out of town.

Eating at the Frances Virginia was heady excitement for a small town little girl.

Ira Aikman (who always had a nose for news, no doubt gained from long happy years with her wonderful columnist husband Leo) sent me a newspaper clipping recently. It was from the *Hampton (Ga.) News,* and featured Margie Kemp Burleigh, daughter of Marietta's Peggy and Henry Kemp. (Henry, former superintendent of our Marietta Schools, has just retired from the U.S. Dept. of Education.)

The article told how Margie has a heritage of good food in her family because her late grandmother, Marjorie, was a sister of *the* Frances Virginia—and eventually became her partner.

It seems that Frances Virginia was the dietician at Piedmont Hospital in Atlanta before she founded her tea room. Her two sisters joined her in the venture. In fact, for a while Peggy Kemp was a hostess and a partner.

Said the article, "All food was freshly prepared by staff that grew to 125. A thousand people were seated for lunch each noon, in addition to the 400 who were served downstairs in the cafeteria."

I was so glad to learn of Peggy's connection with this delightful tea room. When I told her the other day about my happy memories of the Frances Virginia, *she* had a memory to share with me.

It seems that Peggy and Henry got married on a Saturday. They spent the first night of their honeymoon in Gainesville . . . and on Sunday morning went to the Presbyterian church and heard my daddy preach!

I forgot to ask her where they stayed in Gainesville. I'll bet it was the Dixie Hunt Hotel.

OCTOBER 17, 1980

A Case of Mistaken Identity

Ginger is a small stray dog we found 11 years ago, wandering around Marietta High School. In exchange for our Gainesburgers and a spot in our basement on cold winter nights, she gave us her whole heart.

Her sole objective in life seems to be to protect us. As a self-appointed watch dog, she barks and darts menacingly at all strangers within our gates, including the mailman, the dry cleaning man, and others we try to explain to her aren't really strangers at all.

She even chases off Hotshot, the white cat that belongs to the Ligons across the street, whenever Hotshot gets close to our cat, Wendy.

But Ginger has never actually bitten anyone.

Or so we thought until last Friday.

Picture this: the phone rings. It's a young man named Mike Barrett who tells me he's a new neighbor down the street. He asks politely if we own a dog named Ginger. I get the same feeling I get when I see my child's teacher at PTA. I admit we do.

Mike says his wife, Lorraine, was out jogging that morning and a dog bit her. The neighborhood children waiting for the school bus told her the dog was named Ginger. Asking around, they learned we had a dog by that name.

I start making stumbling apologies. Ginger is getting old. She had a trying morning. It began at 6:15 when the whole squad of Marietta High School cheerleaders came to our house for breakfast. After that the garbage truck came around, and Ginger had barked herself hoarse with excitement. No doubt she was nervous and testy from all these goings on.

I offer to pay for Lorraine to have a tetanus shot. Being new in Marietta they don't know a doctor. I call my own doctor and he agrees to give Lorraine a tetanus shot, even though he doesn't take new patients, because it was my dog that bit her.

The Barretts have two small children, so I volunteer to babysit. We finally agree that Lorraine will come by and pick me up, and we'll go together to the doctor's office.

She is a lovely person, and seems almost as embarrassed as I am over the situation. I sing nursery songs and tell Mother Goose rhymes with her cute little girl and boy while she's inside.

On our way back home again, the little girl asks me, "Why did your great big dog bite Mommy?"

I start telling her that Ginger is old, and that she's getting cranky, even though she's so little that many people think she's a puppy.

"Little?" asks Lorraine. "Isn't your dog a big collie?"

Mistaken identity!

The dog that bit Lorraine that morning was a dog named Ginger, all right, but *not my Ginger!*

We finally discover there's another dog named Ginger, just a little further down the street.

Next time, will the *real* Ginger please stand up and bark?

OCTOBER 13, 1978

Meals on Wheels Deliver Love

Miss Lily is a charmer. Propped upon the pillows of her big four-poster bed, she looks like a storybook grandmother: a round, merry face, snow-white hair pulled back in a soft bun, a radiant smile.

But life for Lily is no fairy tale. Her needs are all too real. She is elderly, bed-ridden, and most of the time alone. (She shares her house with a roomer who is away at work throughout the day.)

The spunky little lady doesn't indulge in self-pity.

"My get-up-and-go has done got up and gone," she laughs, and struggles gallantly to make it on her own regardless.

Thanks to Meals on Wheels she's doing it.

Meals on Wheels is a program funded partly by the government, partly by private donations. It's administered in our community by several agencies working together through Marietta-Cobb Community Service. This is a triumph over red tape if there ever was one! Joan Green and Pat Stevens are the two coordinators who direct the program, assisted by many volunteers.

Right now 193 volunteers give their time regularly two hours weekly or once or twice a month, to deliver hot meals to those unable to prepare them at home. Because of this wonderful program, 100 senior citizens in Cobb County are assured of one good hot meal a day, and can continue to live in their own homes despite difficulties.

As Pat says, "By helping them remain at home and function as normally as possible, we feel we help to maintain their dignity as well as their nutritional level."

Funding has recently been increased, so Joan hopes more volunteers can be found and the service can be expanded.

She also hopes other Cobb businesses will follow the lead of Marietta Federal Savings and Loan, which extends an employee's lunch hour if he or she volunteers for Meals On Wheels. (Obviously, C. W. Marlow, president of Marietta Federal, knows how wonderful Meals On Wheels is . . . his wife Kitty was formerly the program coordinator.)

Last Wednesday I met my friends Lucille and George Soukup at the Calico Cat (the distribution point in Marietta—there are others in Acworth, Mableton, Powder Springs and Smyrna.) I wanted to learn more about the program and see it in action.

A commercial caterer prepares the food. Volunteers are given an insulated chest with the hot foods and an ice chest with the drinks, salads, desserts, and butter.

Since George retired from Lockheed, he and his charming wife volunteer for Meals On Wheels every other Wednesday.

They introduced me to another couple who also help on Wednesdays, the Ray Millers. One Wednesday seven weeks ago the Millers missed coming—that was the day little Brenda Miller was born. Now Brenda and her sister Janice Tiffany, 16 months old, go along with their mother and daddy, to the joy of those they take meals to!

The Soukups have their system down to a T. While George drives their van (one he rebuilt from an old bus), Lucille works in the back of it setting up the next delivery, referring to her small "route notebook" for special diet information such as low salt or low sugar. She sets out an aluminum tray of hot food, a cup of cold salad, wrapped rolls and a carton of buttermilk.

Between 11:15 a.m., when they start out, and 1:00 o'clock, they'll deliver dinner to Miss Lily and nine other senior citizens. They will also write notes to a couple who are deaf mutes, give a pat on the arm here, a hug there, brighten up each home by their obvious caring and their friendliness.

"You fall in love with each one; it's hard not to stay longer," says Lucille.

"That's my job—to help Mama get away," teases George.

They have to stick to a fairly tight schedule or they wouldn't make the rounds fast enough for their hungry clients' lunch hour.

"Meals On Wheels"—three words—just like "I Love You." In fact, they're different ways of saying much the same thing.

OCTOBER 24, 1980

ALTA's Back in Town

ALTA's back in town again. And that means I'll be lonesome all fall.

None of my friends will have time for me. They can't meet for lunch. They're busy with ALTA. They can't come over for coffee. They have to get ready for ALTA.

When I first heard of ALTA, I wondered who she was. Someone new in town? She was already the most popular woman in Cobb County.

Then I discovered ALTA wasn't a person at all: it's the acronym for the organization people join when they play tennis—ALTA, for Atlanta Lawn Tennis Association.

I discovered something more: when people join ALTA they undergo a personality change. Tennis is not just a hobby. It's a cause, a crusade, a supreme reason for being. And when a man or woman is a serious Tennis Player, he or she is a disciple, a radical convert to the Tennis Way Of Life.

They're everywhere. Have you noticed? At the supermarket, in the hamburger place, even at meetings or parties—dressed in their "tennies," they stop by only briefly before moving on to the courts for their main role in life.

Some days I have a terrible feeling I'm going to look around and discover that I'm the only non-tennis playing person alive on planet Earth. Future historians will sift through our ruins, studying artifacts like moldy old sweatbands, shredded little wrap-around skirts, and crumbling ALTA charts to learn what life was like in the late 20th century.

I'm not against being a Tennis Player myself. In fact, I've tried, but I can't meet the qualifications.

First, there's attitude. To be a bona fide Tennis Player, one must promise to play tennis every single day. Weather is no excuse. Last summer was our hottest and driest on record—virgin trees fell in the forest and crops withered in the fields. But those Tennis Players were out there, boy, sweating, panting and dehydrating on the dusty courts. Last winter just after our big ice storm, I saw a woman with her arm in a sling. Had she slipped on the ice? Yes . . . as she was running across court to return a serve. And no one but me thought that was funny!

Pregnant tennis players time their serves between labor pains. Brides and Mothers of the Brides plan their weddings around ALTA schedules. Surgeons set their operations around tennis games. And the first thing patients ask when they come out from under the anesthetic is not, "When will you take out the stitches?" but, "When can I play tennis again?"

Golfers have an old joke about pausing a moment on the golf course to show respect when a spouse's funeral procession drives by. Tennis Players aren't joking.

There's another reason I can't be a Tennis Player—the wardrobe and equipment requirements.

For years I've owned a tennis dress. I see no need to buy another since I can only wear one at a time (even though it's an off-white color now, it was on-white when I bought it.) Real Tennis Players have whole closets full—dresses, shorts, tops, velour warm up suits, jackets, and cute little skirts with "LOVE" appliquéd on them.

I have a tennis racket, too. It belonged to my father in college, and it says Big Bill Tilden on the handle. Tennis Players snicker when they see it. They buy the latest in rackets every year. They weigh them in their hands and count the strings tenderly. They keep them in custom made covers with their initials printed on them.

They don't stop there. In their kitchens they hang up potholders and plaques about tennis, serve you with glasses and napkins about tennis, carry purses that say, "Tennis Is My Bag."

The only thing that isn't cute and sharp-looking about them is their shoes. Tennis Players wear awful looking shoes. They're always a dirty gray with a split up the back. I think they can't do without them long enough to wash them or get them repaired.

But the biggest difference between me and the real Tennis Players is conversation.

No matter how hard I try, I really can't find very much to say about tennis. On the other hand, Tennis Players can't talk about anything else.

These are some of the things they discuss: their forehand, backhand and service (they don't say "serve," they say "service"), their partner's forehand, backhand, and service, ditto their opponent. Then they talk about their pro—what their pro wants to change about their game, why they can't do it and what their pro says about their not doing it. Also the latest news from everyone on their team, and on all the other teams in ALTA (they all have names like airplanes—C-5, B-2).

It's unbelievable. I am astounded at their verbosity. Someone should hold a Tennis Talking Marathon. It would be a great fund raiser.

I guess I should also mention that I'm not a Tennis Player because I can't do the things with my body that they do. The only tennis ball I can hit is one that bounces just to my right and slightly in front of me. Any efforts to re-position myself to return a ball result in chopping motions that fan the air. It's very embarrassing. My serve could best be described as dainty. And if by some fluke my racket ever hits a ball, it's a pop fly that goes into the next court or over the fence.

And so—when ALTA comes around, I'm left to my lonely devices. I play the piano. I read a lot. I guess I'm lucky ALTA doesn't last year round.

SEPTEMBER 19, 1980

Kindergarten Teaching: Not Much Glory but a Lot of Love

Sometimes my phone rings early in the morning and a low voice whispers with desperate urgency, "Can you help me today?"

I know who it is without asking: not a kidnap victim; not a Weight Watcher on a chocolate binge; just my good friend, Ann Hildreth, needing a last-minute substitute at kindergarten.

Ann directs the weekday kindergarten at the First United Methodist Church, and since I taught a class there for five years, I'm on her substitute list.

There aren't too many of us, you know. You can't send just anybody in to face a roomful of four- and five-year-olds alone. It would be as indecent as sending someone off to fight in a bloody war without basic training.

Kindergarten Teachers are a very special breed. No one knows it better than we do.

You can tell who we are at first glance. We're the ones with runs in our hose, paint under our nails, and an extra layer of dry skin on our hands (actually it's Elmer's Glue.) Also we go around smiling a lot through clenched teeth.

The biggest differences between Kindergarten Teachers and Regular People, though, are inner differences. We may look fairly normal, but inside, we're a composite of so many personalities, we border on schizophrenia. Next to us, *The Three Faces of Eve* seem normal.

Consider these paradoxes. To be a good Kindergarten Teacher, one should:

• Be tough enough to break up a wrestling match before blood is drawn . . . yet gentle enough to relate to the shyest child.

• Have eyes in the back of her head and all the way around, to keep up with 20 active, moving children at one time . . . yet still give complete attention to one.

• Have a lesson plan prepared each day . . . yet be flexible enough to ditch it if something better pops up, from a bulldozer working nearby to a creepy crawler a child brings for Show and Tell.

• Speak softly . . . yet penetrate the room's noisy din, which is equal to the engine noise of a C-5 cargo plane.

• Give each child a chance to speak at Circle Time . . . though no one else wants to listen. (They all want to talk, none want to listen.)

• Know when a child needs lap cuddling . . . and when his independence needs encouraging. (Emotional needs vary from not getting his fair turn in a game to wondering why daddy doesn't live at home any more.)

• Plan art that lets a child be creative and do his own thing . . . yet hope the mother still puts it on the refrigerator door.

• Be a Bionic Woman. Be able to kick, crawl, stoop, skip, jump, hop and slide. The only physical requirements Kindergarten Teachers don't have to fill is being still. ("Rest Time," contrary to popular opinion, is not a time of rest at kindergarten. It's a time when children place a towel on

the floor and squirm near, around, over and under it, while teachers say things like, "Come out from under the table, Bobby," and "Don't flip Jill with your towel, Ricky, you're hurting her.")

• Maintain some semblance of dignity . . . while engaged in undignified pursuits. Once I had to pursue a rebellious child around the outside of the building, while 19 delighted little spectators cheered me on from the windows, "He went that way, Mrs. Ryle—through the shrubbery!"

• Help each child have a happy, unpressured year and develop at his own pace . . . yet satisfy anxious mothers who want to know why he can't read yet.

• Include the following in your curriculum: current events, history, meteorology (we talk about the weather a lot), math and reading readiness, religion and philosophy, music, drama, art, science and health, large and small motor skills . . . but expect most people to call your job baby-sitting.

• Cardinal Precepts for Kindergarten Teachers:

(1) Never be boring. These kids grew up on Sesame Street and Star Wars heroes. You can't just tell them a story. You have to tell a story, throw in a song and dance, juggle if possible, and play the piano while your head is swiveled backwards—which leads to the other Cardinal Precept:

(2) Never turn your back on four- or five-year-olds. It's suicidal. And never, of course, leave your room. (Kindergarten Teachers must have stronger kidneys than Regular People.)

Why do we do it?

Because little children show pure love in ways others never approach.

Once when I was substituting, a little girl named Darby, a four-year-old pupil of mine the year before, saw me from the hall. Without saying a word, she walked into the room, opened her tiny purse, took out a dime (probably a prized possession), handed it to me, and walked out.

No wonder Kindergarten Teachers hang in there year after year, underpaid and under-appreciated.

With so much love, who minds a little spilled paint and Elmer's glue?

OCTOBER 2, 1978

Hugh Spears . . .
What One Man Can Do

"A good man," as Flannery O'Connor said, "is hard to find." A man so good that he doesn't want to be noticed or thanked is even harder to find. I want to tell you about such a man.

His name is Hugh Spears. He and his wife Mary (his partner, also, in "goodness") live on Sandy Plains Road. They don't know I'm writing about them and I hope they won't mind.

Right now Hugh is sick and it seems appropriate to let him know what he means to so many of us.

With the world going crazy, with pain and tragedy and evil everywhere you turn, it helps to think about Hugh. If it's better to light a candle than to curse the darkness, then maybe Hugh won't mind being a "candle." Then he can help us see with what meaning and beauty one life can shine in the worst darkness when someone lives it the right way.

I don't know much about Hugh's background except that he was a career Marine, and that he, Mary and their son lived many places before he retired as a captain and came home to Marietta.

He went into business at the Cobb County Tractor Company with Pat Cristie.

Then in 1970 something special happened.

Hugh heard a visiting preacher say that folks should find something exciting to do to serve the Lord—something they really *liked* doing. Rather than wait for the church nominating committee to ask you to fill a position just because it's needed, you should seek something that fills you with enthusiasm.

Hugh knew what he wanted to do. He wanted to help little children.

At that time Marietta Place was a large public housing project on Clay and Fairground Streets (now the South Marietta Parkway). It was filled with women and children with low incomes—80% of the families there were without fathers in the home.

Many had come to Marietta from the mountains or rural areas. They knew nothing about urban life. They needed food, clothes, jobs—all kinds of help. And most of all, the children needed love.

Hugh and Mary decided to teach in a small mission Sunday School our church had just begun there. Soon Hugh was asked to be chairman of the mission—and the project took off and flew.

The Spears visited in all of the apartments in the project, learned the people and their problems, made helping them their top priority in life.

Today the young men associated with Hugh at the tractor company speak of how contagious Hugh's enthusiasm was. Frank Wiginton says, "When he started the mission work, all he had to say was he needed us and we were ready—because Hugh did so much for everyone. You could write a book just talking to the guys that Hugh helped at the tractor place."

A whole crowd of young bachelors began doing something they never thought they'd do—getting up early on Sunday morning and teaching Sunday School! Frank, Eddie Williams, Henry Raper, Johnny Barrett.

Hugh also enlisted some high school girls from our church—Lynn Sutton, Becky Thomas, and our daughter Patty. For good measure he recruited Lib Meiere, a wise and warm-hearted school teacher, to join the team.

Soon 50 or more children each Sunday morning flocked to the community room for juice, doughnuts, and Bible stories. But that was just the beginning.

On Sunday nights Hugh and Mary drove their new van (bought solely for that purpose), collected the children and took them to the evening worship service at our church, First Baptist.

Frank says, "He enticed them by promising we'd all go to McDonald's afterwards."

During the week you could find Hugh at the housing project almost as much as at work. The people would phone Hugh first if they needed something, before they called Child and Family Services. Groceries, shoes, a father in jail, a sick mother, tutoring for school—Hugh helped. One little boy needed an artificial leg. Hugh bought one . . . a new one every year to keep up with his growth. He helped pay for dental care—and even for braces for some of the children.

Each summer he took them all out in the country to Ernest Bentley's farm on Villa Rica Road for a big cook-out, hayride and fishing in the lake.

At Easter there was a huge egg hunt at Marietta Place.

And Christmas . . . well, Christmas was so special the mission workers still miss it now. There would be a big chicken dinner for everyone, presents under the tree, and a nativity play performed by all the classes from the youngest up.

"I'm sure everyone at Marietta Place thought of Santa Claus as a bald-headed man about five feet five, who looked exactly like Hugh Spears," laughs Frank.

Then, after six years of the mission, Marietta Place was torn down. The inhabitants were relocated in many places.

Today the Lockheed Credit Union and a new office park exist where once women in print house dresses and tots on broken trikes spent their days in tiny yards and crowded apartments—and where Hugh Spears moved among them as a friend, surrogate father, and patron saint.

Lynn Sutton Wiginton (a romance that began at the Mission) says Hugh is the most loving, compassionate man she ever knew. So does my Patty. Eddie says, "All he cared about was helping those people. That was his life."

The little boys and girls who snuggled by him in church and fought to sit near him in the van are grown. Wherever they are, I'm sure they remember the man who loved them when they needed it most.

And I hope today Hugh Spears knows they remember.

NOVEMBER 3, 1983

Vigil at Scottish Rite

It's my turn to stay with little Ben.

He's been in Scottish Rite Children's Hospital a week and his mama and daddy need a break from their nightly vigil on the leather couch in his room.

Ben has just now decided he's hungry. He wants a bottle and he wants it *now.* I press the little white button over the crib to call a nurse.

Ben says, "Who needs a little white button?" He's announcing it loud and clear to the entire third floor of Scottish Rite. If the windows were up, he'd be telling everyone in North Atlanta.

His cries of angry outrage bleat and gurgle in his throat because he's too mad to stop for breath. His big blue eyes are shut tight in concentration. When you're only five months old, it's not easy to fight for your rights!

Tiny clenched fists flail the air, telling the whole world, "Put up your dukes!" How vulnerable they look, one little wrist encircled with a hospital identification tape and the back of one little hand bearing a bruise where needles drew blood.

His screams shatter the hushed atmosphere of this place, where behind closed doors parents wind up music boxes and sing lullabies to calm fretful children, and nurses hurry on crepe-soled shoes from one emergency to another.

I rock my darling little grandson trying to calm him down . . . but I give silent thanks to the Lord for every loud cry. I exult in each push of his small, bucking, squirming body.

Last week Ben couldn't act rambunctious. He could only cuddle sweet and helpless on our shoulders, feeling entirely too feather light, accepting whatever the world dished out to him.

I've never been so glad to hear a baby cry!

Go to it, Ben. You tell 'em, Tiger.

His bottle finally comes (how long four minutes can seem!). Ben's silky eyelashes close over tears. His head snuggles on my arm. His hands—tiny stars with dimples—clutch the bottle as he puts all his energy into swigging down the magical concoction they've devised, based on many lab tests, to take care of Ben's needs.

His young specialist, Dr. Saripkin, tells us that a few years ago feeding problems like Ben's (which can start with a virus or allergies) couldn't always be treated. Babies who kept losing valuable nutrients, losing weight, often died. Now they have more ways to break down the nutrients so babies can assimilate them through formula or a tube and overcome the problem.

Chalk up one more victory for modern medical science.

We'll have a very special Thanksgiving this year—for the medical knowledge that makes little Ben's recovery technically possible . . . and for the caring people who help it to happen.

Scottish Rite is just as wonderful as we heard it was. Since 1915 this institution has cared for sick children in Atlanta. It moved a few years ago to a modern facility near Northside Hospital.

Babes in arms, toddlers clutching their Garfield, teddy, or baby doll and holding a parent's hand, other children manipulating their own wheelchairs—they all come to Scottish Rite. And here they find the best possible care, both physically and emotionally.

The bright colors in the hospital symbolize the courage, hope and personal attention waiting for them here. There are purple doors, gaily striped curtains of red, purple, bright blue and green, a sun-and-moon sign on each patient's door ("Benjamin is awake," "Benjamin is asleep").

Ben's young student nurse Laura is in school at Georgia Baptist Hospital. She hopes to work here after graduation. I hope she can, too. Laura is a super nurse—and she's more qualified than most to understand the hopes and fears of these young patients. Laura walks with a cane.

It seems appropriate that the Tech-Georgia freshman football game on

Thanksgiving weekend benefits Scottish Rite. I don't even care which team Ben roots for when he gets older.

If he can just keep hollering this loud, it couldn't matter less!

NOVEMBER 15, 1984

Our Lady of Perpetual Help—A Very Special Place

For years my neighbor, Barbara Glover, has been telling me about the cancer home in Atlanta, Our Lady of Perpetual Help. It's operated by the Hawthorne Dominican nuns and Barbara is one of their most dedicated volunteers. Barbara wanted me to visit the home.

And for years I'd been giving Barbara excuses for not going.

Finally I ran out of excuses. This week when their Auxiliary invited me to an "Awareness Day," held to acquaint social workers, nurses, hospital chaplains and others about the home, I accepted.

Wednesday I drove into Atlanta, turning off the downtown expressway at Georgia Avenue. I parked and walked inside the high fenced grounds to the entrance of the home, dreading what I would find inside.

Incurable cancer brings such dread, sorrow, and despair. How could a place that cares for patients with incurable cancer be anything but dismal?

What I found there was—well, peace and beauty and love.

The grounds of the place are lovely, with tall oaks (the building was planned right around one tree, which must be the oldest, biggest oak tree in Atlanta), a fountain, swings, and inviting walkways. In one corner of the lawn is a small grotto with a rich blue stained glass window—a quiet prayer retreat, within a stone's throw of the Atlanta Stadium.

Inside the home are statues and other art, a chapel, and modern facilities for the best possible patient care—but not in the antiseptic impersonality of a hospital—in the warmth of a real home.

My friend Barbara is right: the service being given to mankind at Our Lady of Perpetual Help is so incredible I wish everyone would go and see for themselves.

Jack Spalding of the Atlanta Newspapers once wrote about it, "It is one of the most remarkable places here or anywhere. It is testimony to the best in man. Each visit there has buoyed me and strengthened a shaky belief that mankind is worth saving."

Rose Hawthorne, daughter of the famous novelist Nathaniel Hawthorne, founded the Sisters of St. Dominic when Rose became so concerned with destitute cancer patients in New York City that she left her comfortable society life, moved into a tenement on the lower East Side, and began caring for them.

Today the nuns operate seven cancer homes in the United States. This is the only one in the South.

They're financed entirely by donations. *No* contributions are accepted from patients. And all are served, regardless of race, creed, or color. Most of their patients in Atlanta are non-Catholics. Laughs a woman named Carolyn, the volunteer guiding us through the home, "It's not because Catholics don't get cancer—it's because here in the Bible Belt, most people are non-Catholic."

Carolyn points out that until you see the place for yourself, "You may think it's the absolute pits—a charity hospital for incurable patients in southwest Atlanta!"

I can tell you: it's not "the pits" at all. It's a real home, cheerful, comfortable, and caring. Enthusiastic volunteers like Carolyn and Barbara say the morale of every patient improves amazingly a few days after entering.

The nuns are the nurses. The only paid workers are a few orderlies and cooks. Each patient is assigned to one special nun and she is his only nurse. She does his laundry and prepares his meal trays according to his wants and needs. "Maybe he wants baby food, or syrup on everything, or a hot dog at 3 a.m." Sister does it.

There are attending physicians, and pain medicine is administered, ("We use medicine which keeps the patient as alert as possible, but comfortable,") but cobalt, chemotherapy and other such treatments should be completed before a patient enters the home.

The rooms are huge and sunny. Sheets on the beds are gay plaids and prints, with colorful quilts and afghans. African violets and other pretty plants and several parakeets (a green one named Mike is quite a character) add to the cheerful environment.

In the beauty salon, "Chez Marie," Marie—a beautician—and other volunteers, including a stewardess, come regularly to give shampoos and manicures.

The chapel in the home is one of the most beautiful I've ever seen. The patients (Catholics and Protestants and those of whatever faith) worship there as well as the nuns. Sister Mary, administrator of the home, says simply, "We are sustained by our prayers and by our community life."

That, of course, is the biggest gift the home offers its patients—faith. I love the little quotation they use on their stationery and other printed material: "Death is not putting out the light, it is extinguishing the candle because the dawn has come."

One of the volunteers told me, "We are not trying to compete with the *next* place our patients are going, which is of course the ultimate."

I came away feeling that Our Lady of Perpetual Help, however, is not only an ideal last earthly home—but a fairly good foretaste of the one to come.

NOVEMBER 16 and NOVEMBER 23, 1979

What's It Going to Be . . . Buddy or George

Dear Buddy,

Congratulations and best wishes up there in Washington!

We're proud of our new congressman. Even my Republican friends are admitting you'll do fine.

As for me, I've peeled the Buddy Darden bumper sticker off my car and pulled up the Buddy Darden sign from the yard, happy in knowing the Seventh District of Georgia is served with intelligence and integrity by one who knows us well.

Hey, but Buddy, there's one little matter we need to talk over.

I hate to bother you when you already face tough decisions, like where you and Lillian will live, where little George and Christy will go to school, and how you stand on every issue from A for abortion to Z for Zimbabwe.

But this is a biggy, Buddy. Your entire future could hang in the balance. You need to resolve this matter quickly and courageously—it can affect your clout in Congress more than which side of the aisle you sit on, or whether you're a liberal or a conservative.

It's the very basic issue of your name.

Now that you're a U. S. Congressman, what's it going to be . . . Buddy or George?

Will you continue to be the same warm, friendly Buddy Darden we all know and love? Can a Good Ol' Boy named Buddy win fame and honor in our nation's capital?

Or has the time come to switch to the dignified, earnest, rather stuffy name of George? (Stuffy isn't all bad, you know. That name worked well in the presidential election of 1789.)

There are delicate nuances and subtle implications in this choice that boggle the mind. If you keep on being Buddy, you embarrass the voters of swanky, high-toned East Cobb. If you switch to George, the good folks up in Cartersville and Acworth will say you've gone high-hat. It's a risk either way.

Let's consider the pros and cons.

Inside the state of Georgia, Buddy is no problem. In fact, it's a decided advantage. Anyone wanting to make it in Georgia politics needs a nickname or a double name, like Joe Mack or Joe Frank. Otherwise forget it.

Where else but in Georgia would you find a beautiful new office building like the Veterans' Memorial, just across from our state capitol, with tall shiny towers, a lovely garden—and an inscription on the entrance, "Dedicated to the memory of James H. '*Sloppy*' Floyd"?

Any state that puts the name "Sloppy" on its public buildings will always love any politician named Buddy.

Demographically, Buddy is good for the youth vote, the truckers' vote, and liberated women's vote. ("I Only Want A Buddy, Not A Sweetheart, Buddies Never Make You Cry.")

However, when Georgia sends her men to Washington, we like their regular monikers more than their nicknames. Exceptions are Jimmy and Mac and Newt . . . but think about Senator Walter George and Senator Richard Russell. No one called them Wally or Dicky and look at the long run they had.

And look at Sam Nunn—a solid 10 on anyone's list. You'd no more call him "Sammy" than you'd call the Pope "Father Johnny Paul."

All in all, it seems to me you should hang on to both names if you can do it without being accused of straddling the fence. That way you can go with what's best at the time.

When you're on the MacNeil-Lehrer News Hour, or mingling with suave types at black tie embassy parties and White House concerts, by all means be George.

When you wear your plaid shirt and eat barbecue at the Cobb County Fairgrounds, be Buddy.

Ask Lillian what she thinks. That lady is such a winner, that if she agrees to being called Mrs. George Buddy Darden, you'll have it made.

November 17, 1983

Old Movies

Do you ever watch old movies and hear dialogue so corny you can't believe they said it?

Don't get me wrong. I love old movies. Some of those movies of the '30s and '40s will never be surpassed. They don't make 'em like they used to.

I even like some of the grade B oldies. The old westerns were great. Right was right and wrong was wrong, by golly. The only old movies I turn off are those gangster pictures where Bogie or Cagney wears a dark shirt and light tie, and the background music is in a minor key and wavers a lot.

My favorites, though, are the old musicals. You know each step of the plot before it happens. They're totally predictable. You feel secure and okay because of that old happy-ever-after world on celluloid.

The plot goes this way:

A. Boy meets Girl. Boy (rich playboy in disguise—Girl never suspects even though he has a Harvard accent and clean fingernails) falls madly in love with Girl, right off.

B. Girl discovers Boy has duped her. She gets furious (this shows how dumb she is—so who minds rich?)

C. Boy tries ploys to win her back, such as (1) roses, (2) singing telegram, (3) intervention by goodhearted manager (Jack Oakie), Girl's roommate (Ann Miller) or the landlord ("Cuddles"—what was his last name? That lovable old fat fellow who looked over his glasses and never knew what was going on?).

D. Boy sings a love song. He smiles a lot while singing, and moves toward Girl in little bitty steps because it's a long song. Usually this is on a stage because the Girl is a musical star. But no one ever yells, "Get him out of here," and the band always knows his key.

E. Girl looks startled. (Actually she's mad—why is he spoiling her big number? Is all that money worth it?)

F. Girl succumbs, remembering his Cadillac, Park Avenue penthouse, and big blue eyes. Girl puts her head on Boy's shoulder, careful not to muffle her voice as she joins him on the final chorus.

G. Boy kisses Girl. Everyone looks happy. Jack Oakie or Cuddles gives a wink. THE END.

Those old movies, of course, have lines so trite and hackneyed you groan out loud.

One of our good friends, Jerry Vandeventer, has decided they're so awful, they're wonderful. He's started a collection of Really Terrible Old Movie Lines.

Many of you know Jerry's voice—if not Jerry. For years he announced for WSB Radio (Night Beat was his special show). Now he freelances doing movies, commercials, special radio and tv programs—editing, producing and speaking much of his own material. As a wordsmith himself, and as a fanatical movie buff all his life, he really gets a kick out of cornball movie lines. We jot down any we hear and pass them on to Jerry.

Here are some he's collected:

"Gee, honey, I think you're swell."

"There's always tomorrow, Janice. Always tomorrow."

"I'll take that chance."

"I'm afraid your little game is over, Beauchamp. Consider yourself under house arrest."

"Somehow, Baron, I always knew it would come to this."

"Listen, Tonga! The drums speak war."

"Pick up your sword, kinsman. Let us see if your blade is as sharp as your tongue."

"Now I understand . . . You loved him, too . . . didn't you?"

"Now, if nobody makes no funny moves, nobody's gonna get hurt."

"My, my, Ellen. It's been a long time and you're no little girl any more."

"Quickly, Markham—fetch me some brandy."

"Okay, Louie, drop the gun."

"I didn't mean to hit you so hard, but I'm particular how people talk about my sister."

"You're going out on that stage tonight as a nobody, but you're coming back a star."

"I gotta go for the championship, Scotty. Gimme a chance."

I called Jerry with a new one the other day. John Wayne said it to his leading lady, just before he rode off alone into the sunset: "I love you, but I'm too old for you. Why ma'am, my saddle's older 'n you are."

THE END

DECEMBER 7, 1979

Saint Jude—A Man After My Own Heart

The organ at St. Joseph's Church in Marietta is in the balcony, behind the sanctuary. I have learned to be very grateful for this location.

It makes it easier to hide. When I make a mistake, while playing for services (like I did two Sundays ago, when I came out with a resounding chord just as Father began the Gospel reading) and heads of the worshippers swivel around and eyes turn upward in my direction, I just duck behind the music rack. That way, they don't know who made the blooper—me, or Phil Malonson or David Hall, the other organists (though I think they have a pretty good idea!).

The top of the organ is big and wide, and has become a catch-all for lost gloves, old bulletins, pencils, and other flotsam and jetsam of church life.

It was there that I recently found a fascinating little card. I've kept it to ponder over. It's about one of the saints of the church, St. Jude, whose feast day was October 28.

St. Jude is known as The Saint Of Hopeless Causes.

Don't you love that?

From information on the card, and from reading I've done on him since then, (*Saint Watching* by Phyllis McGinley and *Saints for All Seasons* by John Delaney,) St. Jude is ready to help in desperate situations and hopeless cases, things almost despaired of. He is sometimes called "The Saint Of The Impossible."

You may know him better by his other name—Thaddeus. Remember, he was one of the Twelve Apostles, and the author of one of the books of the Bible, the small book of Jude. A verse in there says, "Use your holy faith as your foundation and build on that."

According to tradition, St. Jude was clubbed to death by a mob after his last missionary journey.

"The Saint Of Hopeless Causes"—what a beautiful charge for a saint to be given! And how it fires the imagination.

My own list of "hopeless causes" could keep him busy:

There's my diet—which I can handle okay until my chocolate craving takes over.

There's the matter of my closets and cabinets. I clean them one at a time but never all at once, since the only thing I know to do is move stuff from one to another.

More hopeless causes: buying groceries without writing an extra check, being ready for Christmas by Christmas, getting to the bottom of the ironing basket, getting ahead of columns before deadline, my tennis game. Oh yes, and all of those awful mistakes on the organ.

I could tell St. Jude about the traffic in Cobb County. Seeing I–285 finished in our lifetime. Having a railroad underpass on the north side of Marietta.

There's the Atlanta Braves—who obviously haven't talked to St. Jude yet.

To be less flip about it and far more serious, St. Jude could help with many "things almost despaired of": abused children, broken marriages, crime, disease, poverty, and finding a way for peace among men.

If you look at the life and writings of St. Jude you will know that he would not ever confuse real hope with glib, slick answers, but he would advocate ultimate solutions that call for time, faith, and perseverance.

Katharine Hepburn says, "The only failure is not to fail once, but to quit trying again." Hope is buoyant, easy, natural in the young, but not so easy as we grow older.

I can imagine that St. Jude smiled when Annie Sullivan met a little girl both blind and deaf named Helen Keller; and when three diverse, but earnest, men came together at Camp David.

Surely he is the patron saint of every cancer research lab, and coronary care unit, and children's hospital.

St. Jude would have to be a special friend to each pastor dealing with an apathetic congregation, every teacher of exceptional children, each member of Alcoholics Anonymous.

Ann Kiemel would love St. Jude. She writes, "I love the word" *impossible* . . . It's the joy after sorrow, people being friends after being enemies, rainbows after drenching rain, a wound healed, sunset on quiet evenings after hot, noisy days . . . I love the word *impossible* because my God believes in adventure, because He is love, and love always finds a way through, in time."

Hopeless causes? Impossible situations? Who's to say?

NOVEMBER 17, 1978

From Prison in Cuba to Thanksgiving in America

It's not often you get to meet a real hero.

Two weeks ago the Rev. Benjamin Valdes came to Marietta, and we've met a hero, face to face.

The basic facts about him you already know from news accounts: a Cuban Baptist minister . . . arrested by the Castro government . . . imprisoned 12 years . . . released last April . . . finally coming to join his wife and children in America.

It was a dream come true for the Valdes family, their Cuban friends and relatives, and the members of my church, First Baptist of Marietta. We had "adopted" Carmen Valdes and her children when they came to the United States nine years ago (many churches have such support programs for refugees). With them we had waited, despaired, prayed and hoped, year after year, for Benjamin to be released from jail.

It was a jubilant reunion for the family that Thursday night two weeks ago at the Atlanta airport (you may have seen it on television news).

Sunday morning brought another emotional moment.

Regardless of what our Episcopalian and Presbyterian friends think, our Sunday morning services at First Baptist are reverent and dignified (It's Sunday nights when we slip in a few good old Baptist "amens" now and then!). But Sunday morning, Nov. 6, was an exception. When our pastor announced that Mr. Valdes was with his family in the congregation, we rose as one man and broke into long, spontaneous applause (the first applause in our church that I can remember).

It was a very moving and fitting tribute to him and his family.

Carmen and Benjamin met when both were seminary students in Cuba. They served several pastorates in Cuba, had two little boys, then two little girls.

It was an April evening in 1965 when they heard the knock on the door. Mr. Valdes was "wanted for questioning." Government officials drove him away.

It would be twelve long years before he would be free again.

The actual charges brought against Benjamin were "trafficking in exchange of currency and helping a fugitive out of the country." He admits assisting more than one fugitive to leave, including his own brother.

There were 50 other Cuban Baptist pastors imprisoned during Castro's revolutionary takeover. No one knows the total number of political and religious leaders arrested then, but 2300 were in the first prison to which Benjamin was taken.

It's easy to see why Castro would consider Benjamin Valdes a formidable adversary. He is a man with strong leadership qualifications: intelligence, speaking ability, dynamic personality, and strong religious convictions.

While he was in prison he set up programs to maintain physical and mental health, took daily exercises, began learning English hoping he could eventually come to America, and refused the government's offer of leniency in return for taking a "re-education" program.

In a recent article in the *Christian Index*, he said his imprisonment was meant to teach others a lesson "but it taught me a lesson, too. I'm not bitter about my experiences. I think that time helped develop my testimony." He feels that God helped him love, not hate, his captors.

When Benjamin finally came to Marietta to re-join his family, we expected to see someone frail, subdued, perhaps embittered. But the sparkle in his eyes, quick way with a joke, and friendly personality show he's a man who appreciates life in a special way after his long prison experience.

I'll never forget the news photos of his reunion with his family—that joyful embrace. When he last saw them, Ben, Jr. was a boy of 13, Otteil ("Otto") was 10, and the little girls, Carmita and Ruthie, were 4 and 5 years old with long dark curls and ruffled dresses.

Now Ben, Jr., is in graduate school at Vanderbilt, Otto is a sophomore at Mercer U. in Macon, and Carmita and Ruthie are pretty teenagers at Marietta High and Marietta Junior High Schools.

Carmen Valdes, in her own way, has shown as much faith and courage as her husband, and endeared herself to us all. Her expressive dark eyes, vivacious personality, warmth and charm overcame the language barrier from the moment we met her (she can speak English now but her Spanish accent is pronounced and lovable).

She and Benjamin, thanks to the Home Mission Board, spent a week together in Spain while waiting for his clearance to enter the states. Future plans are uncertain. The Board will locate him in a Spanish ministry, but 'til January they want him to take a vacation and become re-acquainted with his family.

When the rest of us name our blessings this Thanksgiving, we may mention home, our nation, freedom, our faith . . . but none of us could know the same feelings the Valdes do, or celebrate quite as joyfully.

They have twelve years to make up.

NOVEMBER 18 and NOVEMBER 25, 1977

At Thanksgiving, Listen to Both Sides of the Record

Celestine Sibley writes in her book *Small Blessings*, "The greatest waste in life is not to know when you are happy."

Sometimes we grow so accustomed to the blessings of life that we take them for granted. This Thanksgiving, I might do a little better than I do some years—I've had a bizarre, O. Henry sort of situation happen to me recently that made me realize how easy it is to overlook some of the best gifts of all!

Let me tell you about it.

Dallas and I were riding in the car with the radio on, when some gorgeous music came over the station. It was classical music, but it had folktune qualities: melodies you felt you already knew, they were so simple and singable; lilting rhythms that made you want to dance. The orchestral arrangement was rich and luscious.

When it ended, we listened carefully to hear the announcer's identification. It was something called Rumanian Rhapsodies by Enesco.

The next time we were in the record shop we were delighted to find it! We played it over and over at home, and each time it lifted my heart and made me happier the moment it began.

Eventually, out of curiosity, we turned the record over to see what was on the other side. It was the Liszt "Hungarian Rhapsodies." Since we already had them on an older record, the next time Patty came over we gave our old Liszt record to her.

Later, when Patty was with us, we were playing the Enesco music.

"Oh," she said, "I have that, too. It's on the back of that record you gave me of the 'Hungarian Rhapsodies."

We'd had it the whole time!

How often do we fail to turn the record over to the flip side, and see what is ours in life all along?

On the *Today Show* recently a young man was photographed as he walked in the autumn woods with his wife on their estate near Nashville. He was a country music star who seemed to have it all—a huge mansion, attractive family, fame, wealth, talent, youth.

Then he said, "I like to walk outdoors, especially at this time of year. My wife describes the leaves to me, and I know they must be beautiful."

Ronnie Milsap smiled, and his eyelids quivered over sightless eyes.

How often do I forget the wonder of seeing: the leaves in autumn, the sparkle of frost in winter, the tender green buds of a willow in spring, the radiance of a sunset, the faces of my family?

Another television show this week—Cambodian refugees: the ones who made it by crawling into camp, are being handed their small daily bowls of food. Old people whose flesh barely covers their bones, babies with huge eyes peering hopefully at a world which offers little reason to hope.

How often do I, in this land of plenty, grumble over prices and shortages, enjoy abundant food and never remember the hungry people in the world or think seriously about my own stewardship and sharing of our bounty?

My mother enclosed in her letter this week a letter from my Aunt Louise, a widow in her 80's. She writes of her chrysanthemums, of Sunday dinner each week with eight widows after church, of her D.A.R. luncheon, of her children. She doesn't mention her loneliness without Uncle Barber, or her health problems. Self-pity is not her style—and I guess that's one reason all of us love her.

I hope when I start counting my blessings this Thanksgiving, I can remember not only the big ones, but some I often overlook, on the flip side of the record. Often they're some of the best!

NOVEMBER 21, 1979

Giving Thanks for Love, Beauty, and Giblet Gravy

One of the worst problems about writing a column is the timing.

This column, my Thanksgiving column, won't come out for two days but I have to write it today, Wednesday, since the newspaper office will be closed tomorrow for the holiday.

Whatever I want to say in the spirit of the season must be said early.

To get into the spirit of things would be easy if I were a hermit, or a nun in some nice, contemplative order. I could stroll about the woods, enjoying the deep autumn colors, hearing only the crunching of leaves and the skittering of squirrels overhead, and thinking about how beautiful the world is . . . or I could sit in a hushed and lovely chapel, meditating in stained glass seclusion. Surely then my expressions of praise and gratitude would well up and overflow.

Even if I were a full-time journalist I'd have a place in the office, with my own desk and coffee mug and green eye shade. (Well, all right—they don't use those any more, but it makes such a nice touch.) And I could pound out my Thanksgiving column in single-minded concentration.

But what am I doing? I'm writing this at home in my usual hopeless dichotomy: as a columnist with a deadline, and as the wife and mother of a hungry horde expecting a big Thanksgiving dinner tomorrow.

I'm not contemplating the beauties of the earth, the glories of the sky, or the joys of human life. I'm contemplating giblets and gravy.

Right after breakfast this morning I made the cornbread for the dressing. (Southern style dressing, unlike "stuffing," evolves in complex stages, beginning with crumbled up biscuits and cornbread. You don't find it in any cookbook. You have to get the recipe from your mother.)

Now I've boiled the eggs for the gravy, to go with the chopped up liver and gizzard. The cranberry sauce was made last night since the longer it chills, the stiffer it gets and the less likely to slosh out of the cut glass bowl onto the white tablecloth.

This afternoon I'll take the turkey out to thaw, make up the dough for icebox rolls and bake the pies. We always have pumpkin pie since the children are traditionalists and "hams," and someone has to yell "Hurrah for the pumpkin pie!" But we make apple pie, too, because they like it more.

Tonight after our church prayer service, I'll arrange the fresh fruit centerpiece on grandmother's ironstone platter. At one end of it I always put fresh pineapple, and over it a red felt turkey head my mother made for us years ago. The greenish brown pineapple spikes make the turkey's tail.

Tomorrow morning while the boys and their father go squirrel hunting at Lake Allatoona, I'll set the table with our good silver and our white and gold china. (Going hunting was traditional for my husband on Thanksgiving Day when he grew up . . . but in Perry it was quail hunting. Here we have no place to hunt quail, no bird dog any more.)

No, there really is no time yet to contemplate the meaning of Thanksgiving. If I did now, my praise litany would surely center on my electric blender, double oven, Mr. Coffee, and—most important—our dishwasher.

Not 'til we gather around the table tomorrow night will I have a full awareness in my heart of the blessings of home and health and each loved one far and near.

'Til then I'm taking comfort in a wonderful poem by Caroline Rhea, called "Patchwork Quilt":

The many blessings for which I thank God by day
Are multi-colored patches in my quilt of prayer.
At times I'm prone to shiver,
Feeling urgent need for something more,
But nestled 'neath my patchwork quilt
Of God's remembered blessings,
I find I'm truly warm enough.

It reminds me God understands when a woman's gratitude is not a full, richly designed tapestry, woven in quiet seclusion. It's a homely quilt, put together in bits and pieces.

Yet each day brings new pieces.

Thank you, Lord.

NOVEMBER 24, 1978

Rehearsal Pianist for Alliance Theatre—Wow!

"Nancy, this is Robert. Your next call is for Tuesday night from 8:00 til 11:00."

Now, before you get the wrong idea, let me explain.

The message was about my temporary, very exciting job last month as a rehearsal pianist for Alliance Theatre's "The King and I."

I've been playing the piano for one thing or another most of my life—ever since I was eight years old and my father drafted me to fill in at prayer meeting for the lady who usually played and was sick.

We picked out easy hymns, I remember—with flats, not sharps. I even remember what they were: "What A Friend We Have in Jesus" and "Jesus Calls Us O'er The Tumult." The latter was especially appropriate due to the tumultuous racket I made, heeding my mother's advice. She had said "keep the tune going, no matter how many mistakes you make in the left hand,"—and keep it going I did, through one terrible dissonance after another!

From that early start I've played for many choirs, choruses, orchestras, and musicals. (I was the envy of all my girl friends in the tenth grade at

Orlando High when I was the only girl in the class 5th period, playing for the boys' glee club.)

But this new job at Alliance would be an exciting first in my career—for the first time, I'd be working with a professional theatre group. They only needed me for rehearsals when they divided for dancing and singing groups. Michael Fauss, the musical director at Alliance and a marvelous pianist, would play for all of the performances.

So what? I was in show business! Having been stagestruck since Shirley Temple dunked animal crackers in her soup, I was ecstatic.

As I drove to the first rehearsal, I wondered what it would be like in the real, honest-to-goodness, behind-the-scenes theatre world. I had definite notions of what I would encounter.

The actors and actresses would be temperamental creatures who would wear weird pants and black turtleneck shirts and call everyone "darling." They would never be on time. Out-sized egos, of course—especially the leads in the show. The children ("The King and I" has many children) would be bratty. The director (would he wear a beret?) would yell and scream, in a heavy foreign accent.

I hoped I wouldn't cry when he screamed at me.

I had a lot to learn.

Take all my notions, turn them around, and you'll get the true picture.

A professional theatre company is exactly that: professional. The members of it are totally committed to their craft, intently studious and serious, honing and polishing each scene 'til it glows with the magic of a quality performance.

If they can't, they bust their guts trying.

No artistic temperaments. No weird outfits (well, creative sometimes, but practical, comfortable rehearsal togs to move around in). Definitely no late entrances—I've never seen any activity run on such clockwork—each run-through timed to the split second, each rehearsal organized in careful blocks of time and adhered to fanatically.

No prima donna egos or bratty kids—just attractive, courteous young men, women, and children, who happened to have such fantastic talent that I cried only because they performed so well, not because anyone yelled at me.

The director, Charles Abbott, shaped the production with a sure hand and witty style that combined understanding of the problems with competent solutions. (How to turn, how many steps to take, what feeling do you have, what inflection works best, how many inches is this from the end of the stage, what scenery goes here, how many measures from the end of the song do we start again?) I never saw such attention to detail. The Marines could learn.

No one else seemed surprised. They were as involved as Chuck Abbott was in putting together a perfect show.

Robert, his assistant Pat Waldorf, and the production crew kept giant notebooks and charts, scribbling with the precision of a Lockheed engineering team.

Michael, my musical boss, who played for simultaneous rehearsals in another room, ran an equally tight ship, starting and stopping his sessions on the dot of the appointed time with Chuck.

At the end of my two weeks, the show left the rehearsal hall and moved to the theatre for the final week of rehearsals with Michael at the piano. My show business career was over.

If you've seen the reviews of "The King And I," you know by now it's a smash hit. We're going next week, and I'll be as enthralled as though it were the first time with the heart-tugging songs, the charisma of Linda Stephens (Anna), the compelling charm of David Pendleton (the King), and the entire cast of this unforgettable musical.

I hope Michael will call me again. I'd like to play for their next musical, and the one after that, and the one after that. As the King would say, "Et cetera, et cetera, et cetera."

December 5, 1980

CHRISTMAS

My Christmas List—With Thanks to Andy Rooney

Christmas is a season of lists. Santa isn't the only one who's making a list and checking it twice. December is ticked off, list by list: shopping lists, gift lists, Christmas card lists . . . lists you don't have time to even write down, much less check off.

Andy Rooney had a good idea. In his latest book he made a "Christmas List Of Ideas"—thoughts and observations about the season: Such as "If your Christmas tree fits in the living room easily, it's not big enough." And, "Lunch doesn't fit very well into the Christmas Day schedule."

It's a fun way to vent some of your frustrations about Christmas and remember some of the special joys.

Here's mine . . .

• You know you're late with your Christmas shopping when you find a parking place right in front of the post office—and it doesn't have a picture of a wheelchair painted on it.

• It's nice to remember when Christmas cards and stamps weren't so expensive, and you could send them to everyone you wanted to.

• Mimeographed Christmas letters don't bother me. Maybe it's because it's the only time most of my friends write. However, a friend who brags about her trip to Europe and her child's Rhodes scholarship and her new vacation condominium should also say something humble in her letter—even if she has to work at it.

• Mimeographed Christmas letters and Christmas cards with names printed on them should have something on them written by hand. "Love" will do.

• Two types of people can spoil Christmas for the rest of us:

Type A: People who diet in November. They always tell you how much weight they lost in time for the holidays—just after you've piled your plate with goodies and you're praying your hook and eye will hold.

Type B: Early shoppers. You discover them when you say, "Finished your Christmas shopping, ha ha?" (The ha ha signifies this is a joke.) And they answer, "Yes, I bought the last thing I needed August 17th."

Dieters and early shoppers should keep their mouths shut and not ruin Christmas for everyone else.

• Pay the store to assemble it for you. Pay them anything. One Christmas Eve Dallas had to assemble one tricycle, two bicycles, a parking garage and a doll house. He finished at 5:00 a.m. The children woke up at 5:15. Now if anything comes in more than two pieces he blinks and twitches like the chief inspector in the Pink Panther movies.

• You'll forget to buy the batteries every time.

• You may remember to buy film, but you'll forget the flashbulbs. Or—if you do remember both, you'll forget to take the pictures.

• People always think they want to sing "Chestnuts Roasting By An Open Fire" at Christmas, but when they get started all they know is the first line. The same for "The Twelve Days of Christmas." After five golden rings, it's a disaster. Some of the nicest people get belligerent over which comes first—lords a-leaping or maids a-milking.

• When you put out all the Santa Claus stuff Christmas Eve night, one child will end up with less than the others. Don't worry about it. Next year it will happen to a different kid.

• We have ambrosia and fruitcake every Christmas because they're traditional in our families. I feel guilty using frozen coconut in the ambrosia and a bought fruitcake. I'd like Dallas to grate fresh coconut like my father used to. But I'm afraid he'd ask me to make a fruitcake like his mother used to.

• We'd probably enjoy chocolate cake more than fruitcake and ambrosia at Christmas.

• Some of the worst catastrophes at Christmas become some of the funniest memories. One year when our children were 3, 5, 8, 11, and 13 we were asked to be in the pageant at our church. We were supposed to be a typical family at home on Christmas Eve, gathered around the fire. Dallas would read Luke's Christmas story from the Bible and we would sing "Away In A Manger" together. Simple.

We were afraid the youngest Stephen would get stage fright. So we gave him a pep talk about not minding all the people watching us—just sing out good and loud.

The night of the pageant came. Dallas read the Bible story o.k. Then we tried to sing. We were terrified. None of us could sing. When we tried to, we choked up. Only one voice could be heard in the auditorium—a clear, high piping little solo—by Stephen!

• Families should be together at Christmas. An airline ticket home is worth it, even for just a day.

• Christmas should be shared with someone needy or lonely.

• You don't need perfect decorations, perfect food, perfect anything for a wonderful Christmas. What you need is: the smell of fresh greens, the light of candles, and people you love, including small children and grandparents if possible. And carols, the Luke story, and "The Night Before Christmas" read by the fireside.

• Christmas is a miracle. It celebrates a miracle, and what it does to us is a miracle.

• A final thought—this one comes from Andy Rooney: "The only people who don't like Christmas are people who don't like anything else either."

DECEMBER 9, 1983

Fernbank Planetarium Lets You Choose a Christmas Star

Sometimes the innocence and joy of the Advent season is almost crushed by commercial overkill. You're sick of tinny, warped recordings of "Have a Holly Jolly Christmas" and "Rudolph" blasting through the stores in torturous, never-ending cycles. And sick of pushing through crowds, fighting traffic, and hurrying, always hurrying.

Before the Scrooge Syndrome gets you and you hate Christmas, take a night out and attend the planetarium program at the Fernbank Science Center, located just off Ponce de Leon Avenue near the square in Decatur.

Our family discovered several years ago that the annual Christmas program at Fernbank is a perfect antidote for December delirium. We go every year we can.

It costs almost nothing ($1 for adults, 50¢ for children). The seats are soft and comfortable and if you catnap, no one minds. The background music is soothing, not the sort that assaults your senses. An hour spent gazing at the "stars" through the skillful special effects of the planetarium can lift your earthly tunnel vision to soul-stretching vistas of time and space.

It's wonderful preparation for Christmas.

The annual program varies from year to year, but it always culminates with a presentation of the Bethlehem Star. This year two characters in the dramatization—a modern astronomer and one from ancient Babylonia—discuss with one another what the Bethlehem star could have been. A comet? A meteor? A super nova (a dying or exploding star)? A conjunction (two planets so close together they appear to be one bright star)? Probably, they agree, one of the latter theories.

When the modern astronomer says wistfully that he wishes he could have seen the Star of Stars, the Babylonian tells him he can—not physically in our 20th century, but spiritually within the heart at Christmas.

Not long ago Dr. Art Ulene said something on NBC's *Today Show* which impressed me. He was giving basic rules of good health, and he said, "to avoid stress and live a long, healthy life, think more often about things like *clouds* and *stars*."

Robert Frost said the same thing in his poem "Choose Something Like a Star":

> The Star (the fairest one in sight)
> Asks a little of us here,
> Asks of us a certain height,
> So when at times the mob is swayed,
> To carry praise or blame too far,
> We may choose something like a star
> To stay our minds on and be stayed.

To look at a constellation and know the light you see left its source while earth was still in the Ice Age . . . to concentrate a little while on planets and moons, constellations and galaxies . . . . to think how black holes and gaseous matter are always expanding into endless space . . . suddenly makes such cares as an overloaded Rich's charge account or the number of shopping days left 'til Christmas seem very trivial indeed.

At this season "there's a song in the air, there's a star in the sky." And if you fail to hear the song or see the star, you miss the real Christmas.

DECEMBER 15, 1980

Christmas Comes in One Special, Magical Moment

Christmas, in the end, comes down to one special, magical moment—one personal experience during the season that transcends all the clutter, busyness, holiday trappings and commercialism and fills your heart with the amazing wonder of Christmas.

For each of us it's something different. From year to year it's not the same. If you tried to plan it, you never could.

It may be an idea you suddenly have for doing something spontaneous and loving for someone else.

It may be when you listen—really listen—to a carol, and suddenly the words make a vivid scene for you, and the music infuses you with its sweetness and beauty.

Whatever the moment, it's your own epiphany. I love that word, now that I finally know what it means! It's the coming of the Wise Men . . . but it also has another meaning: "a manifestation, especially of divinity."

Your epiphany is your special moment of Christmas when you feel your sharp edges softened, your anxiety gentled, your self-centeredness turned inside out, into caring for others. And it has to be a miracle!

I'd like to tell you a true Christmas story about such a moment as it happened to one of our friends.

DeVant Crissey, a close friend of ours, lives on Atlanta Road in Smyrna. He and his wife Jeannette own a framing and art restoration gallery that many of you know about because it's one of the best anywhere. We belong to the same small group in our church where we share some of the things that happen to us—and DeVant says I can tell you his bike story, too.

Two years ago on Christmas Eve, DeVant felt unusually despondent for some reason. He had enjoyed all the special music programs at church, dinners with friends, the usual shopping and preparing for Christmas. But that day he asked himself, "Is this all there is to Christmas?" He felt a strong urge to do something else. But what?

Part of the joy of Christmas, he remembered, had been the happy times watching the wonder of their children Laura and Mark (now adults) when they were small. He thought of bringing joy to a little child in need.

He remembered the old three-speed bicycle of Mark's in the basement. Mark had talked of selling it. DeVant decided to buy it from Mark, buy the needed parts, and fix it to surprise a child for Christmas.

When he asked Mark, Mark told him, "I'll give you the bike and help do the work this afternoon, if you just buy the parts." They knew the stores would be closing early, so they worked fast.

DeVant says, "By 5 o'clock that 12-year-old bike was clean, polished, had new knobby tires, was almost like new. The transformation was unbelievable!"

They began searching for a child.

DeVant called a friend, Terry Moncrief, who works with the Techwood Mission in Atlanta . . . but Terry didn't know of a child who needed a bike. More phone calls failed to locate a child.

DeVant says, "As Jeannette and I sat by the fire about 9:30 Christmas Eve night, we prayed again—somewhere, there had to be a boy who needed this bike!"

Suddenly he thought of Christian City Children's Home. (Christian City is a retirement center/convalescent home/children's home complex in College Park, where the elderly and children interact in a helpful way—a wonderful concept for such facilities.)

The rest of the story is fantastic.

Says DeVant, "After several calls, I reached houseparents Ray and Cindy Elder, who care for 20 children in Southwest cottage. They told me about Chris.

"Chris had come to live there several weeks earlier, along with his younger sister and older brother. To Chris, Christmas was doubly important: Christmas Eve was his birthday! A middle child sometimes gets lost between a baby sister and an older brother, and to have a birthday lost in Christmas is not easy for a 7-year-old boy in a new place.

"He was also the only boy in Southwest Cottage who didn't already have a bicycle and he sure did want one! The sponsor who bought the toys for the children had tried hard to find a bike for Chris—and couldn't find one within their budget.

"No words were adequate to describe the joy Mark and I felt as we delivered a bicycle at 11:30 on Christmas Eve night to a 7-year-old boy who was fast asleep. Driving home that night, my son and I silently shared one of the closest moments of our lives."

May all of us find such a moment this Christmas.

DECEMBER 20, 1984

Cabbage Patch Dolls—Only One Part of the Garden

I can remember when little girls told Santa they wanted a doll at Christmas.

Just a doll.

They didn't care what kind. Maybe they would say one that could open and shut its eyes. It could be a small baby doll with a sweet china face, a large cuddly baby doll, a pretty old-fashioned doll, a bride doll wearing sumptuous satin, a little girl doll with hair to comb and brush, a Raggedy Ann with bright button eyes.

Little girls left it up to Santa. And somehow the one he put under the Christmas tree, the one you found waiting in its new box, arms outstretched to you on Christmas morning, was always the perfect doll.

This week *Time* magazine says, "What are we to think about the great Cabbage Patch Kids madness of 1983? What are we to think of a homely, vinyl-faced cloth doll that has become such an object of desire that 5,000 people staged a near riot in a department store in West Virginia, a woman suffered a broken leg and a store manager armed himself with a baseball bat when another crowd turned violent after waiting eight hours to get into a Zayre's in Pennsylvania?"

I know what I think. I think it's a crying shame.

Forget the conduct of such adults. Forget a society where children for whatever reasons feel such a need to belong that they want "official adoption papers" for their dolls. I'll leave it to the sociologists, preachers and psychologists to comment on that.

What bothers me is that little girls have been manipulated into wanting the very same consumer product: dolls exactly alike for Christmas.

What's special about a doll like all the other dolls? I know—theoretically every Cabbage Patch differs slightly from all the others, but not really that much.

What's fun about having a doll tea party when all the guests are the same? Or asking friends over to play if their dolls are just like yours? The mystique of loving a doll has to do with the doll's uniqueness—just as the little girl herself should feel unique and special to her parents, so should her doll to her.

I'll admit that the Cabbage Patch Kids are adorable.

Their homely little puckered faces and huggable bodies are a credit to their designer, a young Georgia man named Xavier Roberts.

But the stores are full of adorable dolls, hundreds of them, of all descriptions.

Children should be encouraged to choose freely—or to let Santa surprise them. They should not be stampeded by manufacturers, marketers, and unwitting parents into wanting the latest craze just because it's a fad.

Status symbols and designer labels imposed on the young violate childhood. Do we have to take the hard sell that far?

Another problem—and this is a joke on adults. Doesn't everyone know that children don't need official adoption papers to adopt a doll?

The bond between a little girl and her special doll, or a little boy and his Teddy bear, is instantaneous and everlasting. Who needs adoption papers? When a child loves a doll it's "adopted" and cherished forever, from the simplest carved wooden doll to the finest Madame Alexander.

I'm thinking of some dolls in our family that didn't need adoption papers to become a permanent part of the little owner's family . . . The two cloth dolls made for Dixie and Patty by a darling little lady in Orlando whom everyone called Grandma Wharton. She named each doll that she made "Jincey." (I never heard that name elsewhere 'til Celestine Sibley's book, *Jincey*.) We still have our Jincey dolls, pale, tattered and beloved . . . Dixie's first doll. She named it "Girl Doll," but pronounced it "Dirl Goll," dragged it by the hair and adored it . . . Tiny Tears, in her long baby dress hand-embroidered by a great-grandmother . . . Shirley Temple, dimples and all . . . Mary Poppins, still holding a dusty lavender umbrella on Katie's shelf . . . Raggedy Ann, who lost one arm but went with Patty to college, and joined her and David when they married!

Dolls are as magical as childhood itself.

We should no more intrude into that world than frighten away a unicorn or deny the existence of Tinker Bell. The song "Toyland" has a line in it that makes me choke up every time:

> "Once you pass its portals you may never return again."

It's such a fragile kingdom. And it lasts such a very short time. Let's not spoil it any more than we have to.

DECEMBER 15, 1983

Don't Let a Computer Do Your Christmas Shopping

I heard a news story the other day that sounded terrific at first—the end to all my Christmas shopping woes!

The article said that computers will soon be able to answer that perennial question: "What to give him (her) for Christmas?"

The idea is that you can walk up to a computer in the store, punch in the right data for each person on your list, and presto! The computer hands you your Santa ideas. If you tell it the person's age, weight, size, hobbies, interests, etc. it can tell you what to give.

Well, maybe.

I've been thinking about it some more.

It seems to me when I look back at the most perfect gifts, the best surprises, the ones that meant the most to us—they're things a computer would never, never come up with.

The best Christmas gifts are:

1) Gifts someone bought because "it looked just like you."

2) Gifts someone chose instinctively, intuitively . . . not rationally.

3) Gifts someone made for you by hand—cooked, sewed, painted, or in some way personalized.

Such gifts are created with love or chosen with love. They are often something you never even thought of wanting—but once you got it you couldn't do without it. They're things you use with pleasure . . . and get a glow . . . just from remembering.

They'd never factor into a computer program at all.

I've been thinking about some of the very best Christmas presents we've ever had. A computer would never come up with these, some of our All Time Favorite Christmas Presents:

• Kitchen magnets—made from shells. Peggy, our son's lovely girl friend, collected the shells at the beach and glued them to magnetic bases. We use them on the refrigerator and they dress up the most prosaic grocery list.

• A sand dollar Nell Abbott brought me, from a special two weeks spent at a writers-artists colony. (Her way of sharing this rare treat with me.) Her name, the place and date are written in gold ink on the back. Shellacked and worn on a chain, it's one of my favorite necklaces.

• A large, desk model dispenser for Scotch tape. Ted and Vel Dansby thought of this handy gift. It makes using Scotch tape infinitely more convenient, and this way you don't lose it. They usually come in boring gray or tan, but Ted painted ours a soft antique green.

• A kitchen calendar—with a blown-up photo of our little grandson, Gary! A surprise given us by cousin Charles Watson. Sure to please any new parents or grandparents.

• More photograph ideas: a plastic cube already filled with snapshots . . . wooden curtain rings with paper glued inside, as frames for snapshots; my cousin Nancy Neighbors gave us five one Christmas, painted gold with red bows, for our children's pictures as tree ornaments. (School pictures just fit.) Now we have them hanging in the upstairs hall. . . . Another great photo surprise: my friend Diana gave candid shots of each couple in our supper club group, on fabric covered poster board.

• Magazine subscriptions. You can individualize this and it's a gift to enjoy year 'round. Some we like: *Smithsonian*, *American History*, *Georgia Journal*. For older people you can give large print monthly subscriptions of *Reader's Digest* or *Sunshine* magazines, or a *Guideposts* daily devotional book.

• Goodies from the kitchen. You never go wrong here—and store stuff can't compare! We give jelly, if it's been a good year for muscadines or blackberries. Nell Hall's jar of vegetable soup, left at the back door one busy week before Christmas, was perfect. Some friends are known for the same delectable goody they make each Christmas. It wouldn't be the same without Ann's fruitcake cookies or Kathleen's cheese roll.

• Arts and crafts. I'm no good at this but some folks are. Nell Hall (who does many things well) one year left a brown paper sack at the back door with a large rolled up piece of paper inside. When we unrolled it, we found a family portrait in caricature. . . .all seven of us. I'm playing the piano, Dallas is practicing his golf swing, Buddy is off to Georgia with his suitcase, each member of the family—down to the cat and the dog—are there! A hilarious, sentimental gift to treasure.

• Family keepsakes. My mother now shares something special each Christmas with her children and grandchildren, writing the story of each one—the alphabet mug Great Aunt Ada got on the country school Christmas tree when she was in 1st grade, the old dough tray from Grandmother's home, a lace cloth bought in Venice from a countess after World War II . . . priceless treasures because of family memories.

• Bookmarks. These can cost only 50¢—but the fun is choosing one that just fits the person. Evelyn Ransom gave Dallas one because he hates to talk to strange seatmates on airplane trips. It says, "Shhh! Don't bother me—I'm reading." Hand-made of felt, crocheted or embroidered ones are deluxe and personal.

• The scrapbook a thoughtful friend, Merrilyn Eastham, gave me: she had cut out, week by week, the columns I wrote my first year as a columnist, and put them in a scrapbook for me.

• Presents our children made—the lopsided vase of clay from our creek, baked in our oven, when Stephen was 6; the coffee table Buddy made for his Dad last year, with a glass inset to display his prize arrowheads; the poems and sketches by Dixie and Patty; the original cross-stitch designs by Katie.

Would a computer ever come up with these? I guess there's no substitute for old-fashioned love. Especially at Christmas.

DECEMBER 1, 1983

Treasured Memories of Christmas Past

Our couples' Sunday School class is having our Christmas party tonight.

"Be thinking of a favorite Christmas memory. We'll share them at our party," the social chairman said.

So while I slap Scotch tape on packages and hope I can dash to the post office before closing time, I block out the chaos of my household this week before Christmas and do some remembering.

The drafty old manse in Gainesville is icy cold except for the living room, where the fire is kept going in the fireplace. My little brother and I sit close by the hearth on Christmas Eve and listen as Daddy reads "'Twas the Night Before Christmas" and then the lovely story from Luke—"And there were in the same country shepherds . . ."

We hang up our stockings (two of my father's long silky black socks that will bulge tomorrow morning with oranges, Hershey bars, and a dime in the toe), put a piece of fruitcake and a glass of milk on the mantel for Santa, and then run through the cold house to our bedroom at the back.

Tonight we don't whisper long. We're scared to death that we'll hear Santa's sleigh bells before we get to sleep—he mustn't find us awake!

My last waking thought: "I wonder if the carolers will come again this Christmas."

They do! They wake us from deep sleep in the hushed darkness before dawn begins to break. We hear muffled sounds as they come under our windows and then begin to sing. We don't know them—this small group of black men and women who come caroling each Christmas morning—but their singing is a magical part of Christmas.

My brother and I kneel on his bed to peek out the window, and our parents come in the room to listen with us. It's so dark we can't see the Bensons' house next door.

The voices are rich and full, blending in perfect harmony and that innate rhythm black musicians communicate so well. As I hear their "special" carol (one we never heard before they started coming on Christmas morning), somehow I feel the baby Jesus has *just now* been born!

Go, tell it on the mountain,
Over the hills and everywhere,
Go, tell it on the mountain
That Jesus Christ is born!

Fort Worth, Texas—our first Christmas as newlyweds. Living far from home in a tiny matchbox garage apartment.

Dallas and I decide on Christmas morning, after we get up, that we will cook a traditional dinner, the kind our mothers always had. Turkey, cranberries, dressing, the works. We'll even make homemade candy.

We don't know anything! We don't know that you don't *start* Christmas dinner that day—you start it days ahead. Or that you have to make cornbread before you can make dressing. Or that cranberry sauce needs time to set.

We find a candy recipe in Mrs. Dull's cookbook called Seafoam Delight. We make it, set it in the kitchen window to cool. It runs over the plate and down the wall—an oozing, sticky river of caramel.

By nighttime the kitchen is a disaster, we're exhausted and starving, and nothing is fit to eat.

Our landlady, Mrs. Tandy, calls and invites us to join them for dinner in the "big house." She becomes our Christmas angel.

Christmas with our children.

A new stocking every other year, until there are five hanging between ours.

Trips to see Santa at downtown Rich's, ride the Pink Pig, eat at the Varsity or—if we're splurging—in a restaurant.

The Night Before Christmas and the Luke story, read by the fire.

Staying up late Christmas Eve finding the Santa things we've hidden in out-of-the way nooks and now can't remember . . . putting them together, setting them up, laying them out.

The excited early dawn awakening, five tow-heads sitting on the top stairstep 'til Dallas starts a fire and calls out they can come on down—then the mad scramble, shrieks and squeals.

Their childish drawings, homemade gifts and notes to us—priceless beyond measure.

This year our grandson Gary is two years old. His blue eyes sparkle at the sight of the Christmas tree (he calls it the Christmas "treat"). Once more we feel the hustle and clamor and rush of the season brought gently back into clear focus—by the simple wonder and joy of a little child.

"The more things change, the more they remain the same." And never more so than at Christmas, when we celebrate the Alpha and Omega. "In the beginning was the Word . . . and the Word became flesh and dwelt among us."

DECEMBER 19, 1980 John 1:1

Raymond—a Christmas Vignette

His name was Raymond.

He was a small, shabby, ordinary little man—the kind you see without really noticing. Maybe at a lunch counter, carefully fishing out coins for a cup of coffee. Or trudging along the side of the highway, not expecting a lift. The Raymonds don't expect anything.

He wasn't young any more but he wasn't old either—except for the look in his eyes.

He came from Appalachia. He grew up working the coal mines like all the men in his family. Like them, he developed health problems. He left home and became a drifter. He never married; never put down roots anywhere; just bummed around the country doing odd jobs. His lung troubles and his frail size kept him from holding any job very long.

He was near Marietta last Christmas when he hit bottom. The old car he had finally gave out and he abandoned it. He just curled up by the side of the road and went to sleep.

Some truckers found him (at first they thought he was dead) and brought him to Traveler's Aid. The Traveler's Aid office called M.U.S.T. (Methodists United in Service and Training), which gives emergency aid such as temporary housing, food, clothes, and job assistance.

That's how Patty and David came to know Raymond.

David, our daughter Patty's husband, works on the staff of MUST.

They were deeply touched by the plight of this lonely, sick, down and out little man and soon became involved in helping him.

Patty bummed an old suit from her dad. It swallowed Raymond but they made it do. David helped him re-apply for his Social Security which he had lost during his wanderings. They invited him often for meals in their house and visited him at the MUST emergency house, which was right next door.

Raymond began losing his shyness with them and opening up.

"He's so alone, Mother," Patty told me. "He has no one in the whole world. He has no purpose for living." She had never known anyone like Raymond before, nor had we.

As his health began improving, Raymond talked of going to California. Patty and David encouraged him instead to consider going home to Kentucky. By now his immediate family members were all dead, but there would be nieces, nephews, family friends to care about him.

Raymond said he'd think about it.

One day something exciting happened: Raymond's Social Security check came in the mail! He couldn't wait for Patty and David to get home from work that afternoon. He walked into town, several miles, to try to cash his check. In the bank on the square the clerk asked for an identification. He had none. She refused to cash it for him. Raymond was baffled and disappointed.

Later that day David took him back. They stopped in first at the Social Security office . . . which happens to be in the same bank building. David wanted to get the proper forms for Raymond to use.

Suddenly David realized Raymond wasn't with him any more . . . and that outside, in the hall, a terrible commotion was going on.

He dashed out to find an excited clump of people gathered around a small man, who was being led away by the police.

Raymond had tried to slip back into the bank and cash his check again. Again he had been refused. This time he lost his temper and declared, in a very loud voice, that he wished "he could blow up this place and everybody in it."

It was an empty threat, of course. Just a cry of pain and frustration from a harmless little man unable to cope in a world he couldn't understand.

Quite naturally, however, it had made the bank officials nervous. For all they knew, Raymond had a six-shooter in his pocket.

David managed to get Raymond's release by promising the police he would make sure Raymond left town. They cashed his check and bought him a bus ticket, and Patty and David told him goodby. At the last minute Patty put a gift in Raymond's hands—her Bible, the one her father had given to her.

Two weeks later they had a post card from Raymond. He had made it out to California.

That's why when the phone call came a short time later, just before Christmas, it was such a shock.

It was the state patrol in North Carolina. They had found the body of a man, evidently killed by a hit-and-run driver. He was a small man with no identifying papers on him—he had evidently been robbed. The only possession with him was a Bible with Patty's name and address written inside.

Raymond must have decided to go home after all. He was almost to Kentucky. Almost home in time for Christmas.

The officials kept his body in North Carolina for medical research. Two days before Christmas in Marietta a small group of us gathered for his memorial service: Rex Kaney, pastor of Elizabeth United Methodist Church and director of MUST, Patty and David, their friends, Lynn and Frank Wiginton, and me.

David lit candles. I played the piano. We sang several hymns that Raymond may have sung in the hills of Kentucky—like "Amazing Grace," "How Firm a Foundation."

Then Rex spoke of Raymond and the Christmas story: the babe who had no place to be born. . . The Son of Man who "hath not where to lay His head." . . . Who loved all men—but related especially to the poor, downtrodden, forgotten people like Raymond. Who went ahead, to prepare a room for them in heaven.

A funeral is an unusual way to celebrate Christmas . . . but we did.

No Christmas pageant, no great organ or choir performance, no formal pomp or ceremony will ever convey to me as strongly the simple message of Christmas that I felt in my heart at Raymond's memorial service.

Now, a year later, times are even harder. At Dallas's Rotary Club meeting yesterday I heard Colonel Andrew Miller of the Salvation Army tell that Americans are giving more than ever this Christmas, the Army kettles are doing well . . . but they can never meet all the needs. And I noticed most Rotarians looked misty-eyed. So was I.

The Salvation Army knows best about men like Raymond and I'm thankful for what they do. Once you know a Raymond, you don't stop hurting for him.

Our friend, Dr. Charlie Underwood, has shared with me a quote from Henry Van Dyke about this hurting—and our response (that we call the Christmas Spirit):

"There is a higher calling than merely to stand tall in this world—it is to stoop down and lift mankind a little higher."

DECEMBER 23, 1982

What Ever Happened to Baby Jesus?

Something's missing at our house this Christmas. Something pretty important.

If we don't find it, I'm not sure we'll *have* Christmas.

We made the discovery one cold rainy day last week. We woke up to gusty rain beating against the windows. At breakfast we heard our wind chimes by the back door clinking like musical icicles, or a toy xylophone played by Christmas elves.

Obviously it was a wretched day to get out Christmas shopping, as I'd planned to do. I'd stay home instead and get some things done.

I was so far behind. Our Christmas cards were still untouched, pristine pure in their plastic boxes. The family kept hopefully opening cookie tins—but I hadn't yet baked a single sugar cookie.

But I knew what I wanted to do today—decorate the house.

Somehow when you put up the Christmas decorations, it helps everything else along. The sharp, wonderful smell of evergreens gets you in the spirit. The sight of a Christmas wreath on the door reassures you. You feel magically uplifted—no matter how much you still have to do—by the wonder and joy of this special season.

So . . . up to the cold attic. Push aside the footlocker and the pile of *National Geographics*. Drag out the Christmas boxes and get to work.

I unwrapped the Santa mugs and put them on the tea wagon, the snowman on the kitchen window sill, the angels on the piano, the calico wreath my sister-in-law made on the breakfast room wall. It was hard not to dip into some of the favorite Christmas books as I set them around on tables, but that would be a reward later: Dickens' *A Christmas Carol*, Van Dyke's *The Story of the Other Wise Man*, Celestine Sibley's *Christmas In Georgia*, Catherine Marshall's *Let's Keep Christmas*, Tasha Tudor's beautiful Christmas book for children . . . all the old favorites that stir the heart.

I always save the best 'til last: our Christmas nativity set.

Most of our decorations are inexpensive, though sentimental . . . but our nativity set was a special gift my parents brought us from Germany—beautiful Hümmel figurines.

We love their perfect features and soft colors. Every year we put them on the mantel in our living room, in the place of honor, placing them on fresh cedar branches and stringing tiny blue lights over the fireplace. All through Christmas they shine for us with special meaning and beauty.

One by one I unwrapped the figurines and set them out. I knew the children would want to rearrange them some when they came home. They like to handle them, too: the three kings, the shepherds (one a little boy blowing his flute), the cow, sheep, small lamb, and donkey, Joseph holding out a protective hand, Mary with her sweet smile, and the little baby on the hay.

The baby . . . Where was the baby?

All the figurines were there except for that one!

Somehow the little Christ Child was not in the box with all the others. I don't know if it's lost among crumpled papers in the attic or if we inadvertently threw it out last year.

As Stephen said, when he came home from school and noticed the empty place in the middle of the mantel . . ."Mom, the baby IS sort of important, you know."

That empty place continues to haunt us as we hurry through the busy days of December.

The symbolism is appallingly obvious . . .

Are we leaving out the little Christ Child? Is the baby Jesus missing from Christmas?

You hear a lot of sermons on this subject—but it gets uncomfortably real when you see an empty place, literally, in your Christmas decorations!

If we don't find our little baby Jesus soon, we'll have to buy another. Stephen is right—He *is* important!

He's what Christmas is all about.

Robert Raines put it movingly in his book *Living The Questions* (Word Books):

"Lord of all people, you made your home with peasant parents, nameless shepherds, gifted searchers . . . Lord of little me, you made your home in the heart of my world. Make your home now in the world of my heart. Welcome, Little Lord, Lord of little me, once more."

DECEMBER 16, 1980

One More Week 'til Christmas

One more week until Christmas.

One more week of overpopulated, understaffed shopping centers, overfilled datebooks, inadequate bank accounts, snarled traffic and snarling tempers.

Only one more week, and so much yet to do. Eric Sevareid writes in the current *McCall's* that it is not so much the commercialism as it is the complicated "busyness" that has changed the meaning of Christmas, and you agree.

You want to go to the Living Christmas Tree program at First Methodist, hear your own church cantata, take in the historical Christmas program at Kennesaw Mountain National Park Museum, see the Cobb Ballet perform at the Civic Center . . . and of course, you'll be there, nodding your head as doting parents do, at your child's school band or choral program.

You still haven't sent your cards—the ones to out-of-town friends you care about but didn't write last year. You never have ironed the old bow on your front door wreath and it seems as bedraggled as you do. The only Christmas cookies you've baked have already been gobbled up by your family, when you meant them for friends. An unchecked shopping list seems to go on forever.

It almost gets to be too much. There you sit at a dead standstill in rainy traffic with an expressway sign mocking you: "Minimum speed limit 45 mph." Or you run out of Scotch tape with more out-of-town packages to wrap. Or you realize you can't get into the new jumpsuit you meant to wear to the office party.

But sooner or later it happens . . . whatever *it* is, that suddenly causes that perceptible, surging lift to your heart that you call the Christmas Spirit. In spite of all the problems and negatives about the season, some simple act or touch or sound will cause your own personal Christmas wonderment to begin.

It may be your son's carefully rounded writing on the kitchen blackboard: "Everyone, the Rudolph special is tonight at 8." It may be the sweet purity of children's voices singing "Away In A Manger," or the kind smile of a Salvation Army lassie at her kettle.

Maybe it starts when your excited college child calls to say, "I'm through exams and I have a ride home!" Or a Christmas letter arrives from a favorite cousin, evoking memories of childhood Christmases at Grandmother's house.

Whatever inspires the feeling, suddenly it's there for you, as solid as the cold earth you crunch walking to the mailbox, as sharp as the pine needles, as joyous as the bells.

You're transformed as surely as old Scrooge from his "Bah, humbug!" to his "Hello, my fine fellow. Whoop, how are you, Merry Christmas!"

Your fatigue forgotten, you hurry with the lists and chores, giving special priority to cutting out more sugar cookies together, singing favorite carols and, best of all, lighting the candles on Christmas Eve and gathering your family close for the Luke Christmas story.

What really causes "it," of course, is love—the perfect gift from the Christ Child whose Mass this is.

You want to encircle your family with enough love, warmth and joy to last another 365 days in the world outside. You want to give love in abundance, not only to family and friends, but to the lonely, the sick, the grieving ones.

Someone said it well:

Christmas slips back into your life
And touches you
With salve for burned fingers
That had become afraid to reach out again.

Thank God for the Christmas miracle.

DECEMBER 17, 1976

"Did I Miss Christmas this Year?"

This is a true story about a cute little boy many of you know. His name is Whit, he's the son of Hanson ("Happy") and Donna Smith, and this Christmas he's four years old.

One day early in December Whit went to play at the home of his little friend, Mitch Hunter. The friend's mother, Nancy Hunter, had been on the ball and right after Thanksgiving had put up their tree and gotten their house all decorated for Christmas. It was so early Whit's house wasn't decorated yet.

Whit looked around. His eyes got big and solemn and his face looked sad. He turned to his hostess and blurted, "Mrs. Hunter, did I miss Christmas this year?" I know how little Whit felt. Some years I come pretty close to missing Christmas myself. I almost did this year.

I almost missed Christmas by not being ready in time. I can barely squeeze into my place at the typewriter—because my "office" is also the family Christmas room. Bags, boxes, empty cardboard rolls, and ribbons are strewn helter skelter in a glorious mess.

I seem to need help with my attitudes. I could use a good counselor. Every year I do this. I'm at Cumberland Mall the week before Thanksgiving, they're playing carols in the stores, Santa is ho-ho-hoing, and I get angry. It's too early for that. Why do they start so soon? It ruins Christmas.

Then—presto! Suddenly Christmas is almost here and I need two more weeks.

I almost missed Christmas in the traffic.

Cobb County traffic is unreal. The "confluence" of the Galleria and Cumberland Mall is a "non-confluence." Nobody is going anywhere. Powder Springs Road is worse. But my vote for the single worst traffic problem is the downtown post office in Marietta. You want to tear up the cheery Christmas cards you've gone there to mail, and scatter them in tiny pieces in the traffic backed up Lawrence Street.

I almost missed Christmas fooling with our new electric window candles.

We bought them this year to show the world our homey warmth and cheer.

Have you ever used those little candles? From the street they're lovely. From the backside—oh, what a mess.

Their cords are about two inches long. This means you go back to the store and buy dozens of extension cords. Next you find places to plug them in.

Every afternoon as twilight gently falls I go into my act. First I crawl behind the Christmas tree in the living room, trying not to tip it over—and plug in those candles.

Then I reach behind the desk in our bedroom which is too heavy to move—so I have to angle my hand a certain way to get in the crack—and plug in those candles.

Next I march upstairs to plug those in. I unplug the stereo in Katie's room, pull out the cord under the rug in the hall, move dirty laundry and get on my stomach to shimmy under the bunk bed in Stephen's room, eating cobwebs as I go.

When the candles are finally all plugged in, I barely have time to rest before it's time to do the whole thing in reverse, unplugging them—the only way to turn them off at bedtime.

Bah, humbug to electric window candles!

I could miss Christmas in so many ways.

But oh, I hope I don't. "The Light shineth in darkness and the darkness overcometh it not." The good cheer of Christmas seems strong enough to overcome the hassles and confusion of the season.

Katie came in on the plane from New York, Stephen from Tech, Buddy from Texas. My parents will get here Friday from Florida. We'll all be together.

The sugar cookies and fudge are made. The family our Sunday School class is helping have found jobs and should soon get their children back from the Juvenile Home. Our Christmas tree smells fragrant and wonderful.

The music at church Sunday as Jerome Olds sang "In My Heart I Do Believe" from Saint-Saëns' *Oratorio* lifted my heart high. The presence of loved ones at home and friends coming and going helps to keep it that way.

And our little Gary, our red-headed grandson, is five years old this Christmas—the perfect age to enjoy Santa and to remind us that the reason for this celebration is remarkably childlike and simple: a baby was born on Christmas Day, who died to save us all.

I'm not missing Christmas this year. I wish for you the same!

DECEMBER 22, 1983

Grandmother's House

Just after Christmas I took a sentimental journey.

With my parents I drove over to my grandmother's old house in South Carolina.

It was a trip surrounded by memories.

For my father it was a return to his childhood home. I've heard his stories and I know what a happy childhood it was. Three little boys and two little girls, stair-step close in age, stirring up fun and mischief while their tiny, redheaded mother (less than 5 feet tall, less than 100 pounds but a dynamo of energy) taught piano lessons in the front parlor. Climbing on Papa's lap when he came home, "riding a train" as he rocked them and called out the names of the towns he had been to in his traveling job.

For me, too, it was a place where roots go deep. As a P.K. (preacher's kid) we moved often when I was growing up—from Georgia to Tennessee to Florida. It was my two grandmothers' homes (this one in Seneca and the other, a farmhouse in the beautiful rolling country near Anderson) that gave me stability. I always had a comforting sense of belonging. They were places I came back to each Christmas and each summer through the years.

And how I did love to go! My heart would start pounding as we reached Westminster a few miles away, then saw the water tower of Seneca and turned into Grandmother Dendy's street.

The Christmas visits were the most exciting because all the aunts, uncles and cousins would converge at once. We filled up the old house and the overflow spilled into Aunt Jodie's house in the next block. The cousins slept on the floor on pallets.

We cousins—eight of us, just 2 or 3 years apart—had a compatibility that bound us like Shakespeare's "hoops of steel." Now that we're grown and scattered, we still feel the closeness, burst into inexplicable laughter, and share the same rapport when we see one another.

At mealtime we ate at card tables in the bay window of the dining room. The adults wanted us as far away from them as we could be! We were hopelessly silly. We started snickering before the blessing ended and by the end of the meal would be in convulsions.

It was our job to wash the dishes, of course, but we sang 'til we were hoarse and I never minded.

We played in the woods behind grandmother's house ("the jungle,") where we had cleared the vines, swept the leaves in the summer and made a "club house." We kept a Monopoly game going, like a floating crap game, moving it from dining room to living room to parlor. The aunts and uncles played Rook. (Good Presbyterians didn't play bridge!)

At some point in each visit we had to play the piano. All the cousins took lessons, of course, and we had to play our latest recital pieces with sweaty, nervous hands.

After that ordeal came the fun times of family singing and the uncles' barbershop quartets. They never needed music—they just grabbed their own pitch perfectly. The shortest uncle, Clay, sang the bass; the tallest, Barber, the tenor. The one I loved most was "Sweet and Low . . . Wind of the Western Sea."

The cousins each Christmas would put on a show, rigging up a sheet in the archway between the living room and parlor and presenting "original" skits that we thought were terribly clever (how did the grownups endure them?).

At night we shot the fireworks. The uncles lit the sky rockets and helped us twirl our Roman candles. Then we lit the sparklers and drew magic pictures, like designs of golden sequins, in the darkness.

In the high-ceilinged bedrooms upstairs we scared one another with ghost stories 'til we fell asleep.

Last week I sat in the kitchen of the house with my parents and Aunt Jodie. It seemed very still and quiet. We ate her delicious pound cake, drank coffee and talked . . . but not of the past. None of us dared.

Aunt Jodie, whose family moved there after grandmother died, has put the place on the market and plans to move. It would be our last time ever to go there.

The shapes and sounds from the past were all around me. I never knew the term, "extended family," when I grew up, but I'm thankful for mine—each aunt and uncle and the little grandmother who formed a family network of love and good times.

I'll miss the old house, but in my memory it will never change.

JANUARY 11, 1981

AND BEYOND

Miss Jennie: A Loaf of Bread and an Orchid

They were waiting at my front door when I came home from errands one day last summer: a fresh baked loaf of homemade bread, golden and fragrant, and an orchid, delicate mauve, smooth, perfect.

I didn't have to read the note to know who had brought them—Miss Jennie.

It was a hard time in my life just then, and Miss Jennie knew. Though she herself had been seriously ill and now had to pace herself (at least she was *supposed* to pace herself,) Jennie Tate Anderson had done this gracious, special thing for me.

It figured.

She is "Miss Jennie," "Jennie T.," or just "Jennie" to everyone. Never Mrs. Anderson—though she has had a long and happy marriage to one of the sweetest men on earth, Mr. Jimmy T. Anderson. Jennie is so uniquely herself that we have to call her by her first name—and so warm and natural and friendly it would seem strange not to, anyhow.

And we call her, believe me. We have called her for everything of importance that ever happened in Cobb County.

If one woman were chosen above all others for leadership and service to our community, I'm sure it would be Miss Jennie. She is Cobb County's unofficial First Lady.

And what a lady!

The best way to summarize her might be by the two gifts she left at my front door: a loaf of bread and an orchid.

She's a woman who loves home and family, a woman with immense practicality and ability to get things done, sturdy strength and solid basic values—like a loaf of homemade bread.

But that's only part of Miss Jennie.

She's a woman who loves beauty in any form from landscape gardening (which she studied in Italy and England) to all the fine arts—a woman freely committed to self-actualization, daring to learn, be and do when today's liberated young women were babies. She differs from other women as a rare, perfect orchid differs from a common wildflower.

Connie Kirk wrote a great profile of her in *Cadence,* the publication of the Cobb-Marietta Junior League, (Miss Jennie was the League's first Professional Member). Connie said, "(She) sees herself as an 'independent cuss, a maverick and sometimes a trouble maker' but I see her as a confident change maker who should be a role model for others."

Jennie has been a "First" Lady in many ways. She was one of the first co-eds at Emory University, transferring there after two years at Converse College when other women students at Emory were relatives of faculty members. After working towards a master's degree at the University of Georgia in social work, she became the first director of public welfare for Cobb County in 1933. Three years later, she became the first personnel director at Holeproof Hosiery, then employing 1,000 workers.

After Jennie married, she worked for six weeks and decided to quit because she "couldn't get a good breakfast on the table, clean her house and get to the office by 8 a.m."

Her humor shone in a remark she once made to a friend of mine, who apologized for phoning her so early in the morning. "Miss Jennie, did I get you up?" Jennie (a mother of four youngsters, the oldest then 17 years of age) answered, "Honey, I've been up for 17 years."

But she never was merely a homemaker.

She was appointed by Gov. Jimmy Carter to the Georgia Heritage Trust, by Gov. George Busbee as chairman of the trust, by Gov. Joe Frank Harris as the 1983 winner of the Georgia Volunteer Services Leadership Award.

She was the first recipient of the Lilian Sullivan Award by the Cobb Arts Council. She helped restore the Marietta Square as a member of the first Downtown Marietta Development Authority. She helped establish the Botanical Gardens at the University of Georgia, the Garden Clubs of Georgia Headquarters in Athens, the Marietta Garden Center and Cobb Landmarks Historical Society.

Somehow, she found time for things like Girl Scouts, YWCA, the Cobb Symphony, Cobb Ballet and the Fine Arts Club. She served on the committee that established the Cobb Parks and Recreation Department. The list of her other achievements would take pages.

So . . . what can you say about such a woman?

That from her enormous blue-gray eyes, brilliant smile and charismatic personality shines a free spirit and a gracious lady.

That she is a role model for women.

And that we love her.

Last year she became another "first": one of the first cancer patients to try a chemical implant within the body. Now she is back in the hospital at Emory. We hope she is comfortable and will soon improve.

I know one thing about Miss Jennie. She will deal with illness as well as she has all of life.

A description that Amelia Earhart once gave of Anne Morrow Lindbergh seems to fit Jennie Tate Anderson perfectly:

"Under her quiet gentleness lies a fine courage to meet both spiritual and physical hardships with understanding."

JANUARY 17, 1985

Footnote: Miss Jennie died two days after this column appeared. The Cobb County Civic Center Theater has been named The Jennie T. Anderson Theater in her honor.

Easter—the Fulfillment of the Christmas Promise

Easter couldn't come at a better time for me this year.

My mother died last week.

As Daddy said, "She celebrated her own Easter a little early."

Death comes in two ways: It comes suddenly, which is wonderful for the person doing the dying but hard for everyone else, unprepared for the shock of loss. Or it comes slowly, with the opposite effects.

For mother it was as quick and easy as falling asleep.

She and my father had their annual check-ups a week earlier and were pronounced in perfect health. They planned a trip to California at Easter when their youngest grandchild, Mary Jo, would join the church. They booked passage on a cruise in the fall.

Last week my beautiful, vibrant, 80-year-old mother led her usual full, active life, which included a daily two-mile walk around Lake Lucerne near their retirement apartment in Orlando.

On Tuesday she gave the devotional for the women's club. On Thursday she and Daddy went to Disney World. Bishop Ed Pendergrass was being honored at a retirement dinner, and my father would say a few words about his old friend—who had pastored Orlando's First Methodist Church in the 1950's, when Daddy led the First Presbyterian flock across the street.

They were waiting to enter the hotel banquet room when Mother had a sudden massive stroke. Five minutes of intense pain and then life was really over—though machines kept her lungs breathing and heart pumping until my brother and I could travel the miles to her bedside.

It took no brain scan results, no technical reports, no careful words from the doctor—although we were given these—to know instantly that the real woman was no longer inside that still body.

What makes our personhood? What exactly is our soul? At what point in the dying process does it leave the human body and begin life in the spiritual realm?

We don't know. With all our scientific knowledge, we still have these mysteries.

I only know when we kissed our mother goodbye, we grieved for ourselves, for the pain of separation—not for her. She had gone to live in glory forever.

Thank God for Easter.

For the symbolism of Easter, the faith my mother lived by, manifest in her memorial service from those wonderful words of the 23rd Psalm about walking through the valley of the shadow of death and fearing no evil, to the triumphant closing organ tones of Handel's "Hallelujah Chorus."

For the tightly held hands up and down our family pew, her children and her grandchildren, with her sweetheart-husband of 57 years in the

center, singing through our tears, "For all the saints who from their labors rest, Allelujah."

For the love of friends which has surrounded us.

For the glorious rebirth of nature. The dazzling purity of dogwood The tender green of new leaves. The intense, vivid blueness of a bird that has come each day this week to our feeder. I have to think he's the "bluebird of happiness." We never had this bird before! (Actually I think he's an indigo bunting.)

For the violets we found scattered on the hillside as we left Mother's grave in South Carolina. Violets—her very favorite flower! (Always, if it had violets on it—from note paper to a perfume bottle to the coffee mug I bought at the K Mart and planned to give her on my next visit—we got it for her.)

Dallas, Mary Jo and I picked handfuls of the tiny purple and lavender-streaked blossoms and climbed the hill again to sprinkle them on the dirt covering her ashes. (Yes, ashes. Her desire for cremation, at first so hard for us to deal with, finally became the most positive message of faith she could leave us.)

For most of my life Christmas has been my favorite holiday. Now I'm not so sure. The longer I live, the more I know of human hurts and death, the more Easter means.

Christmas promises us hope and joy . . . but Easter guarantees those promises will come true.

APRIL 19, 1984

Don't Look Now but an Angel is Following You

People can be so wonderful.

These past few weeks I've felt the deepest grief I've ever known. My mother's death early last month was followed just five weeks later by my father's.

Both were such special people and perfect parents, so vitally alive until the last day of their lives, that I miss them with a deep, hurting ache.

But these last few weeks I've also felt the deepest love I've ever known.

People have amazed us with their great goodness and kindness, expressed in a multitude of ways. Our family has felt surrounded with love.

I keep remembering those words of Shakespeare about "the milk of human kindness." And that passage in the Psalms: "What is man, that Thou art mindful of him For Thou has made him a little lower than the angels, and hast crowned him with glory and honor."

Human beings are the worst of all creatures when we sink to our most unloving behavior. The news is full of such tales every day. But human beings are like God himself when they reach out in love. To be on the receiving end of such love is a blessing you never forget.

I heard a great story once from a friend of mine who lives in Orlando, Mary Peterson.

Mary was on the monorail at the Orlando airport. When it gave a sudden, lurching jolt as it stopped, she reached out to help steady a woman in a wheelchair, who was beside her.

The woman's attendant, a black lady with a kind face and twinkling eyes, thanked Mary warmly and added:

"You know, God *always* sends an angel when you need one. It says so in the 23rd Psalm."

Mary, being a good Bible scholar, thought that over. She didn't remember anything in the 23rd Psalm about any angels. She asked the woman what she meant.

"Oh yes, don't you know? It says 'Surely *Goodness* and *Mercy* shall follow me all the days of my life.' . . . and those are His angels."

Don't you love that?

Ever since, I've nicknamed Mary and her husband, Clarence, "Goodness" and "Mercy." They've been my angels when I've needed them, in so many ways.

It was Clarence who phoned me last week and told me my father had had a heart attack (so unexpected, no previous heart trouble). Clarence was keeping a vigil in the cardiac unit of the Orlando hospital 'til I could get there. I talked to Daddy's special nurse, learned he was in good spirits, resting comfortably and looking forward to my arrival. They advised me not to visit that night—he would be sleeping by the time my plane got there. I could see him early next morning.

It was Clarence and Mary who met my plane a few hours later, put their arms around me, and told me my father had gone to be with my mother in heaven. Because of their gentle sensitivity, the blow was more bearable.

It was Mary who gathered roses from her own garden and from friends to make a huge arrangement for his memorial service at the church—far more personal and beautiful than a florist's could be. Roses—his favorite flowers, which he grew with such pride and joy and shared with everyone.

Mary and Clarence even thought of taping his service in Orlando, so that two days later, at his graveside service in South Carolina, his brother, sisters, family and friends could draw comfort from the helpful message of his dear pastor, Howard Eddington. (And beside the grave a little mockingbird trilled special music from the magnolia tree).

There have been so many helpful friends.

Friends meeting planes. Offering us rooms. Bringing food. Calling long distance. Sending flowers. Writing letters recalling what my parents meant to them.

My close friend (my old Agnes Scott "roomie") Dot Clements and her husband Lowell didn't just say, "What can we do to help?" They kept three of my children in their home. Lowell cooked a huge breakfast for them. Then they sat in my parents' apartment and refused to leave 'til we gave them jobs to do.

God sends so many angels when you need them . . .

The friends back in Marietta this week who took me to lunch on a dark, rainy day.

The ones who tell me, "Remember, I'm here when you want to talk . . ." Because they know eventually I'll need to talk about my hurt. (How often those who have felt much grief themselves know how to help best.)

The sympathy cards and memorial gifts, many from people we don't know well but who go that extra mile.

Our sadness is not a tragedy, I realize. It's just a normal part of life. If I need comfort, how much more do those with real tragedies? Fatal accidents, premature death, an afflicted child, a lingering terrible illness?

God does send his angels—in the form of helping people. I hope I can remember that. I hope sometimes I may even be "Goodness" or "Mercy" myself.

MAY 31, 1984

Royal Welcome for a New Little Prince

A hospital maternity wing is a busy place.

The loudspeaker at Kennestone Hospital drones night and day: paging a doctor, calling a nurse, answering a patient.

When you're there, you learn to sublimate this noise, like a murmuring stream or soothing rain in the background. Otherwise you'd go nuts trying to get some sleep if you're a patient, or to have a visit if you're not.

Sometimes, though, the announcement over the loudspeaker isn't so routine. Instead it's a royal proclamation, dramatically intoned and surrounded with pomp and circumstance.

It happens every day at 1:00 p.m., 5:00 p.m., and 9:00 p.m. on the dot.

First the loudspeaker crackles as though bristling with importance and clearing its throat for attention.

Then you hear, in loud ringing tones:

"YOUR ATTENTION, PLEASE! YOUR ATTENTION, PLEASE!"

The first time you're there during visiting hours and hear this, you nearly jump out of your skin. What in the world is happening? Is the place on fire? Is there a bomb threat?

You notice everyone in the hall is freezing in place, stopping all activity and waiting for *something* to happen.

Then the authoritative voice continues:

"THE BABIES ARE NOW COMING ON THE FLOOR . . . THE BABIES ARE NOW COMING ON THE FLOOR."

It's exactly the way an announcer sounds when he says:

"Ladies and gentlemen—the President of the United States."

Or "Ladies and Gentlemen, Her Majesty the Queen."

Now a groundswell of background sound comes over the loudspeaker. Not trumpets playing "Hail To The Chief" or "God Save The Queen," but a mighty chorus of high, shrill human voices. "WAH, WAH, WAH!"

Sure enough, the babies are coming! They're hungry, it's feeding time, so don't mess around. Their attitude is clearly Queen Victoria's "We are not amused."

They may seem small and helpless but it's just an act. These little creatures have already caused grown men to go bananas, drive madly through the night and in general act hysterical. They've brought their mothers nine months of ladies-in-waiting duty and a lot of hassle at the last.

What's more they made their royal entrance into the world any day they wanted to . . . not when their doctors and parents calculated they would. They chose their own birth day, thank you.

Now the whole place goes into obeisance as the royal chariot—a big steel cart—enters and rolls majestically down the hall.

At the door of each room a tiny prince or princess, snugly wrapped in pink or blue striped blanket, is whisked from the cart and delivered to the side of the proper mother.

The loud "wah wah wahs" diminish several decibels with each delivery. Finally quiet descends. Contentment pervades Maternity Hall. All is well in the royal quarters.

Nowadays they allow grandparents and siblings of a new baby to remain in the room at feeding time, as well as the new father. This week I claimed my grandmother's privilege, washed my hands, put on a hospital gown, and had a special close-up view of our little Benjamin James Minor.

So perfect, adorable, trusting and innocent.

He is a big healthy boy weighing 10 pounds, 8 ounces at birth. But here in the bedroom with daddy Ken and mama Dixie Nan holding him (and proud big brother Gary waiting for a turn) he looks impossibly small to be a real human being.

Any trouble he made getting here is compensated by just one enchanting pose of his tiny hands, artfully crossed like Baryshnikov's. One touch of his feather soft hair. One clown smile (okay, so maybe it's a gas bubble but it looks like a smile to his grandmother) puffing up his little round cheeks.

Ben was born only two weeks after my father died. The pain of losing both my parents so suddenly, in so short a time, has left me hurting and bewildered. I know I'll feel this way a long time.

Ben's birth has underscored for me forever, in the most astounding way, those beautiful words of wisdom in Ecclesiastes: *for everything there is a season.*

Sometimes the seasons of life overlap and the cycles run concurrently for awhile. When one ends, we have difficulty letting go.

But there's a continuum and a flow.

My first-born child, this beloved daughter who bears my mother's name, has now given birth to my grandson. She will sing the lullabies, tell the stories, pass on the heritage that her grandparents transmitted to her through me.

To everything there is a season. . . .
A time to be born and a time to die. . . .
A time to weep and a time to laugh.
A time to mourn and a time to dance.

Ecclesiastes 3:1–4

Even as I mourn I feel my heart lifted in joy.

With this small, perfect miracle of little Ben in our lives, how could I not laugh and dance?

How could I possibly have a more joyful celebration?

JUNE 7, 1984

Quotations

My appreciation to the following for use of previously published material:

PREFACE "The story of the universe. . . .", Wilfred A. Peterson, *The Art of Living Day By Day* (New York: Simon & Schuster, 1972).

MOTHERHOOD, OPENINGS FOR CHALLENGING CAREER Marjorie Holmes, *As Tall As My Heart* (McLean, Va., EPM Publications, Inc., 1974). "Love alone . . .," Pierre Teilhard De Chardin, John Powell, *Unconditional Love* (Allen, Texas: Argus Communications, 1978).

SUMMERTIME . . . AND THE LIVIN' AIN'T EASY Carol Bartholomew, *Most Of Us Are Mainly Mothers* (New York: The MacMillan Co., 1966).

FATHER'S DAY Churchill and Nash quotes from *Moments With Father* (Kansas City: Hallmark Editions, 1974).

SAINT JUDE: A MAN AFTER MY OWN HEART Ann Kiemel, *I Love The Word Impossible* (Wheaton, Illinois: Tynedale House Publishers, 1976).

AT THANKSGIVING LISTEN TO BOTH SIDES OF THE RECORD Celestine Sibley, *Small Blessings* (Garden City, N.Y.: Doubleday & Co., 1977).

GIVING THANKS FOR LOVE, BEAUTY, AND GIBLET GRAVY Carolyn Rhea, *My Heart Kneels, Too* (New York: Grosset & Dunlap, 1965).

PLEASE REMOVE LABEL Herb Banks, *Prime Time* (Nashville, Tenn.: Thomas Nelson Inc., 1978).

Index of Column Titles

Allergy Sufferers—Here's Looking Atchoo!, 77
ALTA's Back in Town, 173
Another Link in the Friendship Chain, 16
Art of Cooking, The, 128
At Thanksgiving, Listen to Both Sides of the Record, 192
Autumn and Miss Annie, 161

Back to School at Candler Street—Remember?, 155
Beginning Drivers, Hysterical Parents, 55
Being Middle-aged Means Always Needing Your Glasses, 62
Big Band Sounds—Can't Beat 'Em, 20
Budding Journalists at West Side School, 14

Cabbage Patch Dolls—Only One Part of the Garden, 207
Callaway Gardens: Georgia's Beautiful Getaway Place, 137
Car Pool Mania, 164
Case of Mistaken Identity, A, 170
Cat-Astrophic Summer for Liza, A, 114
Christmas Comes in One Special, Magical Moment, 205
Clyde, Our Children's Friend, 159
Cobb Libraries Offer Children the Magic World of Books, 118

Did Anything Exciting Happen While I Was Away?, 45
"Did I Miss Christmas This Year?", 220
Don't Crack No Acorns for No Chickens!, 53
Don't Let a Computer Do Your Christmas Shopping, 209
Don't Look Now but an Angel Is Following You, 231

Easter—the Fulfillment of the Christmas Promise, 229
Enjoy the Journey, 3

Family Reunion, 135
Father's Day, 93
Fernbank Planetarium Lets You Choose a Christmas Star, 203
Formula for Love, A, 37
Friendship Force Comes to Cobb, 112
From Prison in Cuba to Thanksgiving in America, 190

General's Lady, The, 43
Georgia Governor's Honors, 131
Getting in Shape for the Peachtree Road Race, 108
Girls Club, The: Bubbly, Black, White, Short and Tall, 133
Giving Thanks for Love, Beauty, and Giblet Gravy, 193
Grandmother's House, 222

Hate Loses, Good Will Wins, 142
Help Someone into a New Life Through Reading, 86
Hemlock Inn, 158
Home of the Braves, The, 116
How Can You Judge a Little Girl's Doll?, 29
How to Read in Bed, 166
How We Gave the World's Worst Cook-Out, 100
Hugh Spears . . . What One Man Can Do, 178

I Love New York!, 69
I'm a National Public Radio Freak, 22

Joy Is Having Your First Grandchild, 124
June's Sweet Girl Graduates—Then and Now, 91
Jury Duty, 39

Kaleidoscope: The Ides and Arts of March, 57
Kindergarten Teaching: Not Much Glory but a Lot of Love, 175

Leo Aikman, 60
Looking Back with the Bard, 7

Meals on Wheels Deliver Love, 171
Me and the Man of La Mancha, 5
Memories of Lilian Sullivan, 31
Memories of the Frances Virginia Tea Room, 168
Message to the Ku Klux Klan, A, 140
Miss Jennie: A Loaf of Bread and an Orchid, 227
Mr. Ruddell—Sunny Side Up, 144
Modern Good Samaritan, A, 105
Motherhood: Openings For Challenging Career, 81
Mother of the Bride, 103
Mountain Air at Sylva, 120
My Christmas List with Thanks to Andy Rooney, 201
My Husband the Pot-hunter, 126
My Perfect Father-in-law, 97
My Three Fathers, 73

Neonatology Is a Beautiful New Word, 122
New Year, A: Enjoy the Journey, 3
New Year's Dieting: A Slim Possibility, 8

Off-to-College Advice from a Great-Great-Grandmother, 153
Old Friends, 41
Old Movies, 186
One More Week 'til Christmas, 218
Oops, Not My Grocery Cart . . . and Where Did I Park My Car?, 12
Our Lady of Perpetual Help—a Very Special Place, 182

Parents Need Their Freedom, Too, 66
Please Remove Label, 145

Raymond—a Christmas Vignette, 213
Rehearsal Pianist For Alliance Theatre—Wow!, 195
Royal Welcome for a New Little Prince, 234

Saint Jude—A Man After My Own Heart, 188
School Bands—Excellence the Hard Way, 83
September Goodbyes, 151
Side Effects: A House by the Side of the Road, 24
Sidewalks, 79
Six Flags Auditions (The Grit Behind the Glory), 10
Spring Celebrations, 59
Spring Means the Cobb County Symposium, 71
Spring Will Be a Little Late This Year, 51
Strictly for the Birds, 33
Summertime—and the Livin' Ain't Easy, 98

Treasured Memories of Christmas Past, 211
True Confessions of a Crossword Puzzles Addict, 18
Twisted Words and Teen Talk, 25

Under the Spell of Georgia's Golden Isles, 110

Valentine for Garfield, A, 35
Varsity, The: "Three MKO Dogs and a Large PC," 106
Vigil at Scottish Rite, 180

What, Exactly, Does a School Principal Do?, 64
What Ever Happened to Baby Jesus?, 216
What's It Going to Be . . . Buddy or George?, 184
Why Mothers Should Never Get the Flu, 27
Windows Aren't the Only Things I Don't Do, 75

You Know You're a Parent When . . . , 95

Index

Abbott, Charles, 196–197
Abbott, Nell, 8, 209
accidents, car, 24–25
Aguilar, Carlos, 113
Aikman, Ira, 60–61, 62, 169
Aikman, Leo, 60–62, 169
Aikman, Susan, 60–62
allergies, 77–79
Allgood School, 152
Alliance Theatre, 195–197
ALTA (Atlanta Lawn Tennis Association), 173–175
American Academy of Dramatic Art, 69
Anderson, Jennie Tate, viii, 227–229
Anderson, Jimmy T., 227
apple pie, recipe for, 130
archaeology, amateur, 126–128
Armitage, Katherline, 210
artifacts, Indian, 126–128
Atlanta, Ga. 168–169
Atlanta Braves, 116–118
Atlanta Constitution, 60, 61
Atlanta Lawn Tennis Association (ALTA), 173–175
Atlanta Symphony Orchestra, 31–32
auditioning at Six Flags Over Georgia, 10–12
Austen, Jane, 167
automobile accidents, 24–25

Baker, Elsie, 25
Band Banquet, 83–85
bands, big, 20–21
bands, school, 83–85
Barber, Rev. Ernest L., 193
Barber, Louise Dendy, 193
Barber, Murray, 66
Barks, Herb, quoted, 147
Barrett, Lorraine, 170–171
Barrett, Johnny, 179
Barrett, Mike, 170
Bartholomew, Carol, 99–100
Beavers, Helen, 76
Beavers, John, 76
Beloved Invader (Price), 112
Benson, Billy, 79
Benson, Peggy, 32
Bentley, Ernest, 179
Berrong, Lisa, 145
Bickers, Miss Bessie, 157
Bickley, Nancy, 113
bifocals, 63–64
big band sound, 20–21
bird feeding, 33–35
Bishop, Bob, 74
Blackwell, Phil, 58
Blair, L. M. "Rip," 43–44
Blair, Mrs. L. M., 43–44
Boggs, Carolyn, 183
Bombeck, Erma, 168
books, Christmas, 217
Boring, Alice, 42
Boring, Bob, 41, 42
Bowden, Barbara, 8, 29
Bowden, Chip, 85
Bowers, Mike, 72
Brown, Annette, 64
Brown, Melody, 15
Brown, Reid, 14, 15
Brumby, Otis, Jr., 61
Brumby, Otis, Sr., 61
Bruner, Jim, 57
Bryson City, N.C., 158–159
Burleigh, Margie Kemp, 169
Burns, Beverly, 157
Butch Thompson Trio, 22
Cabbage Patch Kids, 207
Cain, Catherine, 68
Cain, Dick, 68
Calhoun, Ga., 144
Callaway Gardens, 137–140
cancer, incurable, 182–184
Candler Street School, 16, 155–158
car, lost in parking lot, 13–14
Carmichael, Jimmy, 43
Caroline (the dog), 59

car pools, 164–166
car trouble, 105–106
Casey, Nancy, 141
Castleberry, Lucille, 157
Catholic Church, Roman, 73–75
cats, 35–37, 59–60, 114–116, 136
Cheves, C. J., 157–158
Cheves, Charles, 157
Cheves, Joanne (Mrs. Bob Davis), 8, 157
childbirth, 124–126
childhood memories, 222–224
Chilton, Pat, 8
"Choose Something Like a Star" (Frost), 204
Christ Church (St. Simons), 112
Christian City Children's Home, 206
Christie, Agatha, 167
Christmas
  dolls, 207–208
  at Fernbank Science Center, 203–204
  gifts, favorite, 209–211
  for the homeless, 213–216
  magic moments of, 205–206
  memories, 211–213
  nativity set, Baby Jesus missing from, 216–218
  preparations, 220–222
  thoughts and observations, 201–203
  the week before, 218–220
Christmas shopping, computerized, 209
Churchill, Sir Winston, 94
Clay, Chuck, 43, 44
Clay, David, 101, 109, 115, 208, 214, 215
Clay, General Lucius D., 43–45
Clay, Mrs. Lucius D. (Marjorie McKeown), 43–45
Clay, Patty Ryle, 3, 33, 34, 46, 54, 101, 108–109, 115, 136, 162, 179, 192, 208, 214, 215
  graduation from college, 91–93
Clay Elementary School, 66
Clements, Dot, 233
Clements, Lowell, 233
Cobb Arts Council, 32, 57, 113
Cobb Bar Association, 72
Cobb Community Symphony, 58
Cobb County Chamber of Commerce, 113, 134
Cobb County Civic Center, 15, 57, 112–113
Cobb County Parks and Recreation Department, 29–30, 57
Cobb County Symposium, 71–72
Cobb County Times, 61
Cobb County Tractor Company, 178
Cobb Literacy Action, 86–87
Cobb-Marietta Ballet, 113
Cobb-Marietta Girls Club, 133–135
Cobb-Marietta Junior League, 58, 72, 114, 228
Cobb Medical Society, 71
Cobb Ministerial Association, 71
Cobb Symphony Guild, 58
Cole, Dr. Jim, 134
Coleman, Johnny, 65, 66
college graduation, 91–93
Collins, Leroy, 146
cooking, 128–130
cook-out, world's worst, 100–103
Cooper, Ruth, 67–68
Copeland, Billy, 53
Copeland, David Thomas, 53, 54
Copeland, Hattie, 53
Copeland, Isaac, 53
Copeland, Janie, 53
Copeland, Johnny, 53
Copeland, Lola Casey, 155–156
Copeland, Martha Adair, 53
Copeland, Sally Hamp, 53
Corley, Florrie, 8
Corn, Joyce, 65
Costa Rica, visitors from 112–114
Coxe Female Institution, 153
Crestview Baptist Church, 163, 164
Crimm, Jo Anne, 114
Crissey, DeVant, 205–206
Crissey, Jeannette, 8, 205
Crissey, Laura, 205
Crissey, Mark, 205–206
Cristie, Pat, 178
Croker, Dr. Frank, 66
crossword puzzles, addiction to, 18–20
Cumberland Island, 112
Cummings, Father James, 74, 75
Cunningham, Rose, 114
Curtis, Nancy, 157

Dansby, Ted and Vel, 209–210
Darden, George "Buddy," 184–185
Darden, George (Buddy's son), 184
Darden, Christy, 184
Darden, Lillian, 184, 185
Davis, Bob, 157
Davis, Joanne Cheves, 8, 157
Declaration of County Conscience, 143
Delaney, John, 188
Dendy, David, 135–137
Dendy, Josie Wilkes, 222
Dendy, Judy, 136
Dendy, Rev. Marshall C., 66–68, 118, 136, 222, 229–233
Dendy, Marshall, Jr., 136
Dendy, Mary Jo, 135–137, 229, 231
Dendy, Nan Copeland, 67, 68, 129, 136, 229–231
  recipe for Sally Lunn bread, 130
Dennard, Bill, 65
Dent, Mrs. E. R., 157

dialogue, movie, 186–187
dieting, 8–9
Dixie Hunt Hotel, 169
Dobbins Air Force Base, 43
doll contest, 29–30
dolls, as Christmas gifts, 207–208
Dotson, Cheryl, 110
Doty, Linda, 11
Dozier, Bishop Carroll T., 75
Drabble, Margaret, 167
drivers, beginning, 55–56
driving, hazardous, 24–25, 55–56
Duncan, Roy, 25

Earhart, Amelia, quoted, 229
Eastham, Dana, 113
Eastham, Merrilyn, 8, 211
Eckerd College, 91, 92
Eddington, Howard, 233
egg man, 144–145
Eisenhower, Mamie, 44
Elder, Ray and Cindy, 206
Enesco, Georges, 192
enjoying the process, 3–4
epiphany, meaning of, 205–206
eyeglasses, 63–64
family misunderstandings, 37–38
family reunion, 135–137
Fant, Dr. Jean, 132
Farrar, Ralph, 41, 42–43, 158, 159
Farrar, Sarah, 8, 20, 42, 43, 158, 159
fatherhood, 93–95
father-in-law, a perfect, 97–98
Father's Day, 93–95
Fauss, Michael, 196, 197
Fernbank Science Center, 203–204
Fields, Liz, 57
Fiji Islands, 73
Fike, Rev. Cecil, 142
First Baptist Church, 95, 190
First United Methodist Church kindergarten, 175
Flores, Sylvia, 113
Flournoy, Bob, 116, 142, 143
Floyd Middle School, 66
flu, and effects on family, 27–28
Fort Frederica, 112
Fortson, Becky, 153
Fortson, Sarah, 153
Frances Virginia Tearoom, 168–169
Francis, Dick, 167
Freeman, Jimmy, 114
Friendship Force, 112–114
Frost, Robert, quoted, 204
Fuller, Bob, 123
Furman University, 152

Gainesville, Ga., 16–17, 79–80
  Candler Street School, 155–158
  Christmas in, 211–212
Garfield (the cat), letter to, 35–37
Garrett Middle School, 66
Georgia Newspaper Hall of Fame, 60
Georgia Press Association, 60
Georgia State University, 31
Gibson, Charlotte, 31
Gilbert, Leland, 155, 157
Ginger (the dog), 136, 170–171
Girls Club, Cobb-Marietta, 133–135
Glaze, Kim, 135
Glover, Barbara, 182
Glover, Irma, 134
Glover Machine Works, viii
Gober, Maureen, 134
Godden, Rumer, 167
Golden Isles of Georgia, 110–112
Good, Dr. Robert, 72
good-bye, saying, 151–153
Good Samaritan, modern-day, 105–106
Gordy, Frank, 106, 108
Goscha, Barbara, 143
Goudge, Elizabeth, 167
graduation, college, 91–93
grandchild, first, 124–126
Gray, Ginny, 8
Gray, Glenn, 165
Green, Joan, 171, 172
Greider, Marilyn, 57, 113
Grizzard, Lewis, 168
Grogan, St. Mary, 134–135
Grogan, Stephanie, 134, 135
Gross, Mike and Laura, 139

Hagemann, Fritz, 8
Hair, Frank, 66
Hall, David, 188
Hall, Nell, 102, 210
Hames, Judge Luther, 119, 162, 163
Hames, Mrs. Luther, 119
Hames, Patti, 119
Hammond, John, 140, 142
Harmon, Sam D., 66
Harmony Leland School, 65
Harrell, Virginia, 20
Harris, Jo Ann, 134
Harris, Terri, 135
Harrison, George, 79
Hawthorne, Rose, 183
Hawthorne Dominican nuns, 182, 183
hay fever, 77–79
Heartbreak Hotel (Siddons), 91–92
Hemlock Inn, 42, 158–159
Hensley, Iris, 96
Highlands Country Club, 42
Hilderbrand, Patty Hames, 95–96
Hildreth, Ann, 29, 175

Hilton Head Island, 41, 43
Hollydale School, 66
hopeless causes, 188–189
Hosch, Heyward, 157
house, unfortunate location of, 24–25
Housman, A. E., quoted, 51–52
Huffstutler, Diana, 8, 9, 210
"Hungarian Rhapsodies" (Liszt), 192
Hunter, Mitch, 220
Hunter, Nancy, 220
Hutcheson, Larry, 96

illiteracy, help for, 86–87
Indian artifacts, 126–128
influenza, and effects on family, 27–28
Inglis, Ruth, 118
Ingram, Sylvia, 8
inns, country, 158–159
Inside West Side, 14–15

Jackson, Felicia, 157
James, P. D., 167
John Sibley Horticultural Center, 138
Johnson, Marge, 86
Jones, Ann, 67
Jones, Margaret, 8
Jones, Millard, 65–66
Jones, Zabrina, 135
Journalism School of the University of Georgia, 60
Junior League, Cobb-Marietta, 58, 72, 114, 228
jury duty, 39–41
jury selection process, 40

Kaleidoscope (arts festival), 57–58
Kallen, Lucille, 167
Kaney, Rex, 110, 215
Keillor, Garrison, 22–23
Kellermann, Father Leonard, 74, 75
Kemp, Henry, 169
Kemp, Peggy, 169
Kennesaw College, 31, 71, 72
Kennesaw House, 61
Kennesaw Mountain National Battlefield Park, 61, 160
Kennestone Hospital, 122–123, 124, 125
Kessler, Jeani, 86
Kiemel, Ann, 189
Kincaid School Chorus, 58
kindergarten teachers, 175–177
"King and I, The," 195–197
King and Prince (hotel), 111–112
Kinney, Bill, 31, 43, 45
Kirk, Adrian, 160
Kirk, Cleve, 160
Kirk, Clyde, viii, 159–161
Kirk, Connie, 228
Kirk, Dempsey, Jr., 160
Kirk, George, 160
Kirk, George Washington Lee, 160
Kirkpatrick, Lillian, 106
Ku Klux Klan, 140–141, 142
Kuralt, Charles, 71, 72
Kuschner, Sue and Harvey, 16–18

labels, 146–147
Lake Wobegon, Mich., 22
language, use and misuse, 25–27
Lathen, Emma, 167
Lawhorn, John, 57
Lay, Bernice, 157
Lee, Billy, 138
Lee, Edna, 46
Lee, Martha and Bill, 138
Li'l Generals, 113
Lilian Bennett Sullivan Memorial Scholarship Fund, 31, 32
Liszt, Franz, 192
Literacy Action, Cobb, 86–87
Living the Questions (Raines), 218
Liza (the cat), 35–37, 114–116
Lloyd, Andrew Philip, 95
Lloyd, Carolyn Sue, 95
Lloyd, Charles, 95, 96, 143
Lockheed Georgia, 43
Love, Lonnie, 132
"Loveliest of Trees" (Housman), 52
Lyle, Lillian C., 15

Macaulay, Jodie Dendy, 223
McBain, Ed, 167
MacDowall, Louise, 68
McGinley, Phyllis, 188
McKeown, Boyd, 57
McKeown, Marjorie (Mrs. Lucius D. Clay), 43–45
McMillan, George, 43
McShane, Father John, 75
Malone, B. J., 66
Malonson, Phil, 188
Manning, Dr. Jim, 32
Maples, Bill, 113
Marietta, Ga., viii
Marietta City Council, 140, 141, 142
Marietta-Cobb Community Service, 171
Marietta Daily Journal, 61, 143
Marietta Federal Savings and Loan, 172
Marietta High School, 20, 61, 162
  Band, 83–85
Marietta Place, 178–180
Marietta Rotary Club, 61, 215–216

Marino, Dr. Brenda, 123
Marlow, C. W., 172
Marlow, Kitty, 172
Marsh, Betty, 17
Marsh, Elizabeth and Herbert, 16–17
Marsh, Ngaio, 167
Marsh, Roberta, 17
Marsh, Sue (Mrs. Harvey Kuschner), 16–18
Martin, Harold, 168
Mathis, Samuel, 14
Meals on Wheels, 171–172
Meeks, Jean, 79
Meeks, "Lit," 79
Meeks, Margie, 79
Meiere, Lib, 179
memories, childhood, 222–224
memories, Christmas, 211–213
Messer, Ryan, 14
Methodists United in Service and Training (MUST), 214
middle age, 62–64
Miles, Susan, 8
Millard, Janet, 134
Miller, Com. Andrew, 215–216
Miller, Brenda, 172
Miller, Janice Tiffany, 172
Miller, Mr. and Mrs. Ray, 172
Miller, Ruth, 8
Milsap, Ronnie, 192
Minor, Benjamin James, 180–182, 235–236
Minor, Dixie Ryle, 46, 53, 54, 55, 131, 136, 151–152, 165, 208, 211, 235
  wedding to Ken, 103–105
  birth of son, 124–125
Minor, Gary Ryle, 42, 123, 124–126, 136, 210, 213, 222, 235
  first day at school, 151
Minor, Jim and Jerry, 125
Minor, Ken, 47, 136, 235
  wedding to Dixie, 103–105
  birth of son, 124–125
Misiaveg, Chuck, 110
Misiaveg, Theresa, 110
Moncrief, Terry, 206
Moore, Rev. John, 73–75
Moore, Kenneth, 66
Moreau, Amber, 15
Morris, Tyler, 14
Morrow, Buddy, 21
Moss, Mike, 58
Mossketeers, 58
motherhood, 81–83, 98–100, 151–155
motherly advice, 154–155
mother of the bride, 103–105
mountain air, 120–122
movies, old, 186–187
Murphy, Allyson Ray, 110
Murphy, Jim, 110
MUST (Methodists United in Service and Training), 214

Nash, Ogden, quoted, 93
Neighbor Newspapers, 143
Neighbors, Nancy, 210
neonatology, 122–124
New Year's resolutions, 3–4, 7–8
New Year's wishes, 6
New York, N. Y., 69–71
nicknames, advantages and disadvantages of, 184–185
Norah, Sheilah, 135
Northcutt, Marvina, 139

Olds, Jerome, 222
Orford, Donna, 29–30
Orlando High School, 112
Our Lady of Perpetual Help Home, 182–184
Owens, Barbara, 143
Owens, Phil, 143

Pagana, Maureen Reeder, 69, 70
parenthood, 96. *See also* motherhood, fatherhood
parents, elderly, 66–68
Parker, Joyce, 133, 134
Parker, Sidney, 15
"Patchwork Quilt" (Rhea), 194–195
Peachtree Road Race, 108–110
Peck, M. Scott, Quoted, 153
Pedro, Nick, 65
Pendergrass, Bishop Ed, 229–230
Pendergrass, Elizabeth, 157
Pendleton, David, 197
Peterson, Clarence, 68, 232–233
Peterson, Mary, 68, 232–233
Phillips, Lucia Hames, 119
pianist, rehearsal, 195–197
Pickering, Susan, 85
Porter, Buck, 68
Porter, Dorothy, 68
Powdermilk Biscuits, 22
"Prairie Home Companion," 22–23
premature babies, care of, 122–124
Price, Eugenia, 112, 167
Price, Rev. Nelson, 7
Prime Time (Barks), 147
principals, school, 64–66
priorities, setting, 53–54
public radio, 22–24
public television, 23
Pym, Barbara, 167

Rachels, Norwood, 86
radio, public, 22–24
Raines, Robert, quoted, 218
Raines, Rupert, 165

Randall, Dr. Henry, 9
Ransom, Evelyn, 210
Ransom, Ron, 116
Raper, Henry, 179
Ray, Ann, 8, 210
Read, Emily, 110
Read, Miss, 167
reading
  in bed, 166–168
  encouragement of, to children, 118–120
  teaching of, to adults, 86–87
refugees, Cuban, 190–191
Renshaw, John, 44, 45
Rich, Virginia, 167
Rhea, Caroline, quoted, 194
Rheay, Mary Louise, 119
Riddle, Thad, 116
Rivers, Herb, 43
Riverside School, 65
Road Less Traveled, The (Peck), 153
Roberts, Xavier, 207
Robinson, Judge Dorothy, 110
Roman Catholic Church, 73–75
Rooney, Andy, 201, 203
Rose, Dr. McCoy, 72
Rose, Margaret Ann, 72
Ross, Stella, 57
Rothermel, Sam, 113
Ruddell, Eugene, 145
Ruddell, J. S., 144–145
"Rumanian Rhapsodies" (Enesco), 192
running, 108–110
Ryle, Buddy, 23, 46, 123, 136, 138, 210, 211, 221
Ryle, Cecile, 46, 129
  recipe for apple pie, 130
Ryle, Dallas M., Jr., 16, 18, 24, 37–38, 41, 43, 45–47, 59, 64, 78, 85, 93, 95, 111, 125, 162, 166, 192, 202, 210, 212, 231
  as amateur archaeologist, 126–128
  birthday, 145–146
  at cook-out, world's worst, 100–102
  at the Varsity, 107–108
Ryle, Dallas M., Sr., 46, 97–98
Ryle, Dixie. *See* Minor, Dixie Ryle
Ryle, Joelle, 122, 123–124
Ryle, Katie, 10–11, 26, 37–38, 46–47, 78, 103, 111, 114, 115, 139, 211, 221
  in New York, 17–18, 69–71
Ryle, Patty, *See* Clay, Patty Ryle
Ryle, Sam and Patricia, 123
Ryle, Stephen, 19–20, 46–47, 108, 111, 118, 136, 202–203, 211, 218, 221
  as beginning driver, 55–56
  at Governor's Honors, 131, 132

St. Joseph Catholic Church, 73
St. Jude, 188–189
Saints for All Seasons (Delaney), 188
St. Simons Island, Ga., 110–112
Saint Watching (McGinley), 188
Sally Lunn bread, recipe for, 130
Sanders, Charles, 64–65
Sanders, Jane, 64
Sanders, Rodney, 64
Saripkin, Dr. Larry M., 181
Satterfield, Kim, 85
Sayers, Dorothy, 167
Schmuhl, Father Lawrence, 75
school, back to, 155–158
school principals, 64–66
Scottish Rite Children's Hospital, 180–182
Self, Mary, 157
September, 151–153
Sessions, Dr. Bob, 145
Shakespeare, William, 5–6
Shaw, Dr. Barbara, 57
Shell, Ella Jo, 42, 43, 152, 158–159
Shell, John, 41, 42, 158–159
Shoob, Judge Marvin, 39, 40
shopping cart, lost, 12–13
Sibley, Celestine, 167, 192
Siddons, Anne Rivers, 91
sidewalk games, 79–80
sidewalks, 79–81
Simenon, Georges, 167
Sinclair, Ryan, 15
Six Flags Over Georgia, 36, 114–115
  auditions at, 10–12
slang, teens', 26–27
Small Blessings (Sibley), 192
Smith, Donna, 220
Smith, Hanson, 220
Smith, Peggy, 209
Smith, Whit, 220
Somerlot, Jean, 32
Soukup, George, 172
Soukup, Lucille, 172
South Cobb P.T.A. Council, 65–66
Southern Tech, 72
Spalding, Jack, quoted, 182–183
Spears, Hugh, viii, 178–180
Spears, Mary, 178, 179
Speed, Flora, 102
Speed, Rev. James, 102
Speed, Sarah, 85
Sprayberry High School, 58
spring cleaning, 75–77
springtime, 51–52, 59–60
star of Bethlehem, 204
Stephens, Linda, 197
Stevens, Pat, 171
Stout, Rex, 167
Sullivan, John, 31, 32
Sullivan, Lilian Bennett, 31–32
Sullivan, Ruth Delmar, 31, 32

Sullivan Memorial Scholarship Fund, 31, 32
summertime, trials and tribulations of, 98–100
Sutton, Lynn (Mrs. Frank Wiginton), 179, 180, 215
Syfan, Linda, 157
Sylva, N.C., 120

Taber, Gladys, 167
Tagore, Rabindranath, quoted, 94
Talmadge, Betty, quoted, vii
Tapp Middle School, 66
Taylor, Bob, 64
Taylor, Elizabeth, 167
teaching kindergarten, 175–177
television, public, 23
tennis, 173–175
Thaddeus (St. Jude), 188–189
Thanksgiving, 192–195
theatre accompaniment, 195–197
Thirkell, Angela, 167
Thomas, Becky, 179
Tisha (the cat), 115
Tommy Dorsey Band, 20–21
Traveler's Aid, 214
Trippe, Judson, 96
Tucker, Linda, 113

Ulene, Dr. Art, quoted, 204
Underwood, Dr. Charlie, 216
Underwood, Mary Kirk, 160
University of Georgia, 60

Vacation Reading Club, 118–119
Valdes, Rev. Benjamin, 190–191
Valdes, Benjamin, Jr., 191
Valdes, Carmen, 190, 191
Valdes, Carmita, 191
Valdes, Ruthie, 191
Valdosta, Ga., 131–132
Valdosta State College, 131
Vanderpool, Dr. Gerald, 77–78
Vandeventer, Jerry, 186–187
Van Dyke, Henry, quoted, 95, 216
Varsity, The, 106–108
Vergowe, Diana, 68
Volunteer Cobb, 29–30

WABE, 22
Waldorf, Pat, 197
Waldrip, Wayne, 110
Walker, Joanne, 101, 165
Walker, Rob, 165
Walsh, Pauline, 8
Watson, Annie, 161–164
Watson, Charlie, 120, 121, 210
Watson, Helen, 120, 121
Watson, Sam, 162
Wayland, David, 143
WCOB, 21
wedding, Dixie and Ken's, 103–105
Wendy (the cat), 59–60, 136, 170
West Side Elementary School, 14–15, 64
Wheeler, Harris, 10–11
Whitaker, Frances Virginia Wikle, 169
Wiginton, Frank, 179, 215
Wiginton, Lynn Sutton, 179, 180, 215
Wikle, Marjorie, 169
Williams, Eddie, 179, 180
WJYA, 21
Woodcock, Harriet, 16, 157
World War II: aftermath in Germany, 44–45
Wright, Kelly, 135
Wright, Mildred, 157

Young, Marie, 135

Zolota, Father John, 75